The Power of
Negative Thinking

The Power of Negative Thinking

Coming to Terms with Our Forbidden Emotions

Gerald Amada

MADISON BOOKS
Lanham • New York • Oxford

Published by Madison Books
4720 Boston Way
Lanham, Maryland 20706

12 Hid's Copse Road
Cumnor Hill, Oxford OX2 9JJ, England

Distributed by National Book Network

Library of Congress Cataloging-in-Publication Data
Amada, Gerald.
    The power of negative thinking : coming to terms with our
forbidden emotions / Gerald Amada.
        p.   cm.
    ISBN 1-65833-125-8 (hardcover : alk. paper)
    1. Negativism   I. Title.
BF698.35.N44A44   1999
152.4--dc21   98-54396
                                                                  CIP

⊖™ *The paper used in this publication meets the minimum requirements of*
American National Standard for Information Sciences—Permanence of
Paper for Printed Library Materials, ANSI/NISO Z39.48–1992.
Manufactured in the United States of America.

This book is dedicated to Amelia Lippi and Donna O'Rourke, my special friends during times of calm and troubled waters.

Contents

There is no crime, however heinous, that I could not conceive committing myself.

— Attributed to Johann Wolfgang von Goethe

There is no such thing as morality or immorality in thought.

— Oscar Wilde

Introduction

Human beings have a strong tendency to disown, deny, and repress negative emotions such as anger, envy, resentment, defiance, and revenge. The inability or unwillingness to acknowledge negative emotions often leads to a variety of psychological, social, and physical difficulties. The purpose of this book is to demonstrate that negative emotions, if properly understood and accepted, can possess enormous potential for producing creative and socially constructive behavior.

This is a book about discovering the true nature of negative emotions in order that they may, where possible, be put to positive use. Most people regard negative emotions such as anger, rage, revenge, contempt, jealousy, and defiance as purely destructive and, therefore, view them as immoral forces. Unfortunately, they don't understand that such negative emotions contain the potential, not only for harm, but also for generating much personal and social good.

How can we transform negative thoughts or emotions into positive forms of behavior and worthwhile accomplishments? Obviously, this is not always a simple or easy task. However, this transformation *is* possible—as this book will attempt to demonstrate—by means of viewing our negative feelings from a psychological perspective that most individuals seem to disregard or ignore. We need to recognize that there are no feelings or thoughts, positive or negative, that are *inherently* evil or destructive. In my view, it may even be harmful to view negative emotions as only sources of social destructiveness. I hope in the following pages to make clear to the reader that negative emotions and thoughts, if properly understood and not automatically repudiated, can produce untold opportunities and avenues for personal growth and fulfillment. Perhaps the following example will help to illustrate this point.

Recently, a community college student, a woman in her early twenties, entered psychotherapy complaining about physical symptoms such as pains in her chest, which naturally puzzled and frightened her. She had been to a physician who had given her a clean bill of health. Suspecting that the origins of her difficulties were psychological, the physician recommended that she undergo psychotherapy.

In the course of only a single session some fascinating facts came to light. In response to careful questioning, the student revealed that she and her quite loving parents enjoyed a very close and warm relationship. However, the student also mentioned that her parents expected a great deal of her and that often their excessively high expectations made her feel guilty and ashamed of herself. She constantly felt that she was disappointing and emotionally injuring her parents if she did not satisfy their unrealistic wishes.

About midway through the session the student tearfully blurted out, "I don't want to hurt my parents. No, no, I'd never want to do that!" Since the student herself had introduced the subject of hurting her parents and seemed to be so terribly appalled by the idea that she might actually harm them, I began to doubt the veracity of her statement. Following the scent of my own suspicions, I gently inquired, "Since you no doubt resent your parents' expectations, aren't there times when you might like to get back at them, you know, make them suffer for putting you through such pain?"

Quite horrified by the image conjured up by my question, the student replied without hesitation, "It would kill me to see them suffer. How can you say such a thing?" I replied with a smile, "I think you perhaps misunderstood me. I didn't say you would actually enjoy seeing them suffer. But perhaps in your thoughts there are times when you could visualize punishing them, making them suffer for the pain they have caused you. Is that such a horrible idea?"

A bit breathlessly, the student pondered my question. She finally replied with deep emotion, "You know that idea occurred to me the other night, but I dismissed it before I let it affect me. You see, I had this nightmare in which I had died and my mother was attending my funeral. She was shattered by my death. You know, there may be something to this idea that I want my parents to suffer. Do you think that might have something to do with my physical symptoms?" The student continued, "So you think my symptoms are my way of making my parents feel guilty and suffer. In other words, if I get sick and die, they'll feel sorry. Is that what you think?" I remained silent.

Answering her own question, she stated, "I'm beginning to agree with you. But it's crazy, how can angry emotions turn into something like physical pain. It's absurd, but it must be true."

Over the next several weeks the student underwent appreciable improvement as a result of her newfound understanding. Her physical symptoms subsided and eventually disappeared. Especially pleasing to her was her increased ability to express to her parents the nature and basis of her negative feelings toward them. They were receptive and sensitive to her feelings and this seemed to put their relationship on an entirely new and positive footing. Thus, from an acceptance and understanding of intense and overwhelming negative emotions emerged physical improvement and a more rewarding family relationship.

Strange? Perhaps. But emotions, both positive and negative, have a life of their own and, if they do not find expression immediately and directly, they will often eventually find their outlets in disguised and "absurd" forms, such as the student's physical symptoms.

The mental life of the ordinary human being is filled, second by second, with a wide range of sensations and emotions. The positive emotions, such as affection, joy, love, and pleasure, are eagerly sought and appreciated by most people. The negative emotions, however, such as anger, rage, sorrow, resentment, envy, revenge, and defiance, tend to be shunned and suppressed at all costs.

In our never-say-die quest to experience only that which produces untrammeled pleasurable feelings, we hide ostrichlike from our negative emotions and thoughts. Not only do we disguise and camouflage our angry feelings in order that they may go undetected by others, but we expend great emotional energy in denying the very existence of such feelings even to ourselves. In this manner we ignore and preclude the vast opportunities given to us by our negative emotions to produce benefits to ourselves and others. By being able to tap the energy and inventiveness of our negative emotions we could not only avoid depression, but also develop creative ways to improve our lives.

Realistically, the average person who lives in today's complex society cannot pass through a single day without periodically feeling some degree of annoyance, frustration, anger, and resentment. Commuters who are stuck in traffic on their way to an important appointment may grow tense and irritable, and, consequently, recklessly speed to their destinations when the road finally unclogs. Parents who have just finished the spick-and-span cleaning of their house in preparation for guests will become enraged to find that their two-year-old has just painted colorful pictures on the dining room tablecloth. Most people will find that if they are in the middle of saying something they hope will be interesting and important to others, it will get their dander well up if their remarks are rudely interrupted, ignored, or contradicted. The following example will illustrate how feelings of defiance and resentment can interfere with intellectual and academic pursuits.

Each semester I am asked to speak to classes of health science students about the subject of mental health. Prior to my visit the students are assigned to read a chapter dealing with the defense mechanisms. When I enter the class I usually begin by saying, "I understand you've been assigned to read the chapter dealing with the subject under discussion today: the defense mechanisms. Correct?" All the students nod their heads in unison. I then add, with a knowing smile, "So, I will just assume that no one has read that chapter. Right?" Invariably, the classes heartily laugh at my weak joke because, with the possible exception of a few students, the class indeed has not read the chapter.

I then inform the class that we'll return to the subject of their unread chapter later in the discussion. Eventually, the discussion comes around to how and why people forget such things as doctors' appointments, textbooks, keys, and taking out the garbage at home. We learn of course that forgetting these items is hardly ever a matter of accident or coincidence. Our investigations reveal that we forget to take out the garbage or keep our appointments with doctors because we simply dislike and, therefore, avoid such tasks.

Now the class is prepared to consider why they did not read the assigned chapter. Immediately, a few hands go up in protest. "Wait a minute," objects an indignant student. "I didn't read that chapter because I've just been too busy this week." "Perhaps," I teasingly rejoin, "but I'll bet you weren't too busy this week to do some of the things you really enjoy." A bit sheepishly, the student will admit the truth of my statement.

I can now convincingly demonstrate my point to the class. I suggest to the students that people generally feel a dislike for work or, for that matter, any enterprises that are either inherently unpleasant or are undertaken involuntarily. Since some reading assignments may be dry or very boring and, what's more, are out of necessity imposed by instructors without the willing consent of their charges, there are many students who will resent and rebel against such "impositions" by not fulfilling their assignments. Often, students will continue to defy their assignments and their instructors by waiting until the last days before an assignment or an examination is due before taking up the challenge. In come cases, unfortunately, it may be too late.

Thus, we can see from the above example that feelings of anger and defiance can find expression in procrastination and in an obstinate unwillingness to fulfill academic responsibilities, even when the timely fulfillment of assigned work would presumably lead to success and a sense of personal accomplishment and gratification. It is enlightening and encouraging, however, to note that many students, upon recognizing and understanding these angry and defiant aspects to their unproductiveness and procrastination, will actually regain their motivation to learn and study. By clearly understanding their anger and defiance of authority they can begin to transform their self-destructive rage into positive study habits and improved academic achievement.

In addition to academic and career concerns, there are broad social issues that have definitely aroused the attention and anxiety of literally millions of human beings. For example, the arms race and the specter of a nuclear holocaust, in themselves, should be enough to raise our hackles. One poll that was taken several years ago indicated that the majority of Americans believe the United States will be embroiled in a war within a few years and that the country will soon be domestically victimized by international terrorism. As well, the fluctuations and unpredictability of the economy arouse in literally millions of people feelings of helplessness, discontent, and anger.

In addition to the awesome problems that result from a troubled society, there are sources of frustration and resentment that inescapably arise from and are embedded in the personalities and relationships of most individuals. For instance, it appears quite clear that all people experience, from time to time, jarring and traumatic humiliations during their formative years as children. For example, one of my patients, a quite attractive woman was often ridiculingly called "Pickle Puss" by her father when she was a child. As an adult, she continued to feel quite self-conscious about her appearance even though she realized that others found her quite prepossessing. Another patient, who as a child had been sexually molested by her father, found it difficult as an adult to trust or feel open with male companions. A male patient, whose mother had abandoned him during his infancy, deserted his wife and son soon after his child's birth, without in the least understanding the reasons for his actions.

As I will later explain, these particular individuals, despite the painful and traumatic experiences of their pasts, were able to gradually transform their negative emotions over those events into positive accomplishments.

Some psychological injuries may be largely overcome or resolved in adulthood, but for many people the emotional scars of those early years will sometimes rear their nasty heads many years later in the form of still-harbored grudges and resentments.

To complicate matters further, irrespective of one's upbringing, there appear to be no close personal relationships in which anger, strife, and resentment do not play some part. As a matter of fact, psychotherapists have come to recognize that personal relationships that are ostensibly devoid of occasional discord and conflict are probably also seriously lacking in genuine intimacy. This insight is derived from an understanding that, if two persons cannot occasionally and freely disagree or lock horns, they most likely do not feel especially safe with each other.

For example, no friends or spouses can always entirely agree about how to spend their free time together. Also, they will inevitably disagree at times regarding which of their friends and family members they like or dislike most. Mary is fond of Jim's father, but Jim hates his own father. Most likely, they will also not consistently see eye-to-eye on how much time each wishes to spend with the other. After a hard week at work, Mary wishes to spend her Saturday afternoons reading. Jim wants to spend them in activities with Mary. If they feel safe and secure with these differences, they will perhaps acknowledge that they sometimes annoy and anger each other. This acknowledgment may enable them to discuss or argue over the bones of contention and, hopefully, they can resolve the dissension while realizing that such conflicts are an inevitable and intrinsic part of marital life.

Because a total lack of open conflict in personal relationships implies a serious lack of intimacy, when I am informed by patients that their parents never fought or disagreed, I will at times respond by saying that I consider that fact to be regrettable.

Being able to acknowledge and accept the fact that some degree of disagreement and discord will enter into all of our relationships is the first step toward resolving conflict and transforming negative emotions into problem-solving and constructive behavior. So, paradoxically, our ability to admit and appropriately express some of our negative feelings for another person will often cause us to feel more positively toward that person. This is the potential positive power of negative thinking.

Well, if negative emotions and thoughts are an intrinsic part of human life, why are they so abhorred and determinedly avoided?

It seems that a major reason negative thoughts and emotions are so troublesome has to do with the thoughts and emotions themselves. Put in the simplest terms, negative emotions feel bad. And, intense negative emotions can feel simply awful. Since most persons would naturally prefer to feel positively about themselves and others, hostile or angry emotions feel disruptive and threatening to one's personal equilibrium and welfare.

Another, and perhaps more important reason why we denounce and renounce negative emotions has to do with the various values we have come to attach to those emotions. We have long regarded such emotions as envy, defiance, and rage as not only abnormal but somewhat immoral. Those who are discovered to harbor these feelings tend to be viewed as sinful, or at least ethically questionable. To a fair extent, our Judeo-Christian heritage has contributed to our judgmental disdain for negative emotions by instilling in us the attitude that a negative emotion or thought is equivalent to a negative or sinful deed.

In the following chapters I will attempt to explain in more detail why I think we are so perplexed, stymied, and overcome by our negative emotions. I will also suggest what we can do about it; that is, how we can convert our hostile and angry emotions into positive actions and endeavors.

At this point I would like to discuss a matter that has concerned me for many years. I have realized that most psychotherapists, including myself, attempt to assist their patients by helping them to accept the entirety of their emotions and thoughts. In other words, it is generally deemed therapeutic for psychotherapy patients to nonjudgmentally accept and come to terms with even their most vengeful and sadistic emotions and to eventually regard this "dark" side of their personalities with as little guilt as possible.

I have naturally compared this therapeutic stance with the attitudes toward the negative emotions I have observed in the larger society around me and discovered the contrast to be astonishingly sharp at times. Most people seem to dogmatically believe that sadistic, wrathful, or vengeful emotions and thoughts are inherently immoral and socially destructive. Based on this contrast, I have been forced to ask myself if I were somehow inadvertently traducing my patients into thinking and feeling in immoral ways and, thereby, causing them to be out of sync with the rest of society.

My self-doubts and concerns over this matter have, however, been clarified and allayed by my patients who have reported to me, not only feeling better, but behaving in a less hostile manner, once they had acknowledged and accepted their angry emotions in therapy.

On the basis of my clinical experiences and observations, I have reached a conclusion about the negative emotions that will serve as the central thesis of this book. It is admittedly a point of view that is not only controversial, but one that is highly subject to misinterpretation and misuse. Therefore, I will try to qualify my viewpoint as precisely as possible.

In my view, negative emotions and thoughts—e.g., rivalry, jealousy, revenge, defiance—are neither inherently evil nor inherently destructive. I believe if people could understand and non-moralistically accept their negative emotions and thoughts by placing them in their proper emotional context (i.e., by establishing their various social and personal origins), they would immeasurably enhance their potential to put their hostilities to positive personal and social use. A genuine acceptance and understanding of the dark underside of our personality can enable us to not only control negative emotions but actually transform them into a source of positive personal fulfillment.

For example, the man who had deserted his wife and child because he had been abandoned as an infant was alleviated of much of his suicidal guilt by understanding his behavior in the context of his own traumatic childhood. His guilt over the harm he was inflicting upon his family had caused him overwhelming impulses to kill himself. When he better realized that he too had been a victim of parental abandonment, he no longer felt quite so self-destructive and, although he did not soon return to his family, he was able to make genuine and significant efforts to assist them materially during his absence. In other words, he was able to use his negative emotions for positive purposes by fulfilling some of his parental responsibilities.

The woman who had been verbally abused by her father with the epithet "Pickle Puss" came to better understand the extent to which she was scarred by his mistreatment and gradually overcame much of her self-contempt and self-consciousness as a result.

The woman who had been sexually molested by her father had been for many years plagued by feelings of guilt because she irrationally blamed herself for his destructive behavior. By better grasping her own helplessness and desperation during the period of her victimization she was able to overcome much of her guilt and self-hatred. This further enabled her to improve her social relationships as well as her career prospects.

I would like to interject one important caveat before proceeding further. When I advocate that we accept, even embrace, our negative emotions and thoughts, I am not referring in the least to human *behavior*. Unquestionably, there are evil deeds, a fact to which the genocidal events of this and previous centuries will tragically attest. Without looking very long or hard we can observe immoral behavior in ubiquitous forms throughout contemporary society. The widespread physical mistreatment and denigration of children, the traditional contemptuous treatment of women in the home and workplace, the harassment and discrimination against gay and lesbian persons, and the racist treatment of ethnic minority groups are all patently immoral. As well, the tendency of a great many people to act out their jealous anger by demeaning and undercutting the needs and rights of others can well be regarded as immoral and cruel.

I do not condone or extend license for acts of insensitivity or unkindness, let alone for acts of brutality and sadism. I merely contend that a wholesome acceptance and understanding of our negative emotions and thoughts would greatly help us in our never-ending quest to overcome personal and social destructiveness.

Chapter 1

The Nature and Origins of
Negative Emotions

Negative emotions can be fired off by an infinite number of situations and events. As a psychotherapist, I am continually struck by the fact that most people enter psychotherapy at a point when an important relationship in their lives has been seriously altered, disrupted, or terminated. Why is this so?

Strong personal relationships naturally engender the most intense emotions. It is quite impossible for most people to love or care about someone else without at times feeling highly contemptuous or hateful toward that person. If we care deeply about another person, we will of course care deeply about how that person treats and feels toward us. In the course of our prolonged and intimate dealings with that person there will inevitably be times when we feel that we are being treated insensitively or unlovingly. After all, no one can or should meet all our needs, expectations, wishes, and hopes.

Mealtimes

Yet, even in the most loving relationships, friends and partners unavoidably disappoint, distress, and infuriate one another. The causes and battlegrounds for conflict can vary greatly. For example, in some families mealtimes are especially problematic. One of the family members is particular about when he or she is fed, another about how the food is prepared or seasoned, yet another about table manners, and still another about the seating arrangement at the table. Food and eating are obviously potential sources of great pleasure and enjoyment, but for many persons they are catalysts of tension and disagreeableness. For this reason, it is extremely common for people to experience their worst crises with others just prior to, during, or soon after a meal.

For example, an otherwise compatible couple reported that their recent fight erupted when he was late for dinner at the restaurant, she (in retaliation) drank too much of the house wine, and he in turn was rude to the waiter.

A woman in her early forties recalled that her father drank heavily at dinner, had slovenly table habits, and tended to hoard and eat the best portions. Although she loved her father deeply, she harbored intense feelings of resentment for the way he conducted himself at the family meals.

Jealousy

One of the most common sources of negative feelings between people relates to their respective and unequal levels of success, in terms of work, income, prestige, and love. Even the best of friends can experience powerful feelings of jealousy and competitiveness toward one another from time to time. Thus, at a time when one has perhaps inherited a large sum of money, landed an exceptionally lucrative job, published a celebrated article or book, or won in a lottery a free trip around the world, friends and relatives might in response experience powerful feelings of envy and rivalry. This is not to say that friends and relatives do not ever genuinely wish each other well. Rather, I am suggesting that side by side with the positive feelings that one's grand success might engender in others there are likely to be feelings of loss, envy, and resentment that are aroused as well.

A young attractive and quite gifted writer entered therapy severely depressed. She held a financially and emotionally rewarding job, had reasonably good relationships with her friends and her employer and seemed to have a bright future. Yet she could not overcome acute feelings of sorrow and lassitude.

In her first hour of therapy the source of her depression became palpably evident. This talented writer had a sister who was also a writer. The sister, who for many years had received no public acclaim for her literary efforts, had suddenly published a book that was very favorably reviewed and would, from all appearances, soon become a best seller. The praise and celebrity enjoyed by her sister caused this woman to experience piercingly strong feelings of loss, envy, and resentment toward her.

Unfortunately, she did not realize or appreciate that such feelings were quite natural, even predictable, under the circumstances. After all, being sisters, the two women would inevitably feel rivalrous toward each other under a wide variety of circumstances. Furthermore, since both were aspiring young writers, the stupendous success of one would unavoidably cause the other to feel diminished and depreciated, at least for a short while. However, since she profoundly admired and loved her sister, she found it painfully difficult to admit her envy and resentment toward her. Thus, she assumed that she herself was a worthless snake in the grass for having such feelings and, due to her guilt, gradually developed a hateful attitude toward herself and became depressed.

Hatred and Resentment

There is a patently mistaken viewpoint taken by many people that all parents must and do love their children. Fortunately, many, if not most, parents love their children a great deal. However, many parents, sadly, hate their children quite passionately. Most certainly, even the best parents feel hatred for their children at least every so often. There can be many reasons for the arousal of intense negative feelings on the part of parents.

One reason that even loving parents sometimes resent their offspring is the great dependency and needfulness of their children. Parents often enjoy feeling needed by and important to their children. Yet there are untold numbers of moments throughout normal childrearing that children sap and exhaust their parents' reservoirs of strength and love.

A young, talented, and creative woman explained in therapy that she wanted to have a child but could not anticipate the prospect without great trepidation. She looked forward to a promising career as a consultant to private industry and, realizing that her career would take up much of her time and energy, she wondered how it would be possible also to be a "good" mother. In addition to concerns about her personal wherewithal to care adequately for a child, she also feared the social disapproval of her peers who might look askance at a young mother who was also devoting herself to career pursuits. Thus, this woman, who possessed many warm and affectionate qualities, was beginning to dread and resent her future child who she assumed would, through its predicted needfulness, interfere with and undermine her career aspirations. Since she and her husband genuinely wanted a child, these negative emotions caused her to think of herself as a poor and unworthy candidate for motherhood and, as a result, she experienced relentless feelings of self-loathing and guilt.

Power Imbalances

The power imbalances that exist in all families often breed and ignite conflict and negative emotions among their members. Children have good reason to envy and quest for the broad and unimpeachable powers of their parents. Children, when compared to their parents, are at a decided disadvantage. They ordinarily possess much less income and earning power, have fewer legal entitlements and prerogatives, and generally possess far less physical strength and prowess than their parents. Considering the many and varied inequities that usually exist between parents and their children, it is small wonder that all children, from time to time, hate and bear grudges against their parents.

The far-reaching effects of unappeasable parental power and authority upon a child are brilliantly delineated by the great novelist Franz Kafka in his *Letter to His Father*. In this document, Kafka painstakingly explains to his father why he feels afraid and oppressed by him. Although Kafka's father admittedly seems to have been an extremely authoritarian character, in describing his anguish and remorse over his many painful dealings with the man Kafka boldly lays down some rather universal themes.

For example, Kafka alludes to the great physical stature and strength of his father, the harshness with which the haughty man disciplines him and the rigidity and self-righteousness with which his father expressed his demands and opinions to him. In reading the various criticisms Kafka levels at his father, it becomes sadly apparent that Kafka is speaking for most, if not all, children. Clearly, almost all children have experienced, at least occasionally, some of the very same attitudes toward their own parents. Most children fall prone at times to envying and despising the physical power, the methods of discipline (however benign), and the (sometimes terribly unrealistic) expectations of their parents. Since childhood is quintessentially a period of protracted and considerable helplessness, no child entirely escapes feelings of rage and jealousy toward those relatively powerful individuals who have assumed the responsibility for their care.

Conversely, even parents who raise their children with the utmost care, love, and devotion will be unable to entirely avoid feeling resentment, jealousy, and hatred toward them from time to time. Why? There are many complicated reasons for this state of affairs.

First, children are usually free of the worrisome responsibilities that are shouldered by parents, such as raising the kids, earning an income, and budgeting for an uncertain future. When parental responsibilities mount and become acute, it is only natural that parents will occasionally blame and scapegoat their children for their own plight. Although most children will undoubtedly incur a fair amount of suffering and travail before they reach adulthood, their parents will nevertheless insist that they live enviable lives and are far better off than they themselves were when they were children.

The envy displayed by parents toward their children may take many forms. For example, a father who considered his work as a waiter tedious and redundant developed an intense resentment for his seven-year-old son who, very appropriately for his age, loved to play, daydream, and tramp about with abandon. Although he loved his son dearly, this man could not help resenting the child's carefree and hedonistic existence.

In my psychotherapy practice on a college campus I repeatedly hear accounts from large numbers of young men and women about their parents' accusations that they are lazy, shiftless individuals. I have given considerable thought to these harsh and hurtful allegations. Have these people all been so remiss and irresponsible that their parents' criticisms are warranted? In many, if not most instances, the answer is an emphatic "No."

Instead, these people often carry a full academic load, hold down a full- or part-time job and, at the same time, pitch in at home by doing household chores such as shopping, washing clothes, and preparing meals. Why, then, are they so often accused of laziness by their parents? The explanation, I believe, is that many parents commonly begrudge their children fun and pleasure because their own lives are devoid of joy and fulfillment. Although they may consciously and wholeheartedly wish the best for their children, they may unconsciously dislike and envy the very fruits of their own labor: that is, their children's comfort, leisure, and enjoyment of the world around them. Thus, the moralistic judgment of laziness is imposed.

For many parents their own aging process becomes a definite source of resentful and rivalrous feelings toward their children. In the movie *The Great Santini* a highly autocratic father demands and expects athletic excellence from his son, a highly talented basketball player. Yet when his son is able to outplay and defeat him in a one-on-

one match, the results are cataclysmic. When the father is faced, not only with his son's superior athletic abilities, but with his own mortality through the stark realization that he has aged and slowed down, he ridicules and debunks his son's skills and, worse, his character. Obviously, the father, without realizing his true feelings, envied his son's youth and vigor. Although his vicious manner of expressing these emotions is rather extraordinary, I suspect his envious emotions toward his own son are hardly unique.

Obesity

In my clinical practice I have encountered many obese patients. In tracing the personal histories of these patients I have often come upon an interesting facet of their lives. Many of them, unfortunately, had parents who berated and denigrated them about their weight and appearance. Frequently, the parents called them by derogatory nicknames, attempted to police and restrict their eating habits, and generally treated them with contempt. In reporting these experiences to me these patients often interpreted their parents' actions in a highly positive and, in my view, markedly distorted light.

In their interpretations they suggested that their parents were simply concerned for their health and welfare; in other words, wanted them to be slim and trim in order to feel good about themselves and to be socially accepted. If the parents' intentions were so benevolent, I would ask, why was it that the patient did not conform to their wishes and eat more sensibly and healthfully? The usual reply was, since the patient's parents extended their "constructive" advice and guidance in such a malicious manner, the patient was forced to defy their wishes at all costs by eating aplenty.

At this point I might inquire about why, if the patient's parents truly wanted her to remain slim, they would persist in their hostile demands, demands that only served to exacerbate her eating problems. Well, the patient would reply, perhaps they simply wanted to have things their own way and having a chubby child was not their way.

After having investigated this matter carefully with many patients I have come to interpret many such situations quite differently. What these patients and I have often discovered together is that their parents were fanatically preoccupied with their own (sometimes deteriorating) physical appearance. That being the case, the slender and comely child was viewed as a rival who might draw greater positive attention to herself than the parents could realistically expect for themselves. Although most parents, fortunately, take pride and rejoice in the attractiveness of their children, these parents perceived their children as potential rivals for the affection of others.

How do parents usually treat their children when they consider them a deep threat to their narcissism?   Often, precisely the way in which many obese children are treated by their parents. The malice with which these parents harped on their children about their weight served a definite purpose. Unconsciously, the parents did not want the child to develop into a physically appealing person. Thus, they badgered and harangued the child to control her diet, while at some unconscious level understanding that, if the child were infuriated enough by their importunate demands, she would rebel by doing the opposite of her parents' verbalized wishes. The child, not understanding the parents' unconscious hostile wishes, played into their hands by overeating and undermining her own personal attractiveness. Although she might find some satisfaction in the thought that she at least had thwarted her parents' irrational demands, in fact, by overeating, she had entirely and tragically conformed to their deepest hostile wishes!

Intergenerational and Marital Rivalry

The hostile and envious emotions of parents sometimes stem from their ambivalence about the educational and intellectual betterment of their children. Those parents, however, who are doubtful or self-conscious about their own intellectual capabilities (and there are myriad such parents), may feel threatened by the intellectual and academic attainments of their children.

I have met and treated many students who have been advised by their parents, both implicitly and explicitly, that they would be much better off if they would disenroll from college and find themselves a job, any job. The parental recommendation, on first glance, seems to be largely motivated by economic considerations. Since the family is in economic straits, perhaps an additional income would improve matters considerably. And, since the student has no absolute assurance of a well-paying job after college anyway, why unnecessarily delay one's entrance into the work force?

In discussing this matter in detail with many of these students, an interesting family dynamic often surfaces. What is often uncovered is the presence of at least one parent who has suffered serious academic or professional disappointments in his or her life. In some cases, the father or mother could not attend or complete college due to the financial hardships within their family of origin. In other instances, the parent may have actually graduated from college but somehow could not find employment in his or her chosen field and, consequently, came to despise the job for which he or she was eventually hired. In still other cases, these parents had parents who themselves cared little about their kids' educational success. Because they received little encouragement or help toward intellectual and academic success during their own childhood, they set shallow or modest goals for themselves, while at the same time resenting how badly they had been shortchanged by their parents.

I have also done therapy with many students who were the first among a large extended family who had ever attended college. In some of these families there was no particular value or emphasis placed upon educational or professional attainment; as a matter of fact, often there was downright disapproval and contempt for the student's efforts at self-enhancement. Many of these students were accused by their families of being snobs and treated as pariahs for deviating from the family's anti-intellectual traditions.

We can see from the above-mentioned examples that the parental disparagement and discouragement of the educational pursuits of many students, rather than being purely motivated by economic considerations, are often inspired by feelings of envy and resentment. Many parents who felt that their own childhood wishes for educational fulfillment were thwarted, dashed, and denied, came to resent the educational promise and hopes of their own children. Pathetically, but understandably, they could not bear to allow their own children to surpass them intellectually, academically, and vocationally. Rather than take pride and pleasure in their children's scholastic attainments, they debased and derogated them.

The role of envy and revenge has been a central one in the lives of many women who, after long years of forfeiting educational opportunities due to weighty maternal and wifely responsibilities, decided to re-enter college. The more fortunate of this group received the blessings and endorsements of their husbands and children. Many, however, were subjected to quite the opposite treatment at the hands of their families.

In our sessions this latter group of women has described to me how their families have taken a belligerent stance against their enrollment in college. The children grouse that they are being woefully neglected. The husbands complain that meals are being served without their usual punctuality and savoriness, the house is a god-awful mess, and, furthermore, their wives are lousy company because they spend all their time studying and thinking about intellectual, rather than important practical matters.   And, to make matters worse, these wives are reminded that while they are "wasting their time" in college, they could be out earning a second, vital income in behalf of their family's welfare.

Sadly, a significant number of these women buckled under the pressure of their family's opposition and quit college.

A close examination of these conflictive situations revealed some interesting emotional and social factors at work. Quite frequently, those husbands who themselves had already completed college and fulfilled their professional aspirations had been quite content to have wives who were their intellectual and social inferiors. Insecure with their own accomplishments, these men preferred to rigidly retain control and dominance in their marital relationships by obstructing their wives' personal ambitions. However destructive this inequality was to the genuine happiness and welfare of the marital relationship, they feared and scorned the academic and professional strivings of their wives. The prospect of achieving a state of equity with their wives evidently threatened their fragile sense of self.

Those husbands who, for whatever reason, could not themselves attend or complete college were sometimes bitterly opposed to their wives' wishes to excel scholastically and professionally. Although they rarely based their opposition upon deep-seated feelings of envy, these men often let it be known that they wanted no upstart woman in their home outshining them intellectually and professionally. One such character was Rita's husband in the touching movie *Educating Rita*. A benighted man with limited formal education and social interests, he was affronted by Rita's passionate desire to learn and expand her visions. When he discovered that she was taking birth control pills in order to prevent a pregnancy that would jeopardize her educational ambitions, he took revenge upon her by burning her books. This act of vengeance exemplified the depth of his envy and hatred for Rita's attempts to enlighten and better herself. Envy of this kind, that is, envy over another person's intellectual progress and success commonly arises in personal relationships, although, fortunately, not usually in such extreme forms as was depicted in *Educating Rita*.

Sibling Rivalry

A favorite place for the incitement of intense envy and even murderous rage is the birth of a sibling. The relationships of children to their brothers and sisters are always tinged with feelings of rivalry and even enmity. Since so much of a child's early life is marked by an egoistic and ruthless quest to have his or her needs met, it should be no surprise that the birth of a sibling is normally experienced, even by the most stable and level-headed child, with a good degree of suspicion and resentment. Even when young children possess fond and altruistic attitudes toward their newly arrived brother or sister, inevitably they will come to view that sibling, at least at times, as an unwelcome interloper who has robbed them of some of their emotional supplies.

The death wishes of children for their siblings are commonplace, if not universal. An eight-year-old boy who had suddenly developed a school phobia entered therapy upon the recommendation of a school psychologist. There seemed to be few clues regarding the onset of this boy's phobia since he had formerly adjusted well to school and seemed to have no aversion to his teachers or classmates. What, then, was disrupting his life and frightening him so devilishly?

In our first encounter, the true nature of this child's profound anxieties became rather explicable. He displayed no apparent fear of school. When the conversation switched to his homelife, he made a passing reference to his mother's need for him to help her. With some prodding he revealed that his mother was now several months pregnant. He mentioned this fact with such stiffness and hesitancy that it was painfully obvious he was in serious conflict over her pregnancy.

I inquired into his feelings about having a younger brother or sister. His face broke into a broad mannikinlike smile and he stated with almost no warmth, "Oh, I can't wait. My mom wants me to help her take care of him" (he expected the child to be a boy). The rigid, mechanical way in which he discussed the upcoming birth of his sibling certainly belied any positive yearnings he may have had toward this event.

After meeting and discussing matters over with this boy's mother, the reasons for his phobia became even clearer. His mother could not at all acknowledge that he might experience feelings of rejection, dispossession, and hatred over sharing her with another child. Instead, she naively and one-sidedly stressed how he must and would love his brother and that he mustn't ever feel that he was not loved by her, even if she had to neglect him at times.

What induced and reinforced the boy's phobia could now be more clearly determined. Colluding with his mother's unwholesome desire that he not harbor any hostile feelings for her and her next child, the boy acted as if the forthcoming birth of a sibling would be his cause for celebration. Therefore, he stolidly disallowed and denied himself feelings of regret or fear of displacement brought on by the impending birth of his sibling.

For a short time the boy's conscious strategy worked and led to personal gratification through the glowing (and ultimately destructive) compliments he received from his mother for his "good" behavior. However, as the date of the sibling's birth drew near and his mother's pregnancy daily grew more visible and undeniable, the reality of his feelings of envy and anger became more intense and uncontainable. As he later admitted to me, he sometimes wished that his baby brother would die. This wish was often accompanied by a concomitant wish that was even more frightening to him: that his mother would die, thus preventing her from having a second child.

As is the case with many young children, the boy feared that his murderous desires would become magically fulfilled. He began to dread that he had cast a deathly spell upon his mother and her next child. After all, he thought, if his mother somehow died, he would not only have perpetrated a heinous crime, but would be left totally bereft by her loss (the father had been estranged from the family for several months). In order to prevent his murderous, magical wishes from materializing, he thought it necessary to steadfastly cling to and protect his mother. In effect, he became her ever-present and ever-dependable bodyguard against his own destructive wishes.

It was no wonder that this boy could not attend school. He had of course little fear of school per se, but suffered enormous dread over the possibility that, during his brief absences from home, his powerful matricidal and fratricidal wishes would be fulfilled and a horrible fate would befall his unwary mother. As expected, as he came to understand and accept his feelings of rage and envy for a sibling who, in his estimation, would usurp his previously exclusive relationship with his mother, this boy gradually felt less vengeful and, consequently, less fearful of leaving his mother to attend school.

Phobias and Nightmares

It is now common knowledge that almost all children experience phobias and nightmares, at least temporarily. The violent and destructive wishes that children sometimes feel for their parents can be extraordinarily terrifying to them. Children are slighted or humiliated by a parent. They go off to bed and, while trying to get some shut eye, a fleeting thought enters their mind that they would enjoy some token of revenge for the humiliation they have just suffered. Among the graphic thoughts they entertain is one that has old Dad being cooked in a pot of boiling water. If they are children who are secure and reasonably self-aware, they will realize that a thought is a thought and that, if push came to shove, they really would not cannibalize and parboil dear old Pop. But children have lively and sometimes self-punishing imaginations. When they experience a vivid patricidal or matricidal thought a helpless feeling of fear and self-hatred may overcome them. They may feel that they have gone too far. Killing someone, your own parent, for a personal slight, even if it is only in fantasy, will feel too extreme, too bizarre. Only a horrible person could have such vile, murderous thoughts, so the vulnerable child thinks.

To make matters worse, the murderous fantasy often leads, as it did in the example of the boy with the school phobia, to terrors over one's absolute and irrevocable abandonment. In the fantasy, which for the time being is the child's only subjective reality, the parent who is being killed out of feelings of revenge will no longer exist and, therefore, will no longer be there to care for and protect the child. It is no wonder that such fantasies scare the daylights out of countless children. Of course it is not only children who suffer from nightmares or phobias of this kind. For this reason, whenever I am informed by child or adult patients that they are victims of recurrent nightmares or phobias, I seek not only to uncover their intense fears, but also their hostile or murderous wishes, especially toward their loved ones.

Gossip

Jealousy and resentment obviously reign as important emotions in every walk of life, including close friendships. Such emotions also serve as the basis and impetus for one of friendship's favorite pastimes: gossip. Even a cursory observation of the personal conversations in which many individuals engage will reveal how much envy and hostility play a central role.

When many social conversations turn to the subject of one's employment, usually much ado is made over the poor working conditions at the office, the scant wages, and the boss's rotten temperament and personality. For good measure, there is usually a scathing diatribe against some of one's co-workers who are described as a bunch of airheads and malingerers.

When the conversation moves on to the subject of mutual friends and acquaintances the level of venom and hostility may escalate considerably. The connubial conflicts and ultimate divorce of Joe and Mary Smith (the couple who always put on a happy face at neighborhood parties), the Hardings' new, overpriced car, the drug abuse and eventual suicide of the Does' son, John, and the million-dollar malpractice suit against Dr. Swindle, who was caught seducing one of his patients, are all grist for the hostility mill of social gossip. Although one may detect some genuine regret and empathy in these conversations for the hapless victims of misfortune, if one listens closely, it is likely that one will also discern strong subterranean attitudes of anger and sadism.

What form do they take? "Those Smiths were such phonies, always pretending to be so happy and better off than the rest of us. And those Hardings, so pretentious in their new car. Now look at them. The car has been totaled and they have to drive their old jalopy. Serves them right. As far as the suicide of John Doe is concerned, what a tragedy, but you just knew the Does were going to have trouble with their son, coddling and overprotecting him all the time. And, as far as Dr. Swindle is concerned, that malpractice suit couldn't have happened to a better guy. Always ogling the women, it serves him right. Let him pay for his sleaze by losing his license and medical practice."

The point of this example is not to suggest that people are inherently or entirely vicious in their attitudes toward others. Rather, it is to suggest that one of the purposes of gossip, one of our favorite pastimes, is to give vent to hostile and vindictive emotions. In the case of the victims who appeared in the above-mentioned hypothetical example, we can detect that they were most likely persons who had been greatly envied or disliked by the gossipmongers prior to their grievous mishaps.

During the course of almost any day the average person accumulates a wide assortment of annoyances and grudges, many of which are triggered by unpleasant encounters with other individuals. Since it is usually impossible to resolve each and every setback and disappointment we experience during the course of the day, our emotions in response to these events intensify, sometimes to the bursting point. Gossip serves as a handy outlet for these feelings.

Revenge

The wish for revenge can be observed in a wide variety of settings and situations. Drivers will note that when they have just been passed by a speeding vehicle they often fervently hope the speedster will be stopped and ticketed by the highway patrol. Why? Well, if a person is generally law abiding, he or she will want others to reasonably conform to the law as well. But there is another dynamic at work: jealousy. When we see another driver breaking the law with impunity we often feel that we ourselves would like be such lawless daredevils, providing of course that we do not get caught. It then irks us that someone else can "get away with murder" while we have to pay the price (in longer commuting time) for conforming to the law. It is no surprise, then, that we gloat when two miles later we find the lawbreaker at the side of the road, parked in front of a patrol car, where he or she is receiving a citation. The capture and punishment of this individual serve two emotional purposes for gloating onlookers. First, it satisfies their need for revenge. Second, it relieves them of much of their jealousy since they no longer feel that the lawbreaker has immunity from the legal authorities.

Feelings of jealousy and revenge are often aroused in relation to persons who are in positions of social authority in our society. It is for this reason, I believe, that persons like myself, who work in the psychotherapy profession, are so frequently asked, "Don't you have your own emotional problems? How can you help others when you have problems of your own? Besides, I know you shrinks have higher rates of alcoholism and suicide than the general population. How do you explain that?" Such questions, in themselves, are obviously quite valid and legitimate and, therefore, deserve responsible explanations.

However, it is important and interesting to note that those persons who raise these relevant questions almost always do so with ill-concealed sarcasm, animosity, and contempt. I have often asked myself why so many people are so angrily determined to establish the obvious, that is, that psychotherapists are human beings with emotional problems that are sometimes so serious they must tragically resort to drinking excessively or killing themselves. Perhaps part of the answer lies in the overly detached and condescending behavior of some members of the psychotherapy profession. Such behavior would naturally arouse widespread resentment amongst the general public. However, I think that is a simplistic and fragmentary explanation.

On a deeper level, the angry challenge leveled at the questionable emotional stability of mental health professionals stems primarily from feelings of jealousy and rivalry. It begins with an unrealistic viewpoint that psychotherapists are infallible persons who possess "all the answers" and live emotionally unblemished lives. Once having been put on such a lofty and precarious pedestal by others, the psychotherapist becomes not only an object of their awe and admiration, but is of course also viewed with a good degree of envy and contempt.

This admixture of emotions is explained by the fact that human beings seem generally quite unable to idealize others without also feeling considerable jealousy and rage for the imagined omniscience, mightiness, and sterling success of those they ostensibly admire. Thus, whenever some psychotherapist is discovered to have toppled from his or her imaginary pedestal into, for example, alcoholism or suicide, there will be some individuals who will inevitably welcome this tragic news with sadistic gratification. Unmistakable hallmarks of this gratification will be such comments as, "That Dr. X. He considered himself such an expert about other people. Considering the fact that he drank heavily and committed suicide, I'd say he couldn't have been much of a therapist. It goes to show you, those therapists are worse off than the rest of us. We're better off staying away from them and dealing with our personal problems on our own." Such comments undisguisedly reveal vengeful and sadistic emotions that have been gratified by the personal downfall of one (the therapist) who had formerly been held both in overly high regard and contempt. By the way, it might at this juncture be apropos to point out that it is exactly this admixture of idealization and jealousy that seems to account for the stalking and assassination of celebrities by their idolatrous devotees that are occasionally chronicled in sensational newspaper stories.

Contempt

The emotions of envy, resentment, and contempt are also commonly directed at persons who occupy the lower end of the social and economic spectrum. For example, the subject of social welfare recipients seems to greatly rile large numbers of people. If one listens only superficially to heated social conversations and debates about public welfare recipients, one might be inclined to think that the source of so much rancor and argumentation over this subject is largely and indisputably economic in nature. After all, the average welfare recipient is repeatedly characterized as a costly, parasitic social dreg that is wantonly draining our national resources at the expense of the rest of us.

Closer examination of these discussions, however, will reveal a considerable range of emotional factors at work. The discussants will moralistically refer to the alleged or real sexual promiscuity of many welfare recipients and to their sometimes overlarge and expensive families. Moral outrage and indignation is further fueled by the fact that the average welfare recipient does not engage in conventional or gainful employment. In other words, receiving public monies (under the federal program called Aid to Families with Dependent Children) for the difficult work of raising young children is not considered legitimate or substantive employment.

I think most people will concede that the daily life of the average welfare recipient is dreary, humiliating, tenuous and, most definitely, unenviable. Most of us who are fortunate enough to have regular work and a decent income would not of course willingly exchange places with those disadvantaged persons who barely subsist on the welfare roles. Why, then, are we not more sympathetic and charitable in our attitudes toward these particular unfortunate souls? Again, we cannot attribute the general lack of sympathy for them simply to the cost of their care since most people do not bemoan and begrudge the costs of caring for other kinds of unfortunate persons, such as the retarded, blind, physically disabled, and aged. No, the welfare recipient is despised primarily for another reason: (as odd as it sounds) envy.

I said in the above paragraph that the life of the average welfare recipient is unenviable and that is generally and undeniably true. However, let us attend closely to the public's two principal complaints about the welfare recipient, namely that she is sexually promiscuous and, to put it politely, not very work-oriented. Why should these particular characteristics of the welfare of the welfare recipient, whether true or imagined, enrage so many people? The complicated and, to many people, disagreeable answer is that the alleged sexual promiscuity and indolence of the welfare recipient mirrors some of the deepest desires of a great many people.

It should not really be difficult for anyone to realize that sexual promiscuity, as unrewarding and dangerous as it often is, arouses the feverish curiosity, interest, excitement, and envy of vast numbers of people. The pornography industry and the enormously popular television soap operas of course thrive primarily on the basis of the vicarious sexual pleasure and dissoluteness of their viewers. Considering, then, the paramount significance that so many persons attach to sex and sexual freedom, it is perfectly understandable that a great many individuals will inevitably resent and envy the welfare recipient, who is perceived to be sexually self-indulgent and uninhibited.

As for the supposed indolence and laziness of the average welfare recipient, we need not search far to understand how they may arouse the resentment and jealousy of others. The search for leisure and idleness is a favorite among a great many persons. Most people look eagerly toward their weekends and vacations for respite from their work. As well, they often anticipate and plan for their retirement years with a good deal of relish, happily looking toward a time when they will finally be disencumbered of toilsome and obligatory labor. When they consider that the welfare recipient already does not work, at least not in the conventional nine-to-five sense, they quickly forget the recipient's generally squalid life, irrationally envy her "leisure" and, consequently, puritanically judge her to be an immoral being. Thus, as strange as it may sometimes seem, we may envy and resent even those who occupy a lower, less fortunate, social and economic position than ourselves.

Thwarted Dreams

Finally, feelings of envy, revenge, and rage can quite naturally emanate from having serious hurdles and roadblocks placed before one's most cherished dreams and desires. Since personal health is usually a matter of urgent and foremost importance to each individual, illnesses, surgical operations, and physical injuries can deliver serious blows to one's sense of self and thereby evoke strong feelings of rage and resentment.

A man who was a highly ranked handball player came to therapy after suffering a mild injury to his back. He was waylaid by the injury for only a few weeks and, although his prognosis was excellent, he fell into an acute, albeit short-lived, depression. The pride, pleasure, and social recognition he had for years acquired from playing excellent handball were suddenly ripped away and he simply couldn't cope with the resultant loss of self-esteem. Until he returned to his former health and athletic capabilities, he greatly envied and resented the men with whom he had been competing.

Sickness and Death

A woman I had known professionally for many years was a standout for her extraordinary warmth, positive regard for others, and joy for living. After not having had contact with her for several years, I called her about a professional matter. She immediately screamed at me on the phone, belligerently demanded to know what I wanted and then announced that she was dying of cancer. The vehemence of her rage and bitterness was at first incomprehensible and overwhelming to me and left me practically speechless. Unmistakably and tragically, her disease in her last days (she died only two days after my call) had irrevocably transformed her personality. She reacted to my call in a manner that was proportionate to the horror she undoubtedly felt over her own imminent death, and, therefore, it was simply impossible for her to speak to an old friend without lashing out wrathfully and pathetically.

The friends and loved ones of a sick or dying patient will also experience considerable anger and resentment during the course of the patient's illness. Seriously ailing patients ordinarily demand and require a great deal of attention and sensitivity from those to whom they are emotionally attached. From time to time their demands are likely to become quite irrational and inordinate. Because seriously ill patients sometimes make extreme and impossible demands, their needs cannot be fully met. As a result, they may cantankerously lash out at their loved ones. Or, in anger, they may withdraw from them and seek revenge for their abysmal plight by sulking and spurning their solicitous efforts.

For these reasons, the care and comforting of a seriously ill or dying loved one is almost always an emotionally devastating experience. And, to further complicate matters, part of what makes the experience so devastating are the feelings of rage, resentment, and hatred that both the illness and the deterioration in the personality of the patient wreak in those who love him or her.

Since so few people understand that anger and resentment are natural reactions to the impending or actual loss of a loved one, they often feel extremely guilty for having such emotions and, as a result, think themselves wicked individuals. Their sense of personal wickedness is of course compounded by their adherence to the powerful social taboo that morally denounces feelings of hatred for those we love, especially when they are ill, helpless, or dying. The sense of entrapment that many people experience within this vicious circle of hatred and guilt, as they courageously strive to care for their ailing loved one, unfortunately, often ends with their suffering severe depression when the feelings of rage eventually and destructively turn inward.

This problem was pervasively shared by a group of spouses and relatives of hospitalized Alzheimer's patients to whom I spoke not very long ago. Because of the shattering effects of this relentless disease upon the patients, these deeply caring and committed relatives were, without exception, grief stricken and forlorn. As we discussed their feelings toward the patients there was, as expected, a rapid and effusive outpouring of acknowledgments of their affection, love, and commitment for their loved ones. This was only natural and entirely expected.

When, however, I inquired about the possibility that they might also harbor more negative emotions at times for their beloved relatives, the group evinced a palpable chilliness and aversion toward discussing such an unpalatable topic. Some members of the group visibly bristled and one in particular thought I was snidely suggesting that they did not genuinely love their diseased relatives.

I stated that I was suggesting just the opposite. Since the group was so devoted to their relatives, it seemed likely that they would sometimes feel worn out by their diligent caretaking, frustrated and aggrieved by the always worsening condition of their loved ones and, therefore, at times they might certainly experience angry and resentful emotions. At first, the group rather forcefully resisted this notion, avidly proclaiming that their love for their grievously ill relatives did not at all permit them feelings of anger and resentment.

I pointed out to the group that it was perhaps possible that they were forced to suppress and deny some of their angry feelings because the Alzheimer's patients were so tragically damaged by their illness it might seem cruel or evil to harbor any negative emotions about them. Yet, I added, it didn't seem humanly possible to me that a person who cared deeply for someone else could watch that person day after day increasingly lose his or her faculties and connection to reality without feeling a profound sense of fury over such a tragedy.

I found it interesting and significant that, as the group discussion proceeded, more and more members began to admit, quite hesitantly at first, that they indeed sometimes felt that the long vigils with their relatives were undermining their own physical and mental health. A few were even able to share brief anecdotes about their Alzheimer's relatives that illustrated quite graphically how infuriating the care-taking experience had become. One stalwart firmly held out against even the faintest possibility of anger entering into the picture. Not surprisingly, she experienced much guilt and endured a particularly acute depression throughout her husband's illness and, sadly, even well beyond his tragic death.

We can see from the examples in this chapter that the sources of the negative emotions—anger, rage, resentment, jealousy, revenge, and defiance—are virtually limitless. The inequalities of power and authority in relationships, the obstacles and setbacks encountered in pursuit of our fondest hopes, physical illnesses in ourselves and our loved ones, and the appreciable success of those we dislike (or like), are among the many sources of our rage, contempt, and envy.

Let us now take up some of the ways that these emotions can be effectively addressed, alleviated, and used for personal benefit and growth.

Turning Points

In almost all human conflicts there is a turning point or watershed moment that serves to instigate or inflame hostile emotions. The turning point might be a subtle form of behavior that is perceived as offensive or dismissive, such as when a person ignores or misunderstands us. Or, it might be a more serious form of mistreatment, such as when someone accuses another of being a liar, malingerer, or clod. A natural reaction to such behavior is to feel hurt and angry and, if our anger becomes excessively intense, to lash out with frothy barbs and accusations.

Let us consider the various options to a screaming match that may escalate into prolonged warfare and serious mutual hatefulness.

Consider the pivotal point at which your anger and resentment were aroused. When did you first become angry, and why? For obvious reasons this may not be possible or even desirable to determine at the very beginning of an interpersonal conflict because our emotions are already running quite high and, therefore, don't permit reflection and restraint. Thus, we may prefer to have the temporary gratification of ventilating our hostile feelings and seeing our "adversary" squirm under fire.

However, if at some point in the conflict we can gain a more precise sense of when and why we became angry, this insight might increase the constructive alternatives available to use. First, it will enable us to express our feelings and thoughts more articulately about the issues that are at stake. Rather than shouting irrationally and unintelligibly about our hatred and sense of injury, we can enable our "adversary" and ourselves to clearly identify why we have become enraged. After all, it is not likely that people in heated disagreement with one another will be able to resolve their differences unless or until they can first identify the issues that divide and estrange them.

Timing

Once having identified the pivotal moment of the interpersonal conflict, what is the ideal time to discuss the reasons we are angry with another person? To be realistic, we must acknowledge that the best time to discuss our resentments toward another person varies from situation to situation and from individual to individual. Despite this variability, however, there are some useful guidelines to consider.

If our negative emotions have reached such a crescendo that there is little likelihood of our expressing them with reasonable clarity, directness, and purpose, it is probably well to postpone the verbal expression of such feelings. However, it is important to recognize that one does not have to express feelings as if they were being adjudicated before the Supreme Court of the United States. In other words, it may be a mistake to wait for a time when angry feelings can be expressed only with supreme logic, calm, methodicalness, and depth of knowledge. Many persons who indefinitely await such illusory moments are often disappointed with the results.

Postponing the expression of negative emotions may provide the advantage of allowing people time to collect their thoughts and identify their primary objectives before addressing a conflict with another person. Thus, this may be a desirable course of action. However, many people find that, by overly postponing the expression of negative feelings, their hostility continues to smolder and burgeon. If this happens, their feelings of hostility may become so intense, sadistic, and guilt-inducing that they are left with little choice but to socially withdraw and wallow in depression. If a person discovers that this is the result of his or her having too long silenced their angry emotions, it is most certainly a signal to take a different course of action. Such a person doubtlessly would benefit more from expressing the intense feelings in some form toward the person who angers them or, if this is not wise or feasible, it might be best to talk the matter over with a psychotherapist.

Expectations

It is quite common for people to be confused over what they truly want from themselves and from others when they are angry. Many individuals want nothing more or less than revenge when provoked by others. Consequently, when they engage in hostile encounters their chief objective is to humiliate, shame, torment, and vanquish their foe. Such persons may indeed derive temporary sadistic gratification from their onslaughts upon others, but it is unlikely that either they or their victims will ever resolve or be edified by their conflicts.

Although winning an argument or outwitting and humiliating someone toward whom we feel angry can sometimes feel uplifting, our vindictive purposes often prevent us from genuinely resolving our hostility. After all, most people do not seem to genuinely enjoy inflicting hostility and emotional pain upon others. Therefore, when the purpose of expressing anger is solely to tell someone off and make the other person suffer remorse or anguish, it is quite possible to incur a backlash of guilt after unleashing great hostility.

It is of course quite possible that someone has treated us so shabbily that a good tongue-lashing and comeuppance is exactly what he or she deserves. It is important to face the fact that there are in this world individuals who are very mendacious, devious, exploitative, and ruthless. Many such individuals do not respond positively to the goodwill, appeals to reason, and respect with which they are treated. Instead, they consider such altruistic efforts on our part to be ludicrous, contemptible, and a sign of weakness. Thus, they use the trust we place in them to further fulfill their selfish aims. In the process, we may unwittingly become manhandled and duped while trying to reach a friendly accord with such people.

If we have exhausted all efforts to reach such a person through kindness and goodwill, it may be high time to switch tactics. With such individuals it may be necessary to exhibit much more forcefulness and intransigence than we are accustomed to showing.

For example, a woman who has been beaten and degraded by an alcoholic husband for many years may have tried to reform her spouse by appealing to his sense of responsibility and love for her. He, in response, makes heartfelt promises to her about giving up drinking and abusing her, all of which he abrogates only moments later. In such a situation, it is obvious that the woman's anger toward her husband, if it is to have constructive value, will need to be channeled into setting strict limits with him. Expressing anger through setting limits might, for example, take the form of issuing an ultimatum that establishes that continued drinking and abuse will result in a separation or divorce, as well as the possibility of an arrest and legal action. Obviously, for many people in such situations, taking such drastic and forceful actions will not come easily. However, if the purpose of demonstrating patience and compliance toward a man who for many years drinks heavily and physically abuses his spouse is to help and reform him for the sake of the marriage, this modus vivendi is obviously not working and needs to be reconsidered and changed.

Asserting Anger

If one is living in such an oppressive, degrading circumstance as I just described but feels helpless to express anger or take assertive measures, it is probably wise to seek legal and psychological assistance.

In any case, what I am pointing out here is the need for some people to use their anger toward those who are extremely abusive toward them by enlisting the help of available law enforcement, legal, and psychological services. Sometimes the threat of using such interventions will in itself bring about a halt to the abuse. However, if threats in themselves do not work, then they may need to be carried out, whatever the consequences.

Persons who are angry over living in chronically abusive situations should ask themselves, "What is the purpose of withholding my anger? Is it to reform or remake the abuser? Will this tack end the abuse? And, has my previous means of handling my anger been effectively fulfilling my goals?" Being able to answer these questions with clarity and conviction should enable a person to consider how to express anger effectively in future situations of interpersonal disharmony and conflict.

The value and purpose of expressing anger toward other individuals should necessarily depend upon the responses we receive from them. If our sole purpose in expressing anger is to affect and change others, we tend thereby to limit our options. Selectively and constructively expressing anger can, in itself, lead to increased self-respect, self-esteem, and confidence, regardless of how other individuals tend to react. Why?

First, as suggested earlier, when angry thoughts and feelings remain unexpressed they sometimes grow more intense and troublesome. Consequently, the mere expression of angry emotions (under safe circumstances) may give certain individuals an opportunity to hear for themselves what their angry thoughts and feelings sound like when out in the open. This not only gives them a better chance to view their hostile feelings with greater clarity but there is a good possibility that, once having expressed their hostile emotions to someone who is sensitive and nonjudgmental (such as a therapist), they will no longer consider these feelings to be quite so fiendish and reprehensible as they once believed.

Second, there seems to be a certain self-validation and consolation that accompanies the expression of angry emotions irrespective of how others respond. People sometimes feel better after expressing negative emotions simply because, in doing so, they gain physical and emotional relief. The relief they feel often finds expression in the form of illustrative clichés such as, "I'm glad I got that out of my system," or "It sure feels good to get that off my shoulders." Thus, it is quite common for a person who has safely and candidly expressed negative feelings to view them as less of an emotional burden.

To whom should one express negative emotions? This is a tricky question that must be answered carefully. Naturally, there is an inclination to express anger immediately toward the individual who has caused this feeling. One might easily think this to be the quickest and most straightforward means of resolving negative emotions. Telling another person how and why he or she has angered us may enable us to feel less helpless and vulnerable in relation to that person. Quite possibly, our expression of anger will help that person "see the light" and take corrective action by curbing injurious or offensive behavior in the future.

By taking up our angry feelings principally with the individual who has aroused them we are of course addressing one of the root causes of our anger. For this reason, our angry emotions often dissipate soon after we have effectively expressed them to that person.

However, I would like to provide the reader with an important caveat: *It is crucial that we understand and anticipate the behavior of the person toward whom we are angry.* There are several reasons why it may be unwise, unnecessary, or even self-destructive to direct our negative emotions toward the individual who has angered us.

First, a person who is angered by someone who possesses far greater physical, intellectual, emotional, or economic power may be unable to safely express angry emotions toward that individual due to a realistic fear of reprisal or retaliation. Small children, for example, are often stymied in their attempts to express negative emotions by the large imbalance of power that exists in their relationships with their parents. If they disagree with their parents' policies or viewpoints they may be bullied or belittled by superior intellectual arguments or physical threats. As we know, many irate and vengeful parents react to the anger of their children by physically hurting and punishing them.

If we have determined that it is reasonably safe and constructive to share our negative emotions with the person who has aroused them, it is probably advisable to take advantage of this opportunity and, for better or worse, face the consequences of our choice. However, if we have deemed it unsafe or unwise to express our hostile feelings toward the individual who has inspired our ire, there are many other possible options available to us.

For example, it is quite common for people to share their daily woes with sympathetic friends. A friend who reliably and sensitively understands our angry feelings can be a marvelous safety valve for our inflamed emotions. Of course, even the best of friends may not be able to tolerate an interminable barrage of angry complaints and grumbling; therefore, in the interest of your friendship it is probably best to first gauge how much your friend is able and willing to absorb your negative emotions before unbosoming yourself.

Although friends and family are often sensitive listeners and helpmates, they may, unfortunately, at times be inept or judgmental when responding to your intense angry emotions. Sometimes, in their zeal to help a friend or family member in distress they may unwittingly impart faulty information and advice that only complicates matters. If a person has had repeated disappointments as a result of sharing negative emotions with friends and family it is probably time to talk matters over with a competent psychotherapist. Psychotherapists are trained to listen attentively, minutely, and nonjudgmentally to the unsettling experiences and negative emotions of their patients. Consequently, those who have been plagued by nagging, recurrent hostile feelings that cannot be resolved through their discussions with personal friends or family members would do well to consult a therapist who can provide the psychological support and understanding they require.

Of course, it may at times be difficult or counterproductive to express negative emotions toward those who are emotionally, intellectually, physically, or economically weaker than ourselves. If we possess appreciable personal power over another individual we then also possess the capacity to easily inflict pain and harm on that person through our expressions of anger. If we repeatedly hurt others with our hostile emotions we would do well to ask ourselves, "Was my display of anger justifiable and, if not, why do I go on causing pain to others?"

A clear answer to this question may enable the angry individual to carefully determine how, when, and to whom he or she should express anger in the future. In general, however, it is sensible as well as humane to modulate or temper one's angry feelings when dealing with a person who is considerably weaker—e.g., psychologically, physically, economically—than oneself in order to prevent anger from escalating into actual sadism.

Readers are now urged to take note of one additional factor when considering which individuals will be the recipients of their angry emotions: the psychological phenomenon known as displacement. By displacement I am referring to the tendency of the individual to direct angry (and other) thoughts and emotions that have been aroused by certain persons, not onto those persons themselves, but to others who, by sheer happenstance, are more or less incidental to those thoughts and emotions.

Because we are often preoccupied and discombobulated by intense angry emotions we tend to lose sight of how they were provoked in the first place. As a result, we often direct our pain and anger onto individuals who serve our emotional needs for a convenient scapegoat. For example, a teenage friend of one of my patients behaves in a nasty and accusatory manner toward her girlfriends whenever her relationship with her boyfriend goes awry. Because she fears disrupting or losing her relationship with him, she tightly harnesses the anger she sometimes feels for him and then deflects and unleashes it upon her various girlfriends. Needless to say, her girlfriends are often quite baffled and miffed by her inexplicable and unwarranted behavior.

Because the tendency to scapegoat others is so prevalent and destructive to relationships, it is generally helpful, when we are angry, to pause a moment to determine whether the person toward whom we wish to express our anger is the true cause of our hostility. Or, are we perhaps feeling angry because of the thoughtless deeds of other persons, including those who most deeply affected us during our childhood? A few moments' reflection may enable us to accurately assess who it is that is actually arousing our anger. This may enable us to avoid using others as human pincushions for our angry frustrations.

If we have belatedly discovered that we have abusively displaced our anger onto an unsuspecting and defenseless individual, hopefully our basic sense of decency and humanity will impel us to repair the harm we have done with an apology, explanation, or some other gesture of goodwill.

Chapter 2

The Effect of Negative Emotions upon Human Behavior

Hostility, rage, defiance, and resentment affect human behavior in a multitude of forms, both subtle and blatant. Let us consider some of them.

Certainly, fatigue, ennui, and listlessness can often be related to suppressed feelings of rage. Of course, lack of sleep and overwork can also lead to physical enervation and immobility. There are, however, many moments in our lives when we have good reason to believe that our physical exhaustion and malaise have psychological roots.

Feigned and Actual Fatigue

Let us consider the simple example of yawning. We yawn when we are tired, of course. If we yawn in the company of someone else, we ask to be excused. Why? Because yawning in someone else's face is generally considered rude. Why? Because our yawn might be construed as emblematic of a lack of interest in or involvement with that other person. Worse, it might be viewed, accurately or not, as a sign that we have become bored or annoyed with the other person's company. Since that is most likely true or we would not have desperately gasped for air in the first place, we must disguise our lack of interest with a glib excuse that the hour is late. The hour may be late, but you may have also noticed that when the conversation rolled around to a topic that especially interested you, you perked up immediately and stopped yawning.

I have observed this very same behavior during psychotherapy sessions with some of my patients. They enter the hour with complaints about lack of sleep, fidget and yawn ostentatiously, and, at the same time, offer all these blatant signs of fatigue as impressive evidence of their general physical decrepitude. Despite the abundant evidence of a sleepless night, I almost always regard this behavior as a form of angry resistance. It is not that such patients are pretending to be tired. They are tired! However, the fatigue often masks and serves as a rationalization for underlying feelings of anger and defiance. My perception of this phenomenon is usually borne out by what occurs when I interpret the yawning and fidgeting as a kind of anxious or angry resistance. The patient will become even more anxious, but also more awake and alive to our interactions. Often, the sleepiness will dissipate almost immediately and the patient will become remarkably motivated and mobilized for therapeutic work.

A psychiatric consultant with whom I met regularly many years ago almost always began our meetings with a pointed reference to his having burned the candle until very late the previous night and thereby lost valuable hours of sleep. He would then yawn repeatedly and flamboyantly as if in deference to the significance of his pronouncement.

This consultant was relatively new to the agency in which I worked. It was evident that he was anxious and hypersensitive over his role as an important psychiatric expert and authority in an agency he hardly knew. He covered his professional insecurities, it seemed to me, with pretenses of excessive fatigue and overwork. Although I was often annoyed by his ostentatious yawning and bellyaching about his lack of sleep, I considered it best to ignore his behavior. As time passed, so did the consultant's constant yawning and Homeric attempts to stay awake. As he became more familiar and comfortable with the agency, he felt less anxious and, in my view, must less resistive to our meetings. Although he continued to burn the midnight oil throughout his tenure in the agency, he gradually gave up the wearisome posturing that he had been using as a defense against feelings of insecurity and hostility.

A man who entered therapy shortly after the dissolution of his marriage complained of chronic depression. During his initial session with me he recollected his childhood years as being bleak and filled with painful adversity. His parents divorced when he was an infant and his mother remarried a man who constantly tyrannized him until he finally left home at the age of sixteen. Shortly before leaving home, he entered into a violent argument with his stepfather. He then sped to his room, loaded a shotgun and went in deadly search of his quarry. He was convinced, he told me, that he would have certainly killed his step-father had it not been for his mother's last-minute intervention.

In discussing with this man his feelings of murderous rage and resentment for his stepfather, he assured me that he had completely gotten over all those nasty feelings and hardly ever felt angry about anything anymore. He seemed to take beatific pride in his outward equanimity and always made it clear to me that he thought I should compliment him for his amazing self-control. I pointed out to him, much to his disappointment and annoyance, that I saw nothing especially commendable about such excessive inhibition and disavowal of angry emotions. Furthermore, I thought his inability to acknowledge his wrath without also feeling severe pangs of guilt had a great deal to do with his long-standing depression. He often responded to comments of this kind by giggling mirthlessly and withdrawing.

It was obvious to me, given this man's tormented childhood, that he would have deep and volcanic feelings of rage, not only for his brutal and authoritarian stepfather, but for other persons in his current life who, in his mind, represented or replicated this despicable man. His present work and earlier military experiences gave undeniable evidence of exactly this kind of difficulty with authority figures.

In his job in a large corporation he was highly anxious, timid, and deferential toward his supervisors and administrative superiors. He acutely dreaded criticism and considered himself praiseworthy for toadying and tightly conforming to the wishes of the higher-ups in the company. However, it was his earlier experience in the military that dramatically brought his emotional conflicts and fury to light.

While in the military, the patient was assigned to guard duty in an isolated area of a base. Several times he involuntarily fell asleep while on duty, but each time his dereliction of duty went undetected. Finally, one evening he was discovered asleep while on duty, summarily reported to the military authorities, and later court-martialed. His attorney referred him to a psychiatrist on the base who evaluated him and subsequently reported his condition to the court. For reasons that were unclear to the patient, he was medically diagnosed as having the condition known as narcolepsy, which is characterized by a transient, compulsive tendency to attacks of deep sleep. He soon after received a medical discharge from the service. The patient stated that he was never told whether the condition was organic or psychological in nature, although medical tests turned up no apparent neurological or physiological basis for his sleep proneness.

The patient further reported that he had never before or since been afflicted with such a strange symptom. I asked him to tell me more about his attitude toward his stint in the military service. He told me that he categorically hated every moment of his military enlistment, finding the entire experience to be excruciatingly oppressive and dispiriting.

"In other words, you hated it and wanted to defy it," I nutshelled. The patient again acknowledged that he had passionately hated his military experience, but, as expected, he assumed a very puzzled and unfriendly attitude toward the idea that he might have somehow defied the demands and orders of the military authorities. He asked to know why I thought him "guilty" of possessing defiant emotions and thoughts.

"Well," I said, "you never suffered from narcolepsy before or after your period of enlistment. You hated the military for its authoritarianism. To make matters worse, the whole vile experience must have reminded you of the sadistic authoritarianism of your step-father whom we both know you despised. You certainly did not want your angry and defiant feelings to be recognized and punished by the military authorities, so you unconsciously disguised them in the form of catnaps that, on the surface, looked fairly innocent. But, if we take a closer look at your selective 'narcolepsy,' we can see that it was an ideal way to get back at the military. They gave you an objectionable order to stand guard duty and you fell asleep. Yet, who can justifiably accuse you of being pissed off and defiant when, after all, it's only a matter of your having taken a brief, harmless nap—caused by narcolepsy, no less?"

Understandably, the patient was not delighted with my attributing to him such hostile and defiant thoughts. Nevertheless, given the life history of the patient and the specific circumstances in which his "narcolepsy" recurred, my interpretation of his behavior in the military service seemed entirely warranted. As the patient made further headway in the therapy, he himself was able to point out various other ways in which he behaviorally disguised powerful feelings of anger and defiance.

Forgetfulness

Along with physical fatigue and sleepiness, another common behavioral means of expressing hostility is chronic or intermittent forgetfulness. In the following discussion of this matter I of course assume that a condition of dementia is not operative.

Forgetting the car keys, a doctor's appointment, important textbooks, or a well-known friend's name can usually be traced to aversive or hostile feelings toward these particular persons, obligations, or activities.

Although we strongly prefer to attribute our occasional forgetfulness purely to distraction or lazy thinking, there are, nevertheless, good reasons to consider the possibility that feelings of defiance are sometimes at work when we forget an obligation or experience.

A common example of forgetfulness that puts parents and their children at loggerheads begins with the rather innocuous request that the garbage be taken out. The child verbally agrees to remove the smelly stuff right away and then sits snugly down to watch television. Twenty minutes later the parent again inquires of her child whether the garbage has been removed and is told, "Oh, sorry, forgot to do it." Another heartfelt promise is made to remove the garbage posthaste and is again mysteriously forgotten almost at once. Later, another, more petulant, inquiry about garbage removal leads to the same response: "Oh, sorry, I forgot. In a minute."

What is happening on the emotional level during this interchange between parent and child? Quite apparently, the child does not want to take out the garbage: now, later, or ever. This is perfectly understandable since only rather exceptional and dubious characters actually enjoy carrying garbage from one place to another. However, the child does not openly admit or express his defiance over the request that is made of him. Instead, he first verbally agrees to comply and then, in a quick turnabout, behaviorally defies the parental expectation. The overtly compliant behavior conceals and belies his true feelings that, if put into words, might run as follows: "Go to hell, I don't want to handle that shit. You take it out!"

Since such direct and explicit expression of authentic negative emotions might very well lead to certain unwelcome consequences, such as the imposition of early curfews or a chop to the back of the head, the child remains polite, promises to carry out the chore, and then blithely watches television instead. Eventually, the parent may intuit the child's feelings of defiance simply by noting the incompletion of the chore and, in retaliation, storm at the child for "forgetting" his responsibilities. By this time she has been angered by the realization that her child is treating her with passive but genuine contempt. As we can see from this example, forgetting our promises, responsibilities, and commitments, can be strongly linked to feelings of resentment, anger, and defiance.

Several years ago, a social acquaintance related to me a rather funny story about an embarrassing gaffe he had committed in his relationship with his wife. He and his wife had originally met at a summer camp and, after a whirlwind courtship, they became engaged. When they returned to the city, they arranged to meet for lunch, just prior to a visit with his prospective in-laws.

After lunch, as they were strolling arm in arm down one of the city thoroughfares, this man noticed in the distance one of his old chums coming toward them. He had not seen or spoken to this friend since he had left for summer camp, so he realized that he would have some quick explaining to do. Complicating matters somewhat was the fact that this particular friend was an enthusiastic matchmaker who had in the past arranged several dates for him. The thought now entered his mind that his friend might somehow ignore the presence of his fiancée and launch into a full-scale rundown of the available and referable women with whom he had recently become acquainted.

To avert a scandalous scene, he decided that the best tack would be to immediately alert his chum to the serious nature of his relationship with the woman on his arm. So, taking the bull by its proverbial horns, he stepped up to his pal and said, "Bob, I want you to meet my fiancée. This is   ." To his dismay, he had suddenly forgotten his fiancée's name. I don't know how he eventually salvaged the relationship with his then fiancée from the ruins of this hilarious debacle, but since he was telling me this story when he had already been married to her over twenty years, I assume his untimely loss of memory did not strike a lethal blow to their engagement or matrimonial plans.

I have discussed this humorous anecdote with quite a few student groups to which I have lectured on the subject of mental health. Together we have conjectured over why this man had shockingly forgotten the name of someone to whom he was soon to be married. The causes, we have concluded, are largely determinable through a review of the few facts at our disposal.

His courtship with his fiancée, as we know, was extremely abbreviated and, therefore, it most likely aroused in him rather tempestuous, conflictual emotions. In a matter of only two months, he and she had made a fateful decision that would most likely have lifelong implications for them both. Although he believed he was solidly committed to matrimony, he was quite likely already having some nostalgia for the relatively carefree days of bachelorhood that would soon be left behind. Then, he fortuitously encounters a friend who had formerly been engineering a few social relationships for him. Consciously, he wants to warn the friend of his fervent commitment to the woman at his side. However, we may infer a quite different set of unconscious emotions at work also.

At the moment when he must introduce his fiancée to his friend, his mind rebels. He defies, disavows, and emotionally obliterates his engagement and his fiancée by forgetting her name. In his unconscious act of defiance he is saying, in effect, "Bob, I don't know this stranger who is hanging on my arm. Don't be put off by the semblance of an important personal relationship here. I'm really footloose and socially available." If we view this man's capricious loss of memory from a dynamic viewpoint, we can see that, at the very moment he felt obligated to introduce his fiancée to a friend, unconscious feelings of regret and defiance unexpectedly surfaced and defeated his conscious intent.

Altruism

Feelings of rage and revenge sometimes cause some people to behave, oddly enough, as if they were paragons of philanthropy and selflessness. A closer examination of the motives of many such people will reveal, however, that this particular form of "generosity" is narrowly self-serving and nothing more than a shoddy pseudoaltruism. One such form of false generosity that I have observed in my clinical practice sometimes occurs when two persons in an intimate relationship clash over their suspected disloyalties to one another. A proposal is then made, usually by only one of the principals, that their relationship would be immeasurably enhanced by a pact between them that would allow both to have extracurricular sexual relationships with other persons.

Usually, only one of the persons, the advocate of course, believes that such an untenable agreement will result in success. However, the other person, confronted by the horrible fear of losing the relationship altogether, grudgingly and resentfully consents. Although she cares deeply and monogamously for her partner, she generously consents to an "open" relationship in the hope that, once having placated her partner, he will appreciate and cherish her all the more. Unfortunately, however, he may instead despise and reject her for her sorry inability to self-respectfully champion her own needs and wishes.

A college student, a man of twenty-four, entered therapy shortly after he had learned that his wife had been involved in an adulterous relationship. He felt murderous rage for the man with whom she had been sexually involved and, rather than act on his feelings, he wisely decided to see a therapist in order to talk things out.

In discussing the chain of events that had led up to his crisis, the student indicated that he regarded his wife's adultery to be his own fault. He indicated that he had actually encouraged her to find and sleep with another man. Why? Well, for some time she had been gaining weight. As a result, he considered her unsightly and sexually undesirable. When, despite his prodding, she couldn't or wouldn't lose weight, he decided to punish her by having sexual relations with another woman. His adulterous behavior then caused him to feel guilty and excessively indebted to his wife. In order to rid himself of his feelings of guilt and indebtedness, he thought it best that his wife also take up an extramarital relationship. This, in his view, would balance the moral scales, so to speak. When, with convincing bravado, he invited her to find another man to sleep with, she took him at his word. When he finally realized the detrimental consequences of his brash actions, it was too late: he was outraged by his wife's affair and wanted revenge.

The earlier personal history of this student helped to reveal the true nature of his rage. His mother and father fought constantly and divorced when he was a small child. He remained with his mother but she had little to do with him, since she spent most of her days out of the home attending to a family business. He saw little of his father after his parents' divorce and the few contacts they did have always fell short of his positive expectations.

The student's mother took rather good care of his material needs and this encouraged the illusion that she deeply cared for him. He sensed, however, that his mother actually took little emotional interest in him and, as a result, he felt sorely neglected by her. In his view, the worst moment of his childhood occurred when he was about five years old.

One evening, while lying in bed, he overheard his mother enter the house with a man. He watched them enter a bedroom and shortly thereafter he overheard his mother uttering pleasurable, sensual sounds from her bed. He knew, even at that young age, that she was enjoying sex with her companion. He recalled, in describing this experience to me, feeling immense murderous rage for the man who was fucking his mother. The depth of his feelings when he described this experience to me was dramatically conveyed by an extremely contorted, wrathful expression on his face accompanied by an almost breathless speech.

The witnessing of a primal scene in itself can be highly traumatic for some young children. For this child, who had already been subjected to severe and ongoing rejection by his mother, it represented a betrayal of vast proportions. It left him overcome with implacable feelings of rage, jealousy, and revenge. Although he often tried to deny and suppress these negative emotions, he could never quite dispel them. When, many years later, he encouraged his wife to engage in an affair, he was again suppressing his feelings of jealousy, disguising them with bravado and an armor of callous indifference. However, when his wife did what his mother had previously done—had sex with a rival—he was again faced with his feelings of despair, longing, rage, and resentment.

From this example, we can see that there are times when certain acts of generosity and altruism can be motivated by rage and vengeance. Unfortunately, we may not always discern the difference between genuine altruism and pseudoaltruism until we experience the effects of an act of (seeming) generosity.

Shyness

Shyness, timidity, and reclusiveness are often reflective of feelings of hostility and suspicious anger. Although shy persons often believe that they are just the unhappy and helpless victims of the hostility of others, there is usually strong evidence to suggest that within their own personalities there are large reservoirs of unresolved rage and defiance.

It is interesting to note how seldom ordinary shyness is associated with feelings of hostility and defiance. Rather, we generally associate shyness almost exclusively with gentleness, consideration, and respect for the feelings of others, and an attitude of honorific self-sacrifice. Shy persons are quite often admired and appreciated for their lack of self-assertiveness and gumption.

Unfortunately, overly unassertive, self-effacing individuals are sometimes appreciated more for their weaknesses and vulnerabilities than for their strengths. Those who deal with them professionally or socially may esteem their shyness because it enables them to dominate and direct the shy person. Since, in our society, there are of course a myriad of people who feel the need to control and dominate their relationships, shy, unassuming individuals are often befriended and lauded by them for their capacity to tolerate domination without clearly articulating their own personal needs. Because excessively shy persons do not adequately express their needs and wishes, they are often mistakenly considered to be not only without needs but to also be miraculously devoid of anger and resentment over their regrettable inhibitions.

Psychotherapists who work dynamically with shy individuals recognize that beneath their conciliatory facades they are often aboil with intense angry emotions. Shy students, for example, will admit that they deeply regret not contributing to lively class discussions and resent the fact that others receive more credit and recognition than they, not because their academic peers necessarily know more, but because they are more aggressive. As one might expect, shy persons often carry with them burdensome and furious grudges against others because they commonly allow themselves to be bested in arguments, conversations, business transactions, and competitive activities. They often think it essential to quell and hide their anger because they have for so long been socially rewarded and valued for their shy and modest behavior.

A woman in her early twenties entered therapy with deep insecurities over expressing aggressive emotions. She was highly tentative in manner and speech, often expressing herself in a rather jumbled flurry of words that usually ended abruptly. For the most part, she started her sentences equivocally, stating that she did not really know what she was talking about, even when it was evident that she knew exactly what she was talking about. Her lack of eye contact and excessive self-monitoring of speech and emotions gave clear indication of an intense fear of losing control of her aggressive emotions.

This patient was raised by highly incompatible and rancorous parents who eventually separated when she was still a child. The patient's father was a rather kind but ineffectual man. Her mother, however, was an extremely disgruntled and irrational person who possessed an insatiable need to control her family's behavior. The patient, more than any other child in the family, bore the heaviest brunt of the mother's wild and unfulfillable demands. The mother allowed her very little privacy or freedom of thought and action. Because her mother supervised and judged her behavior so tightly and relentlessly, the patient, understandably, developed feelings of intense resentment and hostility for her.

Yet, because she felt cowed and entrapped by her mother's dictatorial control, the patient expressed few of her feelings directly or overtly. Instead, she manifested her fears and anger by lying to her mother about her activities and whereabouts. For example, for over a year she misinformed her mother about which college she had been attending.

Perhaps more importantly, the repression and denial of rage and resentment for her mother resulted in a personality trait that markedly interfered with the patient's overall social adjustment. The trait developed in the following manner. The patient's mother would scold and berate her. The patient would, in response, say little, withdraw and escape into a fantasy world of blithe contentment, and pretend through her use of a docile and placid demeanor that she agreed with all her mother's obtuse and irrational opinions. By maintaining a conciliatory and submissive outward stance, the patient avoided open conflict with her mother.

She had concluded long ago that the avoidance of overt hostile conflict took precedence over the risk of alienating her mother by candidly expressing her angry objections to being unremittingly tyrannized. In a certain sense this passive and noncommittal behavior "worked" in that it created the illusion and semblance of harmony between the patient and her mother.

In another sense, however, the patient's reticence and obsequiousness seriously backfired. In her social relationships, her characteristic shyness often caused her to be overlooked and discounted by others. At work, although she was a conscientious, painstaking, and intelligent employee, her employer often took advantage of her willingness to compromise and sacrifice her own needs for the sake of avoiding friction. Thus, the patient came to feel exploited and manipulated in her social and professional relationships. Mistakenly thinking that she would be appreciated, admired, and always treated fairly for her willingness to submit to the wishes of others, it was disappointing and infuriating to her when she discovered that there are many persons who are quite willing to exploit the timidity and unassertiveness of others.

Although fear and anxiety obviously play a large role in causing shyness, as the above-mentioned example illustrates, repressed and inverted anger is also often at the basis of excessive reticence. Frequently, the shy and withdrawn person harbors intense wishes for sadistic revenge and retaliation. Because such feelings are ordinarily perceived or judged to be dangerous and immoral by shy individuals, they isolate, deny, and disguise these negative emotions behind a seemingly frail and vulnerable persona. Psychotherapists who have worked with shy individuals know that as these patients psychologically improve, one of the early signs of their progress is the expression of angry aggression that had long been compulsively denied and dammed up. This unexpected (by the patients) turn of events can, unfortunately, give them and their social acquaintances the false impression that they are actually backtracking and being harmed by their psychotherapy, since the shy person's sudden and uncharacteristic aggressiveness may be viewed as an obnoxious form of behavior by others, especially those who much preferred a relationship with a timid pushover.

Eating Disorders

The negative emotions certainly play an instrumental role in the eating disorders that afflict large numbers of persons. A woman in her early thirties, an employee of a large corporation, entered therapy based upon the insistence of her supervisor. In his view, the patient was a recalcitrant, mistake-prone, and lackadaisical worker who refused to accept the constructive advice or criticism of her administrative superiors or co-workers. The patient herself confirmed without hesitation that her attitude toward work was hostile, devaluing, and self-defeating.

In response to my inquiry regarding her motivation for seeking psychotherapy (other than the prodding of her boss), the patient stated that she had felt depressed for many years and, greatly contributing to her feelings of self-hatred, was her chronic difficulty in controlling her weight. She was indeed quite overweight, her obesity causing her to look and feel much older than her chronological age. She complained of breathlessness and rapid exertion when walking hills or steps and she was already beginning to suffer from the symptoms of high blood pressure.

The patient's personal history revealed that she had been overweight since early childhood, although within the few weeks prior to entering therapy she had put on an additional twenty pounds. She stated that she had been lonely for her family and friends who lived on the East Coast.

An examination of the patient's relationships with her parents revealed many dynamic clues to her eating disorder. The patient's parents had been unhappily married and in rather constant conflict for as long as she could remember. Her father was an unskilled laborer who worked only intermittently and, even when employed, earned scant wages. Her mother was embittered by her marriage and grumbled about her predicament ceaselessly. The patient was the eldest of five children and, as each child was born into the family, she experienced an increasing loss of parental nurturing and material rewards, especially food.

At each meal the patient's mother apportioned the food among the five children with such strictness and exactitude that she usually left the dinner table feeling underfed and cheated. To "beat the system," as she put it, she frequently stole into the kitchen late at night, raided the refrigerator and either ate the purloined food then and there or took it to her room and hoarded it for a later feast.

When questioned about how she felt toward her parents and siblings during her childhood years, the patient readily acknowledged that she frequently hated and resented them. She felt deprived of love and the birth of each younger sibling only served to intensify her feelings of being emotionally shortchanged by her parents. She recalled that she often experienced murderous rage toward her brothers and sisters, imagining them dead, thus allowing her to be the sole beneficiary of her parents' love and affection.

During the course of only a few sessions, the patient disclosed how, as a child, her angry and vengeful emotions originally led to her particular pattern of overeating. One evening, after leaving the dinner table hungry and resentful, she went to her room and made an irrevocable and angry vow to herself. She promised herself that she would never want for food or be hungry again, even if it meant stealing and hiding leftovers from her family. Late that night, after her family had gone to sleep, she crept into the kitchen, pilfered some choice edibles from the refrigerator and set up a secret larder in her room that afterward supplied her with tidbits whenever she became hungry.

Although she recalled feeling guilty over her thievery, she rationalized her behavior by concluding that if her parents were cruel enough to scrimp on food and underfeed her, she could righteously betray and steal from them. In her zeal to outwit and wreak revenge upon them, she gradually began to steal, hoard, and consume increasing amounts of food, causing her weight to balloon, much to the puzzlement of her unsuspecting family.

The patient's surreptitious acts of revenge upon her family enabled her to feel, at least transiently, a small degree of gratification. She certainly felt less deprived and undernourished and, in the realm of her fantasies, she considered herself special and privileged for possessing and eating greater quantities of food than her siblings.

Unfortunately, the patient never resolved her conflicts over the deprivation and anger she experienced in childhood. Thus, even though, as an adult, she earned an excellent income and could easily depend upon having as many square meals as she wanted each day, the patient continued to hoard food and overeat. It was as if she were still carrying out her angry, long-standing vow—her vendetta—to punish her family for withholding food from her. Uncontrollably, she would scurry through a supermarket, indiscriminately plucking bags and cans of food from the shelves to take home to an already overstocked pantry. Arriving home, she often experienced diffuse feelings of deprivation, rage, and resentment, most of which were unconsciously felt toward her parents. So, as she had once done as an angry child in the seclusion of her bedroom, she now acted out her vengeful feelings by gorging herself with immense quantities of food.

This example illustrates how unresolved feelings of rage and resentment can result in an eating disorder of a genuinely hazardous nature.

A few years ago I had the opportunity to observe firsthand the role played by hostility in the development of yet another eating disorder, anorexia, a pathological loss of appetite accompanied by emaciation and other life-threatening symptoms.

A patient who had been in therapy for about two years remarked in passing that her teenage sister had been having some eating problems. She did not elaborate and sloughed the matter off so quickly that I hardly paid attention to it. A few weeks later the patient again alluded to her sister's eating problems but this time with evident concern. When I pressed her on the point, she confessed in a flood of tears that for many months her sister had been undereating and wasting away.

I asked the patient what her parents had been doing about the problem. She stated that her father was away from home on business trips most of the time and her mother viewed the matter with a strange and disturbing sort of complacency, as if it would go away spontaneously. For good reason, the patient feared that, under the circumstances, her sister's life was in danger.

I informed the patient to tell her mother that she must seek immediate professional help for her anorectic daughter. When, in our next session, the patient informed me that her mother was disdainfully ignoring my recommendation, I told the patient to tell her mother that I would report the matter to the appropriate authorities unless she took immediate steps to provide her daughter, who was still in her minority, with the care she required.

That threat seemed to do the trick. In our next session, the patient reported that her mother took her sister to the family physician who, after examining the shockingly debilitated girl, immediately hospitalized her. The patient then unexpectedly asked me if I would pay her sister a visit in the hospital. She said her sister wanted to meet me and, in thinking things over, she, the patient, thought it was a good idea. It might give me certain insights into the dynamics of her own emotional problems.

A few days later I entered a hospital room to find recumbent in her bed a wan, bony, scarecrow of a girl who was looking everywhere about the room except at the food that had been placed on the tray in front of her. Hovering over her was her mother, who greeted me coolly but politely. For the most part, the conversation remained light and there were startlingly few references to the seriously ill patient who was listlessly lying there in the bed, stubbornly refusing to eat her lunch.

I didn't remain long in that room, but what I witnessed there was an eye-opening and unforgettable incident. The mother made a few half-hearted attempts to get her daughter to eat her lunch. Each time, however, the girl stoically refused, blaming her asceticism on lack of appetite. I carefully watched the manner in which she rebuffed her mother's efforts. She displayed a definite angry defiance each time, accompanied by sarcastic remarks about her mother's intrusive pushiness.

Finally, after making one last lame and futile attempt to cajole her daughter into eating her lunch, the mother threw up her hands in overdone exasperation and announced, "Well, if you're not hungry, I am. So if you're not going to eat that lunch, I will." With quiet resignation, her daughter agreed that since she herself wasn't going to eat the food anyway, it was better not to waste it. With that, her mother removed the plate from the tray and smartly proceeded to polish off a sizeable mound of tuna fish.

Although little was said while the mother ate "her" lunch, I closely watched the emaciated girl during their interchange. She silently glared at her mother as the latter lunched on food that was meant to restore her daughter's health. The stolid, resolute, and penetrating way in which the girl watched her mother so greedily feed herself unquestionably bespoke a profound and ineffable rage.

After observing this disquieting scene for only a few minutes, I left the room, sadly enriched with a deeper understanding of the eating disorder that afflicted my patient's sister. An unempathic and oblivious mother had cripplingly neglected the basic needs of her daughter for comforting and nurturance. In depression, rage, and rebellion, the adolescent refused to eat or partake of the joys of life. Feeling punished by her mother's selfish disregard for her personal welfare, the daughter undertook to retaliate by refusing to eat or live healthfully. Although it was obvious that she herself had become the primary victim of her self-deprivation, she evidently derived some form of sadistic gratification from the anguish she imagined her mother suffered as a result of her illness. Tragically, however, as the brief hospital vignette illustrates, the mother remained quite unmoved by her daughter's flirtation with death.

Although rage and defiance may not play a central role in all eating disorders, as the two above-cited examples suggested, these particular negative emotions can be pivotal to the development and understanding of eating disorders in many persons.

Delinquency

Obviously, rage, resentment, and revenge are not always expressed in indirect or disguised forms. Acts of murder, theft, and rape, for example, are patent manifestations of the fury and vengefulness of their perpetrators. That much is clear. What is not always so clear are the reasons some people resort to violence and delinquency and others do not.

A woman in her late fifties, a recent immigrant from a Middle Eastern nation, entered therapy upon the recommendation of her attorney. She had recently been arrested for shoplifting and was soon to appear in court for a hearing. This was her first criminal offense and, therefore, her attorney expected that she would not be treated severely by the judge. However, since she admitted to having repetitively and compulsively shoplifted for many months, it was deemed advisable for her to undergo psychotherapy in order to overcome her delinquent proclivities.

In the course of our first few sessions, the patient described how she had repeatedly gone into large department stores with the intention to shop and, without premeditation, was suddenly seized by an urge to pilfer a commodity. She found her own behavior quite baffling since she had never before acted delinquently and, furthermore, with the substantial savings she had accumulated over the years, she could have easily afforded to purchase, rather than steal, the items. To make matters even more inexplicable, she invariably discovered soon after arriving home with the loot that she had little genuine use for the stolen goods and threw them out almost immediately and with disgust.

This patient suffered great guilt and suicidal depression over her irrepressible urges to steal. She had always prided herself on having high, unimpeachable moral standards and, therefore, she considered her own recent deviant behavior to constitute an unpardonable sin. Several times she had seriously contemplated killing herself and was convinced that if the judge decided to incarcerate her for her crimes, she would certainly have no choice but to do away with herself.

For several sessions the patient and I explored her past experiences for explanations of her perplexing and dangerous behavior. The patient contradicted my speculations that perhaps certain traumatic childhood experiences had left emotional scars that were being expressed through antisocial behavior. Perhaps, as is often the case with kleptomania, she was, by stealing, seeking to symbolically acquire the love and wholeness that had been absent or deficient during her childhood years. The patient vehemently denied my conjectures, stating that her childhood homelife had been happy and wholesome, and went on to describe two completely loving and devoted parents. The earlier history she depicted to me was obviously an idealization but since the patient had ironclad arguments with which to refute my speculations, I thought it best to table my questions about her childhood for the time being.

In our fourth session, the patient revealed many unsavory details about her unrelievedly miserable marriage to a man who had died shortly before she emigrated to the United States. This man had completely and sadistically dominated her for many years. Although he earned a respectable income as a businessman, he imposed upon her a bare bones household budget and permitted her to purchase only proven necessities. In short, he was cruelly repressive and authoritarian in every aspect of their marital relationship.

In an explosive outpouring of rage and bitterness, the patient disclosed what she considered to be her husband's worst character trait. After many years of remaining homebound in order to raise her children, she requested of him permission to attend college in order to better her mind and professional prospects. He flatly and imperiously denied her request and beat her when she protested the injustice. Inconsolably, she wept and railed over how much her husband had stifled her opportunities to attain a college education. With burning intensity, she declared that she was glad he had died and that, free of him at last, she could now pursue her educational and other personal objectives unimpededly.

Although she no longer had a husband who hectored and degraded her, the patient, as she soon began to realize, continued to feel the fury and resentment engendered by her marital relationship. During the many years of her marriage, she was inhumanely deprived of spiritual and material opportunities and pleasures. Despite her husband's death, she could not yet cast off the emotional shackles of the relationship. She spoke of still wanting to take revenge upon him for the brutality and inhumanity with which he treated her.

Now that she had begun to acknowledge her fury and resentment toward her husband, the patient was reminded of a parallel series of experiences that had taken place during her childhood. She revealed that her mother, who was generally a caring and responsible parent, had little respect or use for formal education. Thus, whenever the patient expressed a desire to attain a college education or professional training, her mother would advise her to set lower sights for herself and strive instead to become a clerical worker with a low but secure income. The patient remembered feeling very demeaned, enraged, and discouraged by her mother's apathy toward her educational strivings. She now realized that both her mother and her husband had greatly undermined her passionate quest for personal growth and self-fulfillment.

In a matter of only five or six sessions, the patient acquired a rather solid understanding of her recent delinquent behavior. The feelings of rage and revenge toward her mother and her husband had found expression in stealing. As I had earlier speculated, she had felt cheated and depreciated during childhood largely due to her mother's relatively low expectations for her. When the patient's husband, in tandem with her mother, obstructed her educational ambitions, she understandably felt again robbed of her innermost hopes and desires. She felt that someone or something owed her the personal rewards that had been withheld for so many years. Thus, when she had entered the department stores where an endless assortment of articles were on display, her feelings of entitlement and revenge induced her to steal. Symbolically, the department store (an institutional authority figure) personified both her mother and her husband (hostile and depriving authority figures) and, therefore, by taking revenge upon the store, she, unconsciously, was taking revenge upon the hated figures of her past.

Acts of delinquency are almost always motivated, in part, by wishes for revenge. Since almost everyone has at some time in his or her life committed delinquent acts, we can naturally assume that most of us from time to time have felt vengeful.

The case examples presented in this chapter suggest that the negative emotions—anger, rage, defiance, and resentment—can find expression in indirect, disguising forms of behavior such as shyness or obstinacy or in direct, overt, and sometimes dangerous behavior such as stealing.

In this chapter we have observed how certain forms of behavior are inspired and shaped by the negative emotions and conflicts we have experienced. Now let us consider how we might effectively cope with and constructively use behavior that is generated by anger.

Earlier, we considered the example of fatigue as a possible expression of negative emotions. If we find that we regularly behave in a tired, disconsolate, and dispirited manner, our first step (assuming medical causes have been well investigated and ruled out) should be to regard this form of behavior as a signal of underlying emotional conflicts, often of a hostile nature. If we continually lack interest in what others are saying, yawn exasperatedly whenever we are not the center of attention or highly stimulated, and act as if life itself is a Sisyphean treadmill, it is probably well to take a hard look at our negative emotions.

Looking for Meaning

A first step in the process of overcoming and constructively utilizing such behavioral cues is to avoid simply chalking them up to fate, extraneous circumstances, or immutable personality traits ("Well, that just happens to be the way I am and there's nothing I can do about it." Rather than assuming that your sluggish behavior is meaningless and unalterable, assume just the opposite: that it is most likely a highly meaningful manifestation of angry and defiant emotions and that, with time and introspective effort, it can be changed.

If we can first acknowledge that our negative behavior is an expedient vehicle for the expression of certain negative emotions, we can next usefully ask ourselves, "What negative emotions am I currently experiencing?" It would probably be very helpful to gain as precise a grasp of these emotions as possible. Therefore, we might proceed by next asking ourselves, "Do I seem to be feeling any of the following emotions: anger, defiance, jealousy, rage, vindictiveness, hatred, resentment, etc.?"

If we can even to a small degree identify the negative emotions we are feeling, we have made a significant stride in our quest to constructively utilize them. Now, for the sake of illustration, let us assume that we are indeed feeling defiant and resentful. What next? We are now faced with an emotional task that, unfortunately, many people fail. It is at this juncture that many individuals will say to themselves, "Yes, I do feel angry and defiant but, since I don't know why I feel those ways, there can be no reason or basis for my feelings."

Wrong! No matter how intense, uncomfortable, or alien your negative emotions feel, always assume that you have legitimate, ascertainable reasons for harboring them. This does not of course mean that you will always be able to pinpoint those reasons or that the reasons you eventually adduce to explain your behavior will be the actual causes of your anger. However, even if it is nigh impossible to know what you feel, it is nonetheless extremely important to realize that your negative emotions, no matter how irrational and groundless they may appear to be, do have actual causes. These causes admittedly may be buried so deeply in your past and your unconscious that they have become virtually inaccessible. Yet, knowing that all emotions, including the most intense negative ones, have a definite origin in your personality and in the context of your personal history will enable you to confront the challenge of understanding and using them to your advantage. Remember, knowing that an emotion has a definite cause and origin can in itself open an important pathway to using that emotion to benefit yourself.

Let us now assume that we have discovered that we are feeling very angry and have even located the source of our anger. It is of course quite possible to intellectually grasp the cause of an emotional conflict while at the same time feeling too immobilized to change the self-destructive behavioral patterns based on the conflict.

Let us consider, for example, the problem of procrastination referred to earlier in this chapter. You may be able to fully recognize that the delaying tactics you employ to avoid certain unpleasant or repugnant responsibilities are the behavioral expressions of your feelings of anger and defiance. To carry matters further, you might even astutely trace your defiant and resentful feelings to those childhood experiences when you were chastised and bullied by your father whenever you refused to do your homework. Yet, knowing such things will not always enable your to overcome your tendency to procrastinate.

The Need to Act

If you find that psychological insights in themselves do not sufficiently empower you to resolve and overcome self-defeating behavior, there are usually several means available for dealing with this problem. First, accept the fact that you genuinely dislike or even hate the task at hand and then, if it must be done, do it anyway, despite your feelings of aversion. In other words, don't necessarily wait until your angry and aversive feelings toward a repugnant task eventually subside or transform themselves into positive feelings. You may have an unendurably long wait and in the meantime the task will remain unfulfilled and thereby become an even greater source of disgust and anger for you.

I am not suggesting that you launch into an unpleasant or annoying challenge with enthusiasm or that you seek to complete the task within a circumscribed time frame. Rather, I would recommend that you begin by nibbling at it. Find some part of the task that seems just a bit palatable to you and attempt to complete only that segment.

If, in following this recommendation, you find that you are making poor headway, don't dally or anguish too long; move on and tackle other facets of the task until you are able to make at least a small inroad in your understanding and mastery of the task. Once having made this breakthrough, pursue the course you have taken until you are satisfied with the results. Then move on to another aspect of the assignment. Continue to do this until you have completed the entire assignment.

If, however, you become so enervated or disgusted by a task that it comes to represent nothing but sheer drudgery to you, give it up for awhile, allow yourself respite and time for recovery, and then return to it when you feel more emotionally receptive.

There are a number of reasons why it is useful, if not imperative, to readily and actively attack assignments and responsibilities that we generally regard with distrust and loathing. First, emotional inertia has a peculiar way of feeding on and nourishing itself. In other words, the more we allow ourselves to be emotionally stalemated in our attempts to act and initiate, the more we become demoralized and cynical about our capacity to actuate and achieve. Thus, a vicious circle sets in: fear and hostility toward a given responsibility leads to indecision and procrastination. Procrastination, in turn, causes one to doubt and distrust one's capacity to successfully master the unpleasant challenge and thus leads to even greater hostility and procrastination.

Although breaking this vicious circle may not be easy, it is, as I have emphasized, essential to break it somehow and somewhere in order to begin the process of altering maladaptive behavior. Therefore, to restate my recommendation in somewhat silly sounding and tautological terms, one way to break the vicious circle of hostility-procrastination-more hostility-more procrastination is to break it—somewhere, anywhere.

A second reason to readily disrupt a self-destructive behavioral pattern that is based on hostility is to prevent our perceptions of an unpleasant activity or task from getting nastily out of hand. It is quite common for people who respond to disagreeable or arduous challenges with defiant procrastination to feel over a period of time increasingly menaced by those challenges. The longer they delay confronting the threat of a personal challenge, the more that challenge will be perceived as indomitable, daunting, and larger-than-life.

As the menacing quality of the perceived threat grows and intensifies, it may take on unvanquishable proportions. Thus, the longer one delays confronting a threatening situation, the greater the possibility that the challenge will never be met or overcome. Ordinarily, the sooner one confronts a threatening situation, the more likely the threat will be perceived and approached realistically and, therefore, effectively.

Some people, including myself, best handle dreaded or repugnant challenges by first grappling with the nastiest and most complicated aspects of the experience. The reason this may work well for you is that once the most complicated and unpleasant part of a task is completed, the remainder of the undertaking can be more easily viewed and approached as a "piece of cake." Conversely, the postponement of a complicated and intimidating challenge may cause that challenge to hang ominously over your head like a Damoclean sword. Therefore, you may find it more expedient to cope with an abhorrent task by first defanging its most complex and frightening parts.

On the other hand, there are some individuals who are more apt to fulfill a difficult and disagreeable responsibility by first mastering its easiest aspects. By successively mastering each of the simplest parts of a formidable challenge they gradually acquire a sense of accomplishment and optimism that serves as an excellent springboard to dealing with the harder aspects of a problem.

In short, the reader is advised, when confronted with annoying or infuriating demands and responsibilities, to assume an open, flexible, and experimental attitude. Such an attitude should allow you to test and retest those strategies and coping skills that work best for you. If you find, in the final analysis, however, that a particular challenge infuses you with such resentment, despair, and defiance that you simply find it to be insurmountable, allow yourself to assume a philosophical attitude by unashamedly accepting the fact that you simply cannot conquer this particular challenge. Then move on to other, more palatable and fulfilling undertakings.

Forgetfulness Revisited

I will conclude this chapter by discussing another behavioral symptom of unconscious aggression and defiance that was referred to earlier: forgetfulness.

If you find, as many people do, that you recurrently forget the names of particular people, ask yourself whether you might harbor unconscious hostile feelings for those individuals. The answer might be illuminating and emotionally disencumbering.

If you eventually grasp the fact that, yes, you forgot and avoided the doctor's appointment because you feared his or her diagnosis and treatment, you then have an opportunity to confront the fears and defiant emotions that have animated your behavior. Rather than allowing those emotions to destructively control and tyrannize your actions, by examining and mastering your unconscious motivations you can determine, first, to what extent your feelings are realistic and, second, to what extent you will continue to allow yourself to be dictated to by your negative emotions. After all, if your fearful and defiant emotions are impeding you from receiving essential medical care, would it not be clearly in your interest to understand and resolve those negative emotions once and for all?

Let us shift to the example of forgetting the name of a well-known friend or acquaintance just at the point of introducing him or her to someone else. Why not attribute this momentary lapse of memory simply to chance or to a fleeting state of nervous distractability? Why, in other words, make such a big deal over it? After all, a person need not feel that forgetting a good friend's name is tantamount to committing a capital offense.

Yet, to dismiss an incident of this nature by chalking it up to mere chance or diffuse states of nervousness is to lose a potentially valuable opportunity to learn something important about yourself.

Let us suppose for a moment that you did harbor unconscious hostility toward your friend. Is it not likely that your negative emotions would find occasional outlet through such hostile behavior toward that friend through your forgetting that friend's name? If negative emotions are disrupting your relationship with your friend through your inadvertent acts of hostility toward him or her, why not deal with those feelings constructively by, for example, discussing them with your friend? Why allow hostile feelings and behavior to ruin a valuable relationship? So, to repeat, take regular cues from some of the subtler forms of your behavior such as forgetting a friend's name, assume those cues are telling you something important about your genuine feelings, and then consider ways in which you might express your negative emotions more directly, candidly, and maturely.

Lest I have given the reader the mistaken impression that forgetting a friend's name always and exclusively represents hostile feelings for that friend, I might point out that quite the opposite can be the case. It is quite possible that in introducing your friend to another person your fondness for your friend causes you to dislike sharing him or her with another individual. Thus, your unwillingness to share your friend might conceivably result in an unconscious maneuver to conceal the friend's identity by forgetting his or her name. In any case, negative emotions have ultimately entered into the situation in the form of envy. Again, would it not be preferable to acknowledge this envy, at least to yourself, and then deal with it in a straightforward and mature manner rather than express it through roundabout and surreptitious means? This may be possible if you are willing to take heed of the minute, subtle idiosyncrasies of your behavior that strive to reveal and declare to you the true nature of your negative emotions.

Chapter 3

The Denial and Repudiation of Negative Emotions

This chapter will discuss some of the reasons why people are inclined to avoid, dread, deny, and disavow negative emotions and thoughts. Perhaps the simplest and most direct explanation for the rejection and disavowal of hostile thought and emotions stems from the fact that angry feelings usually cause a person to feel physically uncomfortable. When we feel very angry, our heart may begin to palpitate, we feel overheated and begin to sweat, and an unpleasant physical tension may overcome us.

The slang term for how we appear when we are very angry is quite apt: uptight. Our body may become rigid and, when we attempt to speak, we find ourselves, under the influence of our anger, to be rather breathless, which causes us to sputter and fumble for words. In some cases, a person, when angry, may perspire a great deal. Others experience psychosomatic symptoms such as migraine headaches whenever they are viscerally angry.

Larry, a fifteen-year-old boy, who had been living in a residential treatment center since the age of seven, suffered from chronic and severe migraine headaches. Aspirin and other medications offered him some relief, but generally he found his headaches to be quite painful and enervating. Larry had been placed in an institutional setting shortly after a younger sister had died from cancer. His mother, a widow (Larry's father had died when he was an infant), had become severely depressed in reaction to her daughter's death and could not adequately care for her only remaining child. Thus, she arranged for his care in an institutional setting.

By dint of his superior intelligence, Larry did well academically and was well thought of by his teachers as well as by the staff of the treatment facility. Nevertheless, he was constantly plagued by migraine headaches, tension, and sleeplessness. He often sought and received medical care and examinations in response to his physical complaints, but all tests proved negative. He was sympathetically informed by his doctors that his physical symptoms were psychological in nature and that, with the help of psychotherapy, he might be able to alleviate or conquer them. However, Larry had no confidence in psychological explanations or procedures and instead held out hope that one day a medical examination would finally uncover a physical basis for his difficulties.

Despite his qualms about the value and usefulness of psychotherapy, Larry, at the behest of the institution's administrators, consented to undergo psychotherapy. Although he was able to establish a superficial rapport with me, he remained quite suspicious and aloof throughout many months of therapy. Larry consistently appeared tense, depressed, and tired. Knowing that he had reason to be very angry and bitter over the misfortunes of his childhood, I queried him often about his negative thoughts and feelings. For the most part, he denied angry emotions and devalued my attempts to tap his feelings. Yet, despite his verbal disclaimers, Larry continued to validate the existence of hostile and resentful emotions through his bodily tension and psychosomatic headaches.

It was during a psychotherapy session in his seventh month of treatment that Larry let down his defenses and revealed the true nature of his conflictual feelings. In an unexpected upsurge of angry emotions, Larry described an emotionally devastating experience from his earlier childhood. He recalled that both he and his mother deeply mourned the physical deterioration and ultimate death of his younger sister. He and his sister were fond of one another and her death represented a terrible loss to him. Compounding his feelings of loss was the fact that his mother dramatically withdrew from him and, out of her profound sense of futility and embitterment, refused to acknowledge or support Larry's need for maternal nurturance.

Out of despair, Larry's needs and demands for his mother's attention and affection escalated. She, in turn, estranged herself from him even more decidedly. As a result, hostile and vituperative confrontations between Larry and his mother regularly ensued. During one of these confrontations Larry's mother was especially abusive. In a long and vicious tirade she told Larry that she was sorry it had been his sister who had died, rather than Larry. She irrationally accused Larry of causing his sister's death and then proceeded to vocalize a wish that he too would either die or go away. It was at that point, a juncture at which the mutual destructiveness of their relationship had made Larry's life at home unmistakably untenable, that a decision was made to place Larry in an institution.

In a profusion of tears and angry gestures, Larry expressed his rage over the piercing blows dealt to him by fate. Then he explained with great clarity and poignancy why he had unyieldingly kept his feelings about these events from me for so many months. He said, "You're always asking me about my feelings. I guess that's your job. But you've got to understand that I don't want to tell you my feelings. As a matter of fact, I don't want to have feelings at all. They get you nowhere. Telling my mother about how I felt got me into an institution. Sure, I feel angry and pissed off about the things that have happened to me, but talking about my feelings makes me feel rotten. And I don't want to feel bad. I'd rather they found some organic or chemical reason for my problems so they could cure what's wrong with me, rather than my having to go through talking about my feelings week after week."

Talking about his emotional problems in psychotherapy did eventually help to alleviate many of Larry's symptoms and conflicts. However, in the above-mentioned psychotherapy session he underscored one of the major reasons for the suppression and denial of negative emotions: i.e., angry thoughts and emotions often feel psychologically and physically painful and, if the pain becomes truly unbearable, one is inclined to use any means possible to exorcise such feelings.

Fear of Losing a Love Object

Many persons commonly disown and suppress their angry thoughts and emotions because they fear damaging or losing the intended object of their wrath. If the person we hate is the same person we also love and need, we very likely will feel impaled on the horns of a serious dilemma. Possessed by contradictory wises to both hurt and derive love from the same person, our angry emotions may depress, stymie, and immobilize. To protect ourselves from the specter, imagined or real, of hurting or losing our loved one, we may seek refuge in a denial and renunciation of our rage.

In my clinical work, I have noticed that most patients, at one time or another, develop moderate to acute fears over the angry emotions they periodically feel toward me. If I consider these feelings relevant to the therapeutic process—and they almost always are—I will attempt to elicit my patients' interest in and expression of their negative thoughts and emotions toward me. This is often a delicate, painstaking, but highly worthwhile, task.

Quite frequently, patients who are questioned about their angry thoughts and feelings toward the therapist may initially react as if they were being accused of an evil deed. The resistances to admitting negative thoughts and emotions toward the therapist can be steadfast and granitic. Thus, a therapist's explorations of this sensitive subject with a patient usually must be undertaken gradually, diplomatically, and patiently.

Patients' protestations over being questioned about their conscious or latent hostile thoughts and feelings toward their therapists frequently reflect that above-mentioned dilemma of contradictory feelings. As many patients will readily acknowledge, they need and depend upon their therapists for their knowledge, skill, and support. Thus, they may overly fear the possibility that something they say or do will alienate the therapist, thus causing the therapist to retaliate by withdrawing from or terminating the therapeutic relationship. Although such fears are ordinarily quite exaggerated and without realistic foundation, most patients will not readily test their therapists' thick-skinned willingness to be the object of their hostility.

As patients develop trust and confidence in their therapists, their reticence over expressing hostile thoughts and feelings usually dissipates. It is then, frequently, that they will reveal the reasons they had hitherto avoided discussing their anger toward the therapist. The patient's comments may run as follows: "Of course I've felt angry with you from time to time. I still do. But, not knowing you very well, I couldn't be sure how you would react to my angry feelings. This relationship is important to me and I couldn't take the chance that you might dislike knowing that I sometimes hate you. I realize that such feelings are sometimes an expected part of therapy and that you would not punish me for having them, but it's hard not to fear reprisal from you. After all, in most relationships in the 'real' world, when you express anger to others, they get very defensive and strike back. Worse, they may abandon you. Up to now, I couldn't afford to take that chance with you."

As we can see, the fear of damaging or losing the object of our hatred can cause much anxiety and inhibition of emotion if, at the same time, we need or love the person who is the target of our hostility. Obviously, it generally requires considerable trust to express anger or animosity toward someone who is vitally important to one's sense of personal security.

This point brings to mind an anecdote that I had once heard about a well-known child psychotherapist, Dr. Fritz Redl. According to the story I heard, whenever the children under Redl's care formally referred to him as Dr. Redl, he suspected that they distrusted and feared him. If, on the other hand, a child greeted him with something like, "Fritz, you bastard," he assumed the child rather confidently trusted him. Presumably, this assumption was based upon a realization that children who could flippantly tease and even disparage Dr. Redl had less fear that he would retaliate by withdrawing from and abandoning them than children who rather stiltedly addressed him by his academic title.

Guilt toward the Hated Object

The fear and disownment of angry emotions and thoughts are often induced by guilt in relation to the life-situation or personality of the individual with whom one is angry. For example, it is quite common for people to negate their negative emotions for a parent because that parent has suffered terrible emotional adversities or is mentally or physically disabled.

Ms. G, a twenty-one-year-old community college student, described in her initial psychotherapy session feelings of depression and lassitude. Although of a long-standing nature, these feelings became particularly acute during the time of a family reunion from which she voluntarily excluded herself. Her reason for estranging herself from her family was to avoid contact with her father whom she had not seen in over seven years. During the first session the patient revealed that when she was fourteen her father had expressed a desire to have regular sexual relations with her, for which she would be paid by him. Shocked, dismayed, and humiliated, she immediately decamped, vowing never to see him again, a pledge she had faithfully kept. However, the patient became more depressed each subsequent year and found herself increasingly desirous of a reconciliation with her father.

In discussing how she currently felt toward her father, the patient alternately expressed anger and forgiveness over how he had humiliated and degraded her seven years before. Each time she expressed feelings of anger she would attempt to undo the negative emotions by saying they were unwarranted and unfair. When I asked why, she said that her father was a chronic schizophrenic who had undergone multiple psychiatric hospitalizations during her early adolescence. How, she asked, could she legitimately feel angry with someone who was psychiatrically disabled, out of his mind at the time he had traumatized her. "Quite easily," I opined. I explained that, in my view, although her father was certainly a pathetic and tragic individual, his earlier behavior toward her had certainly been outrageous and infuriating. Although he had obviously been crazy at the time of his mad proposal to her, she had every reason to feel furious and resentful toward him. What I had told her, in other words, was that a person could sometimes legitimately hate an individual who was mentally ill, even if the mentally ill person's offensive behavior was a manifestation of the illness.

Feeling validated and emboldened by my perspective, Ms. G. could regard her own negative feelings in a more objective and condemnatory light. From this growing awareness flowed an increased confidence and determination to see her father once again. She independently resolved that all sexual overtures from him would be dealt with firmly and emphatically. Because she herself could not decide whether to remind her father of the earlier debacle, I encouraged her to totally avoid mention of the incident if possible. The patient then scheduled a second session for a week hence.

Ms. G. reported the following week that she had enjoyed a remarkably unproblematic visit with her father. He was kind and considerate, albeit somewhat disoriented. In parting, they planned to see each other often. Ms. G. expressed the exhilarated feeling that a mountain of emotional pain had been lifted from her shoulders and that her long-standing depression had almost magically vanished. No future therapy sessions were scheduled and none eventuated. A year later, Ms. G. and I met accidentally on campus, affording me the opportunity to learn that she and her father had further solidified their relationship and that she continued to be free of debilitating depression. We both agreed that the turning point in her relationship with her father took place when she was able to accept without excessive guilt the rage and resentment she had felt for him. It was only then that she could begin to forgive him for his uncontrollable cruelty toward her.

Children of alcoholic parents often have acute conflicts over their feelings of hatred and rage. The disorganized and chaotic behavior of alcoholic parents naturally oppresses and disturbs their children. Because seriously alcoholic parents ordinarily behave in a helpless, irresponsible, and childlike manner, their children may unwillingly and quite prematurely be thrust into performing the roles and responsibilities of a parent toward their own parents. As part of this "parentified" role, the children, bearing a stiff upper lip, will feel the need to deny and renounce their feelings of rage for the parents who, through self-abusive drinking, are abdicating their parental responsibilities.

The problem of suppressed rage is often aggravated by a rationalization that is characteristically shared among families with alcoholic parents. A misconception or myth evolves that excuses alcoholic parents' destructive behavior by suggesting that none of their harmful actions are truly preventable or culpable since, after all, they are merely victims of a disease and a drug. According to this myth, the obnoxious and damaging behavior of alcoholic parents must be excused and tolerated, since it is not really the result of their intentions or personalities, but rather the manifestation of their disease or illness. Therefore, anger and resentment toward alcoholic parents must be swallowed and disavowed in deference to the fallacious belief that alcoholic parents lack all responsibility for the harm they cause by their excessive drinking.

A man in his late twenties entered psychotherapy following a sudden outburst of anger at a friend's wedding reception. Prior to this episode he had been getting very little sleep due to a heavy work schedule. His physical fatigue combined with a few drinks on an empty stomach unexpectedly catapulted him into a riotous argument with his girlfriend.

Immediately before the incident occurred, the patient, Mr. D., had been relatively calm and congenial. He soon, however, began to notice that his girlfriend was holding a friendly conversation with a man. She and the man left the party for only a few minutes in order to retrieve an item from the latter's car. When they returned, Mr. D. began accusing his girlfriend of sexual indiscretions and disloyalty. When she vehemently denied his allegations, Mr. D. flew into a rage and a serious, somewhat physical, altercation took place between them.

Mr. D. was subdued by some of the other partygoers and soon thereafter he and his girlfriend left the party together. Throughout the following day, the incident still festered in Mr. D.'s mind. Although he could only vaguely recall the details of his irrational behavior of the previous night, Mr. D. was mortified by his groundless suspicions and his physical mistreatment of his girlfriend who, as he soon came to realize, was an unsuspecting scapegoat for certain hostilities he had long felt toward his parents. Out of an understandable sense of urgency to demystify and gain control over his negative emotions, he entered therapy.

In the first session, Mr. D. expressed deep remorse and self-contempt over his abusive behavior toward his entirely trustworthy girlfriend. He readily acknowledged that she was a sensitive, generous, and supportive friend who in no respect warranted his suspicions or abuse. In response, I suggested to Mr. D. that his eruption at the party most likely made great sense in some other context, perhaps when understood in the light of his childhood experiences. I then elicited the following information from him.

Mr. D. was the eldest of nine children. His mother was a chronic alcoholic whose uncontrollable drinking binges would sometimes require extensive hospital care. At home, her behavior would alternate between a nurturing, loving attitude toward her children and a reckless, dangerous disregard for their welfare, depending largely upon the level of her consumption of alcohol. To make matters worse, when drunk, Mr. D.'s mother would ceaselessly badger her husband with complaints and criticisms until he exploded in a fury and physically beat her into a state of obliviousness. Mr. D. witnessed many of these beatings and, as the eldest child, he assumed the lion's share of the responsibility for halting them (if he could) and for healing his mother's wounds afterward.

These beatings sometimes reached such a ferocious pitch that Mr. D. often thought his mother had actually been killed as a result. Following the beatings, he would stealthily enter her room and minutely inspect her body for signs of life, at times holding a mirror to her nostrils in order to detect inklings of respiration. In time, Mr. D. came to dread, resent, and despise these assaultive episodes with such a passion that he often wished his mother would die once and for all, rather than live such a brutalized and squalid existence. The thought of wishing his mother dead, although acceptable to him on a conscious level, caused him to feel considerable unconscious guilt and self-contempt.

In order to deal with these "contemptible" feelings of hatred toward his parents, Mr. D., throughout his adolescence spent as little time as possible at home. He instead devoted himself, rather successfully, to academic, athletic, and musical pursuits at school.

Soon after his graduation from high school, Mr. D. left home for good. In his early twenties he endured a tumultuous marriage that lasted for only a few years. Soon after his divorce, he met his present girlfriend whose joyful outlook and generous emotional support enabled him to overcome the depression he had experienced over his calamitous marriage. Since its inception, his relationship with his girlfriend had been a mutually positive and enriching one, at least until the time of their recent uproarious conflict at their friend's wedding reception.

Although Mr. D. had since adolescence rather completely estranged himself from his parents, his negative feelings and thoughts about how they had emotionally undermined his life continued to plague him. For the most part, he had been only dimly aware of the intensity of his angry and resentful feelings. However, whenever he visited his (now divorced) parents he was subconsciously alerted to the rage he felt toward them. On such occasions, he would involuntarily treat his mother in a cold and contemptuous manner, followed by feelings of guilt and remorse. In relation to his father, Mr. D., without volition, assumed a passive and subservient attitude, followed by feelings of humiliation and self-debasement.

In discussing his hostile feelings for his parents, Mr. D. informed me that he somehow always knew that he had harbored feelings of hatred for them. To counteract the painful negative feelings, he had for many years assiduously shut his parents out of his life, at least physically. I inquired into what made this so necessary. Mr. D. stated that his mother's chronic drunken behavior during his childhood was so disgusting, humiliating, and scarifying that at times he simply could not tolerate her presence. Yet, as the eldest child, he felt supremely responsible for her. Furthermore, she was like a helpless, pathetic child and, therefore, he had convinced himself that she desperately needed him. In order to deal with the sense of horror he often felt over her alcoholism and the beatings he had witnessed, Mr. D. had attempted to attribute his hatred for his mother, not to her as a real person who was behaving destructively, but rather to her disease—alcoholism.

This diversionary method of dealing with his negative emotions ordinarily allowed him to contain his hostile feelings reasonably well. However, on the evening of his friend's wedding reception, Mr. D.'s long pent-up hostilities for his parents were suddenly set aflame and exploded in an irrational attack upon his girlfriend. Why, one could reasonably ask, did he lose control of his hostile emotions at that particular time and in that particular setting?

Mr. D. supplied the answers to this question through his own later mental associations with some of the details of that riotous evening. In subsequent therapy sessions he recalled that at the reception his girlfriend was wearing an outfit that reminded him of one of his mother's dresses. He then thought he noticed his girlfriend behaving coquettishly toward the man with whom she was talking, a flirtatious mannerism he recollected seeing his mother sometimes affect with men. Very soon and very unexpectedly his girlfriend had come to personify his mother. These largely unconscious associations set his blood aboil. Contritely commenting to me about his explosive behavior that unforgettable evening, Mr. D. noted with a considerable amount of self-insight, that it was interesting and probably significant, that at the wedding reception he had behaved like his mother by drinking too much and acting irrationally and, additionally, like his father by behaving jealously (his father had often accused his mother, probably with some justification, of infidelity) and physically attacking his girlfriend.

Without delving into greater detail relative to the case of Mr. D., suffice it to say we can observe that he obviously had excellent cause for harboring profound negative thoughts and emotions toward his parents. As is the case with many children of alcoholics, he attempted to cope with his hostile feelings by physically and emotionally estranging himself from his parents. A second mechanism of defense was to regard his mother's abhorrent and destructive behavior as merely a symptom of her disease, rather than a despicable aspect of her impaired character. Evidently, these means of defense had enabled Mr. D. to contain and cope with his angry feelings reasonably well for a substantial number of years. However, when his defenses were relatively weak due to fatigue and inebriation, and the social situation was sufficiently redolent with mental associations from his traumatic past, his childhood conflicts were suddenly revivified and his fury for his parents burst forth in a misplaced attack on his girlfriend.

Splitting Love and Hate

For many persons, the denial and disavowal of negative feelings and thoughts is often the result of a tendency to regard the antithetical emotions of love and hate as mutually exclusive. In other words, according to the attitudes of many individuals, one cannot love and also hate another person, either alternately or simultaneously. Hatred is mistakenly viewed as the total negation of love. Analogously, love is one-sidedly and idyllically viewed as an emotion that exists entirely apart from angry and sadistic emotions.

When people view love and hate as mutually exclusive emotions, they may fall prone to certain difficulties in acknowledging and handling their angry thoughts and feelings. Since angry emotions are thought to nullify or obliterate feelings of love, they are considered to be contemptible and even highly dangerous. Obviously, people will ordinarily do whatever is psychologically necessary to avoid destroying their own feelings of love for another person, including denying and suppressing their own angry emotions. Commonly, however, the attempt to maintain a wide and unbridgeable gulf between the emotions of love and hate result in guilt and shame whenever angry feelings rear their nasty heads in relation to a loved one.

In my work as a therapist, I have observed many persons who have struggled endlessly with their conflictual feelings of love and hate. Typically, these conflicts become readily evident in guilt-ridden individuals who attempt to hide and deny their hostile emotions by idealizing their loved ones. When asked about their feelings for their fathers, for example, they might respond as did one of my patients, a nineteen-year-old college student, who said, "He's perfect. We've never had problems between us. My problems are entirely of my own making and

I certainly hope you're not one of those Freudians who will be analyzing or making a fuss about my relationship with my father."

As the therapy unfolded and the patient became less guarded, her personal history revealed that there were indeed times when she and her father had serious disagreements and donnybrooks. When we eventually explored the reasons for the patient's initial concealment of conflict with her father, she expressed the following thoughts: "I thought if I admitted to being angry with him or if it appeared that I sometimes even hated him, I'd worry that he would think I didn't love him. I know I love him, and, although I know in my head that this is irrational, I feel that, because I love him, I can't be angry with him. The two feelings don't seem to go together. I guess it has something to do with how I feel he might react. And if he thought my anger toward him meant that I didn't really love him, that would kill me. That's why I can't accept some of my negative thoughts and emotions, I guess."

In the above-mentioned example, we can see that the patient's strivings to keep separate the emotions of love and hate took a considerable emotional toll upon her. Whenever her hostile or sadistic feelings interpenetrated with her feelings of love and affection for her father, she was overcome with a sense of shame and guilt. Unable to integrate her contradictory emotions and accept the fact that one cannot truly love another individual without at times also hating that person, she tenuously held onto her idealized attitude toward her father and, consequently, considered herself entirely to blame for the emotional problems and pain she suffered as a result of their relationship ("My problems are entirely of my own making").

Mr. B., a thirty-one-year-old college student from a Latin American country, had throughout most of his childhood been severely neglected by his mother who, in order to compensate for her woeful disregard for her son, bought him occasional expensive presents. Whenever his mother materially indulged him, Mr. B., out of feelings of elation and gratitude, temporarily suppressed his anger toward her for emotionally neglecting him. This pattern persisted throughout his childhood and ultimately resulted in an almost total denial of negative thoughts and emotions for his mother.

As an adult, Mr. B. experienced highly problematic relationships with women. Basically, his attitudes toward women were an extension of his long-standing ambivalence toward his mother. He placed women upon a pedestal, considered them beyond reproach, and was grateful for their every attention and interest in him. Conversely, whenever he was ignored or slighted by a woman, he became acutely angry and depressed. As one might expect, his relationships with women seriously lacked intimacy or longevity.

In therapy, Mr. B. steadfastly denied angry or hostile feelings toward his mother, despite strong indications of his contempt for women in general. When, after several months of therapy, he began to grudgingly acknowledge that he deeply resented his mother's depriving and neglectful attitude toward him throughout his childhood, he repeatedly pointed out that he could not "put together my love and hate for her. After all, she's my mother. A person does not hate his own mother. Yet, I know, I sometimes do hate her. But, you have to understand, she was all I had [his father had deserted the family when he was an infant]. So I had to love her. If I felt angry with her, it seemed that I didn't love her anymore and I didn't want to stop loving her. As I said, she was all I had."

For many persons like Mr. B, the fear of loss and abandonment causes them to drive a wide and unfordable hiatus between their feelings of love and hate, leaving them extremely prone to experience guilt and shame whenever anger and hostility appear alongside their affections for a loved one. As we can see, the psychic splitting of hate from love can provide a transient and illusory sense of personal well-being, but in the long run it ordinarily will cause a person to feel inordinate fear, guilt, and shame over the arousal of such negative emotions as hate and resentment.

Magical Thinking

The role of superstition and magical thinking in our everyday lives has been well documented. Sidestepping away from open ladders, avoiding cracks on the sidewalk, and wishing others a "gesundheit" after a sneeze (just in case the sneeze had a diabolical genesis), all constitute well-known examples of superstitious behavior.

Less obvious than the role of magical thinking in warding off evil spirits is its role in the governance of negative thoughts and emotions. It is quite common for many persons, including the unparanoic, to believe in the magical powers of their hostile feelings. The belief that a sadistic or murderous wish will come true can often cause terrifying fears. Children in particular are especially prone to such fears since their relatively undeveloped egos do not always enable them to perceive the irrationality of their angry wishes and fears.

Ms. G., a forty-one-year-old nurse, had suffered since childhood with an unflagging sense of wrongdoing and depression. As she had often stated, she intellectually realized that she had no realistic cause for thinking herself a bad person. Yet, she could not overthrow nagging thoughts that she had at some indeterminable point in her past committed a horrendous injury to others and, therefore, needed to be severely punished.

In carefully exploring Ms. G.'s past, it became quite clear that at no time had she actually perpetrated a seriously detrimental act toward another person. The cause of her guilt, therefore, had to be identified elsewhere. Ms. G.'s parents had married hurriedly, soon after it was discovered that her mother was pregnant with her. Both parents had a strong disinclination to marry but acquiesced to the wishes of their own parents that they provide their child with a two-parent family.

Almost from the inception of their marriage, Ms. G.'s parents bickered constantly, acting out their hostilities for each other by being openly adulterous. Ms. G. helplessly witnessed her parents' daily onslaughts and eventually came to feel great rage and resentment for the way they abused and maligned each other. She intuited that she had had something to do with her parents' conflicts and, to add to her feelings of insecurity, her parents viciously pointed out to her that, if it were not for her, they would not have ever married or had these awful problems. Thus, Ms. G. became the hapless scapegoat for her parents' unhappiness and hostilities.

As her parents' conflicts became more frequent and more violent, Ms. G.'s rage and resentment intensified. She often wished that her parents would divorce in order that peace might finally reign in her home. She felt enormously guilty for harboring such angry thoughts, so when her parents finally did divorce, she irrationally attributed the dissolution of their marriage to her own secret wishes. Her parents, who had few compunctions about blaming their many woes on their daughter, accused her of having caused their divorce.

Although logic and common sense suggested that she had not been guilty of mischief or disloyalty toward her parents, as a vulnerable child she could not withstand or refute their malicious allegations. In pondering the circumstances of her parents' marriage, Ms. G. recalled the many times she had indeed wished her parents would divorce. When her parents actually did divorce, it seemed that her wishes had been magically ratified. As many children are wont to do when their deepest wishes are fulfilled, Ms. G. came to believe in the magical power of her negative thoughts. Although she always maintained a capacity to view her magical beliefs with a large grain of salt, the guilt engendered by her parents' accusations made it impossible for her to completely cast off the feeling that she could actually harm others simply by harboring hostile thoughts toward them. As one might expect, whenever Ms. G. felt the surge of a strong negative thought or emotion, she automatically dreaded its potential for destructive enactment and, therefore, suppressed the thought or feeling.

Lest one think Ms. G.'s emotional difficulties are unique, it may be advisable at this juncture to point out that it is quite common for many psychologically healthy people to believe in the magical power of their own thoughts and emotions. As one might imagine, the fear that hostile or sadistic thoughts and feelings will magically eventuate in a disaster frequently leads to the denial and suppression of angry emotions.

As already suggested, children are particularly susceptible to magical beliefs in their own omnipotent powers. The nocturnal fears and nightmares of children are often the end result of their inability to cope with their own magical beliefs in the power of their negative thoughts. For example, many children will suffer from nightmares following a hostile encounter with a parent. Unable to quell or resolve their resentments over the conflict, they retreat to bed for the evening, only to discover that their anger festers and is soon transformed into thoughts of revenge.

One of the common forms of revenge contemplated by children, evidently considered by them to be of the righteous eye-for-an-eye variety, is the wish that the offending parent would die. Of course, children, generally, would hardly rejoice over the actual death of a parent, but a brief enjoyable fantasy involving the suffering and death of the offending parent is likely to crop up in the mind of even the happiest and healthiest children from time to time. If the sadistic, murderous thoughts fleetingly enter the consciousness of the child, he or she may dismiss them quickly. However, many children cannot dismiss their murderous feelings quite so easily. They fear that their thoughts will magically kill their parents. As a result, they feel tremendous guilt, shame, and dread as they attempt to drive away their "dangerous" thoughts and emotions. The fear that their murderous wishes will be magically enacted horrifies them and sometimes results in such symptoms as sanguineous and violent nightmares.

Religious Proscriptions

Analogous to, but different from, magical or superstitious thoughts in relation to one's negative emotions, is the religio-ethical viewpoint that views sadistic or murderous thoughts and feelings as inherently evil because they are the supposed moral equivalents of destructive deeds. In other words, according to this doctrine, a hostile or negative thought is, in moral terms, tantamount to a reprehensible deed.

In my clinical practice, I have observed that those persons who are strong adherents of the Catholic faith are particularly inclined to abide by the dictum that establishes the inherent evilness of negative thoughts and emotions. To underscore the essential nature of this doctrine, several centuries ago Catholic monks codified in religious handbooks those specific sanctions and penalties to be imposed for the various "evil" (sexual or hostile) thoughts of their votaries.

According to the many Catholics with whom I have spoken about this matter, including several priests, the contemporary Catholic Church has in this century assumed a more relaxed, less doctrinaire approach to the imaginary world of the human mind. According to my informants, although hostile and sadistic thoughts and emotions are still considered tantamount to damnatory deeds, most leaders of the contemporary Catholic Church apparently take a rather moderate, tempered approach to this moral issue. Thus, although a Catholic person's confession of jealous, adulterous, or even murderous emotions may continue to be viewed as a reprehensible form of moral weakness, confessors are ordinarily not so severely admonished or censured for their "evil" thoughts as had been their less fortunate counterparts during the Middle Ages.

Mr. R., a forty-five-year-old part-time college student, entered psychotherapy in a panic over his inability to rid himself of some "nasty," intrusive thoughts. This man had been raised in a strict Catholic home that he described as barren of love and warmth. His mother had been a severely depressed, morose, and aloof individual who preferred to have little to do with her son. Mr. R.'s father was a man who had strong authoritarian traits and in fits of temper would beat and humiliate his son.

Mr. R.'s childhood years were tumultuous. Out of feelings of rejection and desperation, he frequently truanted from school and engaged in delinquent activities. In his late teens he began to drink heavily, a form of self-destructive behavior that persisted over a decade. Mr. R. lived for a few years with a woman he had met in a bar, but their relationship was ordinarily rancorous and unfulfilling. Following the termination of this relationship, Mr. R. led a life of dissoluteness, drinking excessively, working only intermittently, and generally living a hand-to-mouth existence.

Feeling completely out of control of his life, he finally decided to undergo psychotherapy and entered a residential treatment facility funded and administered by the Catholic Church. Over the course of only a few years, Mr. R. acquired almost total control over his drinking, remained gainfully employed on a regular basis, and began to form important and sustaining social relationships for the first time in his life. As a result of his impressive rehabilitation, Mr. R. was justifiably profoundly grateful to the staff of the residential treatment facility and to the Catholic Church for rescuing him from what had been a hopeless and precarious existence.

Out of heartfelt gratitude for the life-saving care he had received, Mr. R. resolved to devote his life to serving the Catholic Church by entering the priesthood. In preparation for entering the seminary, he developed a very close affiliation with a Catholic university and immersed himself in Catholic dogma and teachings. The authority, structure, and cohesiveness of the Catholic Church provided Mr. R. with a deep sense of security and determination. The teachings of the church instilled in him an unwavering commitment to live a life of unassailable probity and devotion to God.

Above all else, Mr. R.'s deepest fear was that he might, as a result of certain untoward events or setbacks, revert to the miserable and perilous life he had once led. In order to prevent such a disastrous reversion, Mr. R. thought it absolutely essential to rid himself of all sinful thoughts and emotions—i.e., lustful or angry feelings. In his view, hostile or sadistic feelings were, as the Catholic Church had instructed, intrinsically evil.

Despite his earnest resolve to purify his thoughts, Mr. R. was continually beset by negative emotions such as defiance, anger, and jealousy. Feeling very guilty and at sea over these feelings, Mr. R. decided to enter psychotherapy. In our initial session, he made it clear that his goal was spiritual absolution and that, if it was possible, he wanted me to find a way for him to psychologically excise his negative thoughts and emotions. I told him at the outset that, in my view, such an objective was neither realistic nor desirable. I suggested to him that his hostile and sadistic emotions were as natural a part of his personality as were feelings of love and devotion to the Catholic Church and God. Therefore, I thought it best that we consider how he could effectively come to terms with his angry emotions—that is, feel less ashamed of the negative feelings—rather than pursue an illusionary means for obliterating them.

Mr. R. openly informed me that my nonjudgmental attitude toward his hostile and aggressive emotions, whether well intentioned or not, was anathematic to him and, moreover, to the Catholic faith. Nevertheless, he considered me to be a person who was competent and experienced in such matters, so, strictly on a trial basis, he agreed to a course of short-term psychotherapy. For a few sessions, Mr. R. complained of acute feelings of shame, aggravated by my willingness to listen to his hostile feelings without morally judging him.

In our third session, Mr. R. was particularly distraught over his inability to shake off or block out intrusive angry thoughts and emotions, especially toward such despised figures of the past as his mother, father, and his former girlfriend. When I empathically indicated that it would take a saintly or superhuman effort to rise so completely above all negative emotions, Mr. R. responded that it was indeed his intention to live his life like a saint, to piously strive to achieve a soterial state of pure holiness; in other words, to disown and transcend all negative thoughts and emotions.

When I again indicated to him that, in my view, such a personal goal seemed neither necessary nor desirable in order to live a devout and morally fulfilling life, Mr. R. somewhat contemptuously expressed his appreciation for my (misguided) opinion. But, he pointed out, I had to understand that he simply could not accept his negative thoughts, as I had suggested he do. He was unalterably convinced that angry or hostile emotions were, pure and simple, as evil as sadistic deeds.

In our fourth session, Mr. R. indicated that, since our last meeting, he had done a great deal of soul-searching. He also indicated that for a brief time he had considered me to be the devil incarnate, attempting to morally corrupt and beguile him with false and irreligious ideas. Eventually, however, he decided to seriously consider the possible validity of my viewpoint. He stated that he continued to find my quixotic ideas about his negative thoughts to be quite objectionable. But, as he put it, I was entitled to my opinions. After all, he said, wasn't it my expert opinion that he had come to me for in the first place?

Mr. R. and I met for a total of eight sessions (the limit set in the clinic). During the last several sessions, he seemed to be less anxious and pressured. Although, as we both expected, his attitude toward his own feelings of hostility continued to be harshly condemning, something I had said about his need to reach saintly heights of holiness had stuck in his craw and caused him to reevaluate his opinions about himself. He stated that he was beginning to realize that he was no saint and that, since he would most likely continue having negative thoughts from time to time, perhaps he had better get used to them. As he viewed it, his hostile emotions were definitely an evil aspect of his moral character, but perhaps he did not have to hate himself so scathingly for having such feelings. Since practically everyone else he knew felt hostilities at least occasionally, he decided that perhaps it would be best to accept his "evil" thoughts as a common human frailty.

As the case of Mr. R. illustrates, the moral concept that establishes a negative thought to be equivalent to an immoral deed can lead to considerable guilt and self-condemnation. Catholics, to be sure, are certainly not the only persons who subscribe to this concept. In my estimation, most people, at least fleetingly, equate their most hostile or murderous thoughts with evil or immoral conduct.

Euphemisms for Negative Emotions

The evidence that many persons attach evil connotations to their hostile emotions is found in the penchant of so many individuals to euphemize their negative feelings. For example, a thirty-five-year-old business executive, Mr. W., described to me that, no matter how hard he tried, he could not feel close to his father. In his view, his father's passive and wishy-washy personality only deserved his disrespect and contempt. Although it made him feel guilty whenever he and his father were together, he could not help but cringe and recoil in response to his father's attempts to be close and affectionate with him.

After listening to Mr. W.'s litany of complaints about his father, I stated what seemed to be the obvious, that is, that he must feel considerable rage for the man. Mr. W. stared at me in disbelief, scowled and then admonishingly informed me that "rage" was much too strong a word for what he felt toward his father. "Annoyed" perhaps, "upset" maybe, but not "rage." Why not rage, I queried. Because rage, according to Mr. W., was a nasty, evil emotion and not one that he wished to feel toward someone he loved, such as his father. Of course, Mr. W. did not see the discrepancy between his words and the harsh, shunning way he treated his father.

It is commonplace for large numbers of persons, in and out of psychotherapy, to use euphemisms to describe intense negative thoughts and feelings. To say that one feels "bothered," "annoyed," or "upset," rather than furious, angry, jealous, resentful, or vindictive, seems to assuage feelings of guilt and moral culpability. Conversely, and unfortunately, the open admission of genuine feelings of rage and vindictiveness, seems to cause many people to feel that, solely by virtue of their hostile thoughts they are actually carrying out a heinous and unforgivable crime. Small wonder, then, that when people equate hostile thoughts with immoral behavior, they will feel guilty and fearful over the entrance into consciousness of even the mildest sadistic fantasies.

Fear of Losing Control

The denial and disavowal of negative emotions and thoughts may be prompted by realistic or fanciful apprehensions that the hostile feelings and impulses will become uncontrollable, all consuming, and actually lead to destructive or sadistic behavior. Such fears are usually quite exaggerated, as evidenced by the strong capacity of most people to suppress, redirect, or socialize their angry emotions and impulses. Yet, as is patently obvious, there are members of our society who possess only tenuous control over their angry emotions and, consequently, are quite prone to behaving in a highly antisocial or even violent manner. Many such persons have excellent reasons for fearing their own negative emotions because, rather than finding socially constructive outlets for their hostilities, they enact their emotions by mistreating others.

However, many individuals underestimate their ability to control their hostile thoughts and emotions. They are unable to appreciate the psychological distance that exists between their sadistic fantasies and the actual enactment of these fantasies. If their hostile feelings become especially intense and their defense mechanisms cannot cope adequately with the emotional upsurge, they may understandably fear that their hostilities will eventually be transformed into overly destructive behavior.

A twenty-six-year-old man, Mr. H., had recently ended a relationship with a woman with whom he had lived for over a year. During the first few months of their relationship, they enjoyed a compatible and mutually nurturing partnership. However, in his attempts to deepen and solidify their relationship, Mr. H. began to materially indulge and fawn over his girlfriend. She, in turn, was highly receptive to his generous overtures and in time began to expect him to cater to her every whim and expectation. Expecting her appreciation and love in return for his generosity, Mr. H. persisted in his bountiful indulgence of his girlfriend.

After several months of pandering to her, Mr. H. began to doubt the wisdom of his actions, especially since he was not only rapidly depleting his limited financial resources, but was slowly realizing that his girlfriend was exploiting and losing respect for him. When he finally decided to pull in his financial reins and curb his gift-giving tendencies, his girlfriend took umbrage with the turnabout in his behavior and began to withdraw and treat him with animosity. He then fully realized that he had been badly duped by her (and himself) into believing that she had really cared about him. Feeling terribly betrayed, he ended the relationship.

In the months that followed the termination of their relationship, Mr. H. began to feel increasingly embittered and vindictive over the manipulation and exploitation he had recently experienced at the hands of his former girlfriend. He began to have vivid fantasies about killing her, many of which entailed various methods of torture and mutilation. For the most part, Mr. H. fully realized that his sadistic fantasies were just that—fantasies. However, there were times when he was frightened by the vividness and ferocity of his sadistic wishes and even began to seriously contemplate the possible consequences of murdering his ex-girlfriend.

Responding therapeutically to Mr. H.'s murderous emotions was a complicated and delicate task. It was important, in my estimation, to validate the extent to which he was entitled to feel murderous anger toward a person who had obviously treated him with disregard and contempt. Yet, as I pointed out to him, it was not only immoral to hurt or kill another person, it would also be downright stupid and self-destructive, since he would obviously suffer greatly for any act of harm he perpetrated against this woman. Mr. H. countered by pointing out that it would give him great pleasure to see her suffer and die, considering the mean and devious ways she had treated him. I, in turn, decisively countered with my own opinion that if he indeed derived sadistic gratification from actually murdering his ex-girlfriend, knowing him as well as I did, I knew that he would hate himself afterward and, regardless of whether or not he would be apprehended, prosecuted, convicted, and imprisoned for such a crime, I also knew that his conscience could never come to terms with the commission of such a deed. In other words, in the final analysis, he would discover that he himself would be horribly victimized by his own crime and, therefore, the murder of his former girlfriend would clearly deliver a ruinous blow to his life. Furthermore, as I added, since he so deeply hated this woman, it made little sense to kill her because this would allow her (albeit posthumously) to go on destroying his life. Why, I asked, would he allow someone he despised so much to torpedo and sink his future? It seemed to me that if he really hated her, his sweetest revenge (if revenge were absolutely necessary) would be to make a genuine success of his life. After all, since she had been bent on turning his life into a failure, wouldn't his success, assuming she learned of it, serve to disappoint her?

On occasion, Mr. H. raised angry doubts about whether I was taking his homicidal wishes seriously. I assured him that I was. His doubts about the seriousness of my attitude stemmed in part from my willingness to nonjudgmentally accept his homicidal fantasies. He often asked me what I thought of those fantasies. Did I think them wrong, evil, immoral? Did they necessarily mean that he would or could kill his former girlfriend? Did these dastardly thoughts make him a vile person?

I told him, sometimes to his amazement, that I saw nothing inherently wrong or evil in the wish to kill another person. A fantasy of that nature was understandable and rather proportionate to the extent to which he was betrayed and exploited by this woman. While he had lived with her he had often felt that she was emotionally killing him a bit each day and, therefore, he was now fantasizing murderous revenge for her psychologically lethal behavior toward him.

I suggested to Mr. H. that he might best deal with his murderous wishes by understanding them as completely as he could in the context of his relationship with this woman. In addition, I indicated that these murderous wishes were important and useful, since they provided vital insights into his feelings and thoughts, but he also needed to understand that they were only fantasies and by all means must not be enacted.

For several months following the dissolution of his relationship with his former girlfriend, Mr. H. was plagued by his vengeful and murderous thoughts toward her. He often felt ashamed of his wishes to wreak revenge, but was incessantly bombarded with such notions. Most troublesome were his doubts that he could contain these wishes. Whenever he was reminded of a particularly humiliating or exploitative experience from the recent past, he felt a resurgence of his homicidal emotions followed by an intense fear of losing control of his rage and committing an irrevocable act of violence.

Repeatedly, Mr. H. described to me his murderous fantasies, sometimes seeming to derive sadistic satisfaction from his own gory descriptions of his ex-girlfriend's dismemberment and harrowing death. Other times, he shuddered and was horrified over the violence of his murderous wishes. He continued to ask my advice about how to view and handle these feelings. Each time I suggested that he attempt to understand them as fully as possible, rather than act them out. I further suggested that he confine his discussion of them to our therapeutic hours in order that he could examine them in depth and detail. As well, in order to buttress his psychological defenses, I encouraged him to call me at any time if he thought he was seriously losing control of his rage. As it turned out, there were several occasions when he took me up on this offer.

The therapeutic tack of encouraging Mr. H. to embrace, understand, and appreciate his own sadistic fantasies (in the context of the double-dealing he had painfully experienced with his ex-girlfriend), rather than seek to disown and disavow them, eventually bore fruit. He began to view his sadistic wishes with greater perspective and even a degree of humor. His progress, however, was uneven and, in his view, inordinately slow. He many times remarked that his violent fantasies could never exquisitely enough match the injustices he had suffered and that his former girlfriend actually deserved the "real thing": physical disfigurement and a painful death. I, of course, steadfastly insisted that, no matter how justified he was in *wishing* her dead, it would be immoral, wrongheaded, and self-destructive to truly victimize her.

In time, Mr. H. was able to neutralize and control his murderous notions, although it seemed that he might never be able to completely dispel them. He has since formed a relationship with a very caring, supportive, and considerate woman who has immeasurably helped Mr. H. to recover from the disastrous encounter he had had with his former girlfriend. They have married and Mr. H., who had always been a first-rate scholar, has gone on to be highly successful in his chosen field.

The example of Mr. H. illustrates one of the reasons for the disownment and repression of negative emotions. When negative thoughts and emotions become so violent, so volatile, that they blisteringly test the self-control, integrity, and inner resources of an individual, their presence is likely to be consciously resisted. Although the psychological defense of disownment may temporarily offer some relief from the unremitting intensity of violent emotions, such a respite from the hellish feelings may be short-lived. The person who exclusively repudiates, rather than acknowledges and comes to terms with sadistic emotions, may be forced to deal with these same impulses over and over again. In other words, simply stanching hostile thoughts and emotions by denying and disavowing their existence can serve, somewhat paradoxically, only to intensify and exacerbate feelings of hostility.

It may be helpful to keep in mind that hostile feelings do not necessarily become all consuming any more than affectionate and loving feelings, providing, of course, that our hostilities are adequately acknowledged, understood, and expressed in a constructive manner.

In this chapter I have explored and explained some of the reasons why people tend to deny and repudiate negative emotions and thoughts. Now let us consider some of the ways in which negative emotions can be regarded with the acceptance and respect to which they are entitled.

A Morally Neutral Attitude

Since you are apt to be horrified and dismayed by some of your hostile, sadistic emotions, it might be quite helpful, at least initially, to consider revamping some of your attitude toward these emotions. In order to do this, see if you can at least momentarily convince yourself that your negative feelings, no matter how intense and vivid, are *in themselves* harmless and morally neutral.

I realize that it may be very difficult to adopt such an unorthodox viewpoint since most your life you have probably been taught that hostile emotions contain the fertile seeds of personal evil.   Nevertheless, consider for a moment how many times in your life you have already harbored highly negative emotions without committing a single evil or sadistic deed as a result. This may help you to realize that usually most of your angry thoughts and feelings remain harmlessly in your head without ever causing you or anyone else undue suffering.   Once having grasped this fact, then try to leisurely reflect upon your hostile thoughts without in the least applying moral values or judgments to them. Better yet, if you can derive some gratification, pleasure, and amusement from your hostile fantasies, by all means do so. Of course, do not at the same time delude yourself into thinking that you can indiscriminately act out your angry wishes without causing harm to yourself or others. In other words, angry, even murderous, thoughts and emotions do not in themselves cause harm, but angry *behavior*, if expressed impulsively and inappropriately, can most definitely inflict pain and harm on others.

A Comical Perspective

In order to derive the greatest benefit from your negative thoughts and emotions you might occasionally attempt to observe their comical or absurd aspects. Obviously, this may not always be possible because acute hostile feelings by their very nature tend to obliterate thoughts of levity and humor. Nonetheless, rather than consistently deny and repudiate your negative thoughts and emotions, seek to find in them some humorous or preposterous elements. I think you will find that even the most wrathful and sadistic thoughts hold the potential to be viewed as comical and amusing, provided you can open your eyes and your heart to that possibility. And, if you can meet this emotional challenge, you will have discovered in your negative emotions a veritable wellspring of positive strength, knowledge, and determination.

The Social Context

Naturally, the tendency to repudiate and deny negative emotions does not take place in a social vacuum. In our everyday lives we often feel quite angry and resentful without suffering a significant loss of self-esteem or morale; that is, until we suddenly encounter a disapproving attitude toward our negative emotions on the part of someone else. When someone whose opinion we greatly value tells us that our anger and resentment are unfounded and irrational we may take such comments to heart and begin to disavow them.

For example, a young man, Mr. U., who was studying to be a computer scientist, grew up in a home with two alcoholic parents. Although he generally did well academically, his ability to concentrate on his studies was seriously undermined by his periodic contacts with his parents, who continued to drink heavily.

Mr. U. usually became justifiably enraged by his parents' self-destructive drinking but was fairly capable of emotionally rebounding from the repulsive contacts he had with them; that is, until he discussed the matter with his brother. Mr. U.'s brother, who himself was a heavy drinker, told Mr. U. that he ought not be so angry and unforgiving toward their parents. Upon hearing this, Mr. U. unthinkingly swallowed his anger, considered himself a scoundrel and a bit crazy for getting so upset with his parents and, as a result, became even angrier and more depressed than ever.

This example is an apt illustration of how one's negative emotions can be misunderstood and manipulated by another individual. Now let us use this example to learn something about the constructive uses of negative emotions. Whenever other persons downplay, ridicule, debunk, or rebuff your negative emotions, try to avoid the almost instinctive tendency to assume that they are necessarily objective and well-intentioned. This is not to suggest that you should assume just the opposite; that is, that they are necessarily being overly subjective and ill-intentioned. Rather, when your negative emotions are criticized or devalued by another person, take time out to inspect the possible reasons for that person's actions toward you. Ask yourself, is that person being reasonable, objective, and fair in his or her assessment of what you feel? If it seems that you are being treated unfairly, is this because you are simply thin-skinned and cannot brook criticism without becoming hostile and defensive? Or, is it possible that you truly misunderstood the actual intent and nature of the criticism directed at you?

If, after carefully weighing these possibilities, you have concluded that a person's response to your negative emotions was definitely insensitive, if not malevolent, then consider some of the possible reasons why you were mistreated in this respect. You may find this psychological investigation quite revealing and even emotionally uplifting, for reasons that I will soon explain.

For example, when I discussed with Mr. U. the possible reasons his brother advised him to ignore their parents' drinking problems and bury his anger toward them, it soon came to light that his brother had a vested interest in having him see these matters through rose-colored lenses. For one, the brother himself had buried and hidden much of his own anger for his parents over the years and, therefore, felt threatened by Mr. U.'s anger toward them. Also, since he himself was an alcoholic, Mr. U.'s brother felt the need to safeguard and justify his own self-destructive drinking by pointing out to Mr. U. that their parents' drinking was nothing to get perturbed about.

When Mr. U. came to understand his brother's ulterior motives for trivializing his anger, he experienced considerable relief and clarity of mind. He realized that his angry feelings about his parents' alcoholism were valid and need not be infringed upon or overruled by a brother who, for his own personal reasons, had to protect their parents from his angry criticism.

I mentioned earlier that the example of Mr. U. would illustrate why it is sometimes emotionally uplifting to determine the motives of another individual who has discounted your anger. By determining some of the motives of a criticizing individual you can better assess the reality of your own motives and emotions. This, in turn, may enable you to better validate your feelings and thereby overcome the tendency to blame yourself for harboring angry emotions that allegedly have no basis. In this manner you can combat one of the common sources of depression and loss of self-esteem: the feeling that your negative emotions are flawed, groundless, and violable.

I have remarked earlier that you might find it advantageous to begin the psychological process of viewing your negative emotions and thoughts from a morally neutral position. I realize and appreciate that for many persons this is a monumental emotional challenge. In a great many respects it probably runs quite counter to the moral teachings with which you have been inculcated since you were a very young child. For example, it seems that it is the experience of most young children when they express to their parents the fact that they hate (even momentarily) one of their siblings, to be told, "Don't say that! You shouldn't think such things! Those are bad thoughts. You must always love your sister [or brother]."

Hearing such things from one's parents, if they are repeated often and stridently enough, tends to cause a child not only to deny genuine hostile emotions for a sibling but, because these emotions must then be involuntarily suppressed and denied, the beleaguered child inevitably comes to feel even greater resentment and hatred for that sibling.

Since the moral attitudes you hold toward your own negative emotions are the accumulation and culmination of a lifetime of absorbing the ethical teachings of your family, teachers, and the religious institutions you have attended, you are apt to regard any major revision in your moral outlook with considerable skepticism. Despite this skepticism, however, allow yourself to engage in the following intellectual retrospection. Begin by asking yourself, "How did I arrive at some of my attitudes toward my negative emotions? What experiences in my life have principally shaped and influenced the ways in which I view my angry feelings? Who are some of the people who have most strongly affected my attitudes toward my negative emotions? Did these people for the most part behave rationally or irrationally when they responded to my anger? Did they at times seem to use fallacious or implausible arguments in order to justify their own attitudes toward the emotions of anger, jealousy, and resentment? If so, which of their arguments seemed sound and which baseless? Why? And, to what extent have I been influenced in my own thinking about negative emotions by what I myself consider to be the faulty notions of others?"

If nothing else, these questions should be thought provoking. But more importantly, they may point the way toward understanding how you have arrived at your own moral attitudes regarding your own feelings. Although you probably wouldn't want to or need to jettison all of your moral attitudes in favor of some new ethical system of thought, this retrospective look at the evolution of your own ethical development can help you reevaluate those particular attitudes that cause you psychological difficulty whenever you are besieged by angry emotions.

Assuming a morally neutral attitude toward angry or hostile emotions will more than likely be viewed as an unorthodox and even scurrilous form of social deviation by many people, especially those who misrepresent this attitude as a license for hostile *behavior*. Therefore, if you are inclined to adopt and give vocal support to this new moral position, expect that you may encounter ardent dissent from others. Therefore, it is important to be patient and tolerant when helping others grasp the meaning of your beliefs. If you are perchance accused of espousing immoral concepts or of advocating, for example, wayward lawlessness, assume that you obviously have not gotten your point across and, with some people, you never will. The point here is not to win moral arguments or popularity contests. Rather, it is to provide yourself with a morally liberating set of attitudes toward your own negative emotions that will enable you to rid yourself of the encumbering symptoms of irrational guilt whenever you happen to have a hostile feeling. Of course, if none of this makes much sense to you or you simply wish to retain a completely antithetical set of moral ideas about anger and hostility, that is certainly your prerogative and I wish you well.

Chapter 4

The Constructive Uses of Negative Thoughts and Emotions

This chapter will discuss the various constructive uses of negative thoughts and emotions. Obviously, there are an infinite number of means by which negative feelings can be put to constructive use. Fortunately, most people seem to have the capability to transform, at least to a degree, negative emotions into positive behavior and accomplishments. One common and effective means of transmuting negative experiences and emotions into constructive behavior is through the pursuit of positive social action.

Positive Social Action

A woman who had been married for thirty-seven years discovered that her husband was afflicted with Alzheimer's disease. For a brief period, this woman, Ms. B., nursed her husband at home, but soon his rapidly deteriorating condition necessitated his hospitalization in a nursing home. During the year in which her husband remained in the nursing home, Ms. B. was his daily and devoted companion and caretaker. As one would expect, the many hours of sitting vigil with a loved one who had become disoriented and oblivious to his surroundings seriously undermined Ms. B.'s morale and sense of well-being.

Watching her husband day after day deteriorate and eventually die left Ms. B. with profound feelings of loss and bereavement. Compounding her feelings of despair and remorse was an issue that unexpectedly and repeatedly arose throughout the course of her husband's illness. Ms. B. discovered that, due to certain bureaucratic snags and limitations, the exorbitant costs of her husband's hospital care was only partially defrayed by state and federal programs. Thus, the nest egg that had been slowly and laboriously accumulated over many years would need to be tapped and depleted in order to pay for Mr. B.'s care.

As she investigated the state and federal programs, Ms. B. learned some disheartening facts. Her husband and she were ineligible for many benefits because they possessed, according to state and federal regulations, too many financial assets. In what has come to be known as a Catch-22, she was told, in effect, that by depleting her financial resources, she could qualify for governmental assistance. Her intensive investigations of state and federal regulations uncovered many ironies and contradictions inherent in the government's methods of (un)assisting the aged.

Throughout her husband's illness, Ms. B. had been an active member of an Alzheimer's support group, a group of relatives of Alzheimer's patients that met on a regular basis. After her husband died, Ms. B. remained a member of that group, attending meetings regularly and volunteering to research the governmental assistance programs for the hospitalized aged. The more she learned about some of these anomalous and inequitable programs, the angrier she became. The angrier she became, the more vigorous and determined she was to redress the injustices and inconsistencies in the programs. The members of her support group, recognizing in Ms. B. a penetrating intelligence as well as outstanding leadership qualities, elected her to the chapter's presidency.

In her capacity as chapter president, Ms. B. has been a creative, dedicated, and innovative leader. She keeps abreast of legislative and statutory developments in the field of geriatric care, doggedly investigating and challenging those regulations that are inimical to the interests of aged patients. With justifiable pride, she champions and lobbies for persons, who, like herself, have been victimized by a governmental system of health care that is often backward and unresponsive in its attitude toward the infirm aged. Although her husband has been deceased for over two years, she continues to commemorate their relationship through her idealism and social activism in behalf of the elderly. She is, in short, the epitome of an individual who has been able to transform and utilize her rage and resentment for socially constructive purposes.

Many persons select careers for which they are eminently unsuited and ill-matched. Unfortunately, for either practical or psychological reasons, many such individuals remain in jobs their entire lives that they consider sterile, tedious, and detrimental to their integrity and mental health. The sense of oppression and hopelessness over carrying out onerously repetitive or meaningless work can of course lead to intense and persistent feelings of hostility and resentment. The disgruntled employees, as is generally recognized, can easily transport their unhappiness from the workplace to their home and family, thereby spreading their misery like a contagious and malignant disease.

Pursuing One's Dreams

Mr. K., a man in his late twenties, had an outstanding aptitude and talent as a musician. As an adolescent, he was a gifted instrumentalist and was, therefore, a highly coveted and appreciated member of his band. After graduating from high school, Mr. K. continued to write and play music with a professional band that exhibited considerable promise. Shortly after his graduation from high school he married a woman who was, he soon discovered, very self-centered and materialistic. She soon became pregnant and when their first child was born Mr. K. realized that his meager earnings from his band's gigs could not support his family. At his wife's insistence, he procured a second job at which he moonlighted while continuing to regularly play in the band.

Over a period of several months, Mr. K.'s heavy work schedule and the all too brief and insufficient opportunities for sleep that he snatched between jobs began to sap his emotional and physical strength. Faced with the inescapable choice between giving up one job or the other, he acquiesced to his wife's wishes by relinquishing his ties with the band. He, however, dutifully, remained with his second job, a well paying position with a large corporation. Despite the fact that he had little enthusiasm for this job, Mr. K. applied himself conscientiously to this assignment and consistently received excellent evaluations of his work from his supervisors.

Mr. K. deeply regretted and resented his severance from the band. His participation in the band had for several years been an essential source of aesthetic satisfaction and social opportunities that were not to be easily found elsewhere. Although the band had not yet completely jelled or reached stardom, it did have considerable promise and much of its budding success could be attributed to the original music written and performed by Mr. K.

Mr. K.'s marriage worsened until he and his wife could no longer tolerate each other. After they divorced, Mr. K. changed jobs, but now that he was the father of two small children and providing for their support, he felt compelled to continue working in a corporate setting where his income was reasonably high and dependable. He often thought nostalgically about his former days with his band but did not seriously consider rejoining that or any other musical group.

Throughout his psychotherapy, Mr. K. spoke disparagingly about his work. He found himself out of place at work, even though he performed his assignments with evident skill and effectiveness. Despite the fact that he had regularly received salary increases and promotions, he regarded his employment as simply a place to drearily put in some time in order to pay his bills. Although he generally liked his co-workers and supervisors, he felt no sense of camaraderie or commonality with them.

During his therapy sessions, Mr. K. lengthily reminisced about the halcyon days of his past when he played with his band, the time before taking a second job and undermining his mental health. With obvious pleasure, he described how he felt especially alive and creative when he performed his music before enthusiastic audiences. The remorse he felt over abandoning his musical career was amplified when he came to learn that his former band had begun to receive widespread recognition and auspicious offers from important recording companies.

As he thought back upon his decision to sever his ties with his former band, Mr. K.'s anger and resentment for his ex-wife's role in this decision grew. He assumed due responsibility for the decision, but also realized that if his wife had been compassionate and supportive during his struggles to earn a living, he could have eventually been happy and successful in pursuing a musical career.

Because of his exemplary performance at work, Mr. K. was offered and accepted an appreciable promotion and salary increase. He was highly ambivalent about this improvement in his status because, in his estimation, this more deeply committed him to remaining in a line of work that was unchallenging and only peripheral to his central interests. So, rather than feeling flattered and inspired by the strides he had made at work, Mr. K. felt entrapped by these circumstances.

As the months passed, Mr. K. felt more and more resentful over his well paying but humdrum job. Then, one day he received an offer from a former acquaintance to join a band that was familiar with his music and musical abilities. Mr. K. was overjoyed and enticed by his friend's attractive offer. Yet the timing of the offer created a crisis in his life. His corporate position had provided him with a lucrative salary, considerable status, and important perquisites such as extensive health benefits. Because the band he was invited to join toured a wide geographical area, he would be required to leave his job if he accepted the offer. Although a musical career might eventually lead to financial success, in order to join the band he had to forfeit, at least temporarily, a considerable amount of economic security.

Even more importantly, going on tour with the band might jeopardize his relationship with his girlfriend. Because her job prevented her from accompanying Mr. K. on his musical tour, they would see each other only sporadically and briefly. Nevertheless, Mr. K.'s girlfriend was sympathetic and favorable to his job change and vowed to stand by him as he put his new career to the test. Heartened and encouraged by her support and stick-to-itiveness, Mr. K. decided to take a leave of absence from his corporate position and sign a contract with the band.

As he indicated to me, Mr. K. had no realistic assurances that he would be successful or happy in his musical endeavors. But he knew full well that he was discontented with his present employment and that he might be afforded few such opportunities in the future. Above all else, he did not want to suffer from lifelong regrets and disappointments because he was too fearful and insecure to take this large but challenging risk.

Because I have not seen or heard from Mr. K. since he has terminated psychotherapy, I do not know how well he has fared in his musical undertakings. However, I think I can safely say that he had made a wise and constructive decision in leaving a type of employment that he considered dreary and meaningless for a profession that offered him creative and aesthetic opportunities. He is an example of an individual who has transformed and utilized past negative experiences and emotions in order to enhance his life.

The negative and unhappy experiences of childhood are commonly the wellsprings of sadistic as well as self-destructive behavior in adulthood. As is well documented, the children of battering parents often, although by no mean always, become physically abusive parents themselves. The children of alcoholics, terribly victimized by the outrageous drinking habits of their parents, disproportionately suffer from alcoholism. These children may be quite determined to live and act differently from their parents, yet they often find it difficult if not impossible to develop attitudes and life styles that are at variance with those of their parents. If these children recognize their parents' weaknesses and self-destructiveness, why do they fall prey to them by repeating and reenacting their parents' mistakes in their own lives?

The answers to this question are rather complicated. Although children may hate a parent's destructive or sadistic behavior, they most likely look upon that parent as a primary source of love and, therefore, as a model worthy of emulation. Consequently, many of the parents' personality traits, including their most negative and destructive characteristics, will be adopted by children as a means by which they can be close to and gain approval from their parents. In other words, children incorporate aspects of their parents' personalities and behavior in order to derive love and nurturance from their relationship with them.

Identification with the Aggressor

However, many children identify with their parents' sadistic behavior not out of wishes for love and affection, but out of feelings of revenge and resentment. Battered or psychologically violated children will often hate the offending parent toward whom they harbor retaliatory and vengeful emotions. Since such children have learned firsthand from their parents that physical violence and sadism can be an immediate and telling form of inflicting harm upon another person, they may quite naturally adopt hostile forms of behavior whenever they entertain thoughts of revenge. Although they may realize that they themselves have suffered greatly from their parents' sadism, they, perhaps involuntarily, adopt these sadistic ways as a symbolic means of redressing the wrongs they have had to endure. Thus, although certain individuals may be earnestly determined to disassociate themselves from the abusive characteristics of their parents, their wishes for revenge and self-vindication may prevail and thereby cause them to adopt those very same sadistic traits they so despised in them. This psychological defense mechanism has been technically referred to as "identification with the aggressor."

Fortunately, many persons who, as children, have suffered severe neglect or physical abuse do not automatically develop into either neglectful or abusive persons as adults. For reasons that are not always explainable, many such persons convert their resentments and hostilities into caring and loving attitudes.

One such person is a thirty-two-year-old woman, Ms. C., who had grown up with parents who were virtual strangers to one another. Ms. C.'s father held a job that required considerable travel, keeping him away from home for long stretches of time. There was weighty evidence that he chose and retained such employment precisely for the purpose of remaining far afield from his wife and family. When he was home, Ms. C.'s father was inconsistent and inept in his attempts to make up for his frequent and protracted absences. He and his wife had constant and acrimonious disagreements, some of which no doubt stemmed from Mrs. C.'s justifiable rage over being abandoned by her husband.

Ms. C. was often caught in the middle of her parents' conflicts and in time became a convenient scapegoat for their marital discord. Thus, her father, who at times could be quite loving and adoring with his daughter, would beat her and maliciously accuse her of being the sole cause of the family's tribulations. Because Ms. C.'s mother was sexually rebuffed by her husband, she was envious of her daughter's sometimes affectionate relationship with him. Her envy, apparently mostly of an unconscious nature, caused her to treat Ms. C. with a denigrating and contemptuous attitude. As a result of these conflicts, Ms. C. was plagued with the chronic feeling that she did not truly belong to her own family. Somewhat predictably, she often doubted her self-worth and her capacity to instill warmth and respect in others.

Despite a rather bruising and tumultuous childhood, Ms. C. developed extremely likeable personal qualities and, as a result, enjoyed many close and rewarding friendships. Yet there remained many doubts about her acceptability to others. Even though she generally received affirmation from her friends, it often amazed her that other people accepted her personal limitations and shortcomings.

Especially problematic to Ms. C. were her gnawing doubts about her friends. Although she realized that she had many genuine and steadfast friends, she often feared that they would resent and reject her if she became professionally successful. When we explored the basis of this fear it became apparent that much of it harked back to her feelings about her father's overriding professional endeavors.

Although her father was a professional success, his fanatical devotion to his work played a central role in disrupting and stifling Ms. C.'s childhood. Because her father could not adequately balance his professional and parental responsibilities, Ms. C. felt sorely neglected and slighted by him. Projecting her own feelings of rejection onto others, she imagined that her friends would resent her, as she resented her father for seeking, first and foremost, professional success.

Because of the depth of her resentment toward her father, she did not realize that her current concerns over her friendships were greatly exaggerated. Unlike her father, she was not seeking professional success to the exclusion of her friends and family. The very fact that she considered it necessary to weigh and investigate this issue in psychotherapy indicated that she genuinely cared about her friends and would not jettison them for a professional career.

Much to her credit, Ms. C. persevered in her quest for professional success. At times her doubts about the wisdom of this decision were undermined by certain friends who envied and begrudged her success, but, with the help of psychotherapy, Ms. C. understood the motives of these individuals and did not allow them to deter her. Others of her friends, those persons who supported her professional pursuits, were appreciated for their loyalty and concern.

At present, Ms. C. holds an excellent position in a small but thriving corporation that has enabled her to develop the full potentialities of her intelligence and determination. Although she occasionally has misgivings over how well she is balancing the professional and personal parts of her life, she has sustained close friendships while establishing a solid foundation for a successful and personally rewarding career. In doing so, she is an excellent example of an individual who has capably transformed negative experiences and emotions into constructive and positive pursuits.

The transformation of negative emotions into positive pursuits does not necessarily manifest itself in tangible or overt forms of behavior. Quite frequently, this transformation may be largely an internal, intrapsychic process that is not always accurately perceived by others. It is quite possible that a person will undergo quite dramatic emotional changes without even their closest friends or relations becoming aware of the transformation. Yet, the internal, sometimes unobservable strides people make in positively changing their attitudes and thoughts can be quite as dramatic and significant as the progress another person makes in attaining more measurable social or professional success.

Molestation

Ms. Y., a twenty-eight-year-old woman, entered psychotherapy as a result of deep and recurrent feelings of depression coupled with highly self-destructive emotions that at times aroused suicidal impulses. Although she usually had adequate insight into and self-control over her self-destructive impulses, she was especially tormented by them soon after having had prolonged contact with her family.

As a very young child, Ms. Y. experienced a terrifying encounter in a movie theater with a man who had attempted to molest her. At the time, no one in her family was aware of this traumatic incident and, because she (rather realistically, it seems) feared they would irrationally blame her for its occurrence, she did not disclose it to them.

Ms. Y.'s parents were themselves quite insecure and depressed individuals. Their marital relationship was relatively devoid of intimacy or mutual regard and they somehow directed many of their personal marital conflicts at their daughter, Ms. Y. Ms. Y.'s father, evidently a man of weak character and terribly poor judgment, began to sexually fondle and molest his daughter during her preadolescent years. In the late evening hours he would invite her to have sexual trysts with him while the rest of the family slept. By blandishing her with avowals of love and affection, he for several years induced her to acquiesce to these incestuous assignations, until she finally developed the emotional and physical strength to stave off his persistent overtures.

Unfortunately, Ms. Y.'s relationship with her mother was no refuge for her. Her mother was a carping, caustic woman who took every opportunity to badger and demean her daughter. No matter how hard she tried, Ms. Y. could find no means by which to arouse in her mother positive feelings for her. Because her mother was so consistently adversarial, Ms. Y. realized that she could not safely reveal to her the incestuous goings-on that were causing her such profound and ineffable grief.

Unable to derive a sense of self-worth and wholeness from her parents, Ms. Y. came to despise and avoid them. A primary source of her resentment was her father's unwillingness or inability to acknowledge his erstwhile incestuous behavior and its deleterious effects upon her. Ms. Y. also deeply resented her mother's elective blindness to her father's behavior. Quite justifiably, she considered herself to be the unwilling victim of her mother's inability to either acknowledge or prevent her father's sexual misconduct. Whenever she visited her parents, her feelings of victimization and worthlessness were reactivated and intensified. Invariably, she came away from these visits feeling demoralized, hateful, and, at times, suicidal.

Like many other persons in her situation, Ms. Y. felt deeply ashamed and guilt ridden over her murderous emotions toward her parents. Also, like many other victims of incest, she baselessly blamed herself for her father's sexual exploitation. Thus, she developed a tendency to internalize her hateful feelings. Her homicidal feelings for her parents, combined with her intense shame, turned inward and transformed into self-contempt and suicidal ruminations. In other words, her guilt caused her to hate herself, rather than the real culprits, her parents.

By minutely examining in psychotherapy the traumatic events of her past, Ms. Y. gradually perceived her relationships with her parents more objectively and with much less guilt. For the most part, she has continued to avoid her parents, but has not suffered from intense backlashes of guilt and shame as she had in previous years. By increasing her understanding of her relative helplessness during the years of her victimization, she was better able to reduce and control her feelings of self-hatred. Although she has occasionally experienced suicidal impulses, especially when she has been under some form of pressure, these are much less common and compelling than formerly.

As a result of her determination to face and understand the traumatic events of her past, the quality of Ms. Y.'s life has markedly improved. She has undertaken employment with a corporation that provides her with excellent training and educational opportunities. As well, she has enrolled in several psychology courses with a view toward undertaking a career as a professional psychotherapist. She and I agree that, given her personal strengths and her commitment to the pursuit of self-awareness, her professional ambitions are quite realistic. She is, in short, a prime example of a person who has transformed traumatic experiences and highly negative emotions into self-understanding, positive objectives, and constructive behavior.

Examples of persons who transform highly negative experiences into active and positive forms of behavior are of course legion. From time to time such examples are so dramatic and stirring that they merit public attention in the mass media.

Political Activism

One such example involves the tragic death of Peter Barry, a junior at Yale University. In the summer of 1985 Peter worked as a commercial fisherman in Alaska. Although he had little experience or preparation for this type of employment, as he indicated to his parents by phone, he accepted the rigors of Alaskan fishing because, as he put it, "I expect it."

Late in August of 1985 Peter's parents, Robert and Peggy Barry, were notified of their son's drowning in the arctic waters off Kodiak Island. Although no remains of Peter's boat, the *Western Sea*, were sighted, it was assumed that it had sunk along with its skipper and crew.

Robert flew to Alaska in order to identify his son's body and to ascertain the causes and circumstances of his death. Upon his arrival, he discovered certain appalling facts. The *Western Sea* was an antiquated, leaky boat with no life rafts, no survival kits, no emergency beacon, and no insurance. Yet, despite its hazardous deficiencies, the vessel did not violate governmental laws or regulations. Upon further investigation, Barry discovered that commercial fishing, by far the most dangerous industry in the nation, was virtually unregulated.

Barry was naturally enraged by his findings. Soon after his son's memorial service, he wrote an article publicizing the horrendous lack of safety standards and regulations in the commercial fishing industry. Each year scores of young men—many of them, like Peter Barry, inexperienced college students—perished in commercial fishing accidents aboard unseaworthy vessels. Thus, Robert Barry directed his energies to bringing "the dangers of the problem to everybody's mind, especially the kids who go up there to fish."

Robert Barry, a former U.S. ambassador to Bulgaria, and his wife, Peggy, further memorialized their son by lobbying congress for legislation mandating minimum safety standards and insuring the seaworthiness of vessels in the commercial fishing industry. As a result of their crusade, other parents of young men who as commercial fishermen had perished at sea joined the Barrys' campaign in behalf of "the kids who go up there to fish."

With a deep sense of idealism and evident courage, the Barrys have transformed a tragic and devastating experience into a vital crusade to reform a major American industry. Although, as Peggy Barry readily acknowledges, "The grief will never go away," the courageous work of the Barrys is for them an important monument and connection to the son they had lost at sea. In this respect, they have transformed their personal tragedy into an inspiring quest to help other young men who may be considering a risky stint in the commercial fishing industry.

Obviously, many persons find it extremely difficult to recover from emotional setbacks and personal tragedy. Often, the trauma, pain, and rage that ensues from a tragedy leaves the victimized individual feeling emotionally disarmed and immobilized. Yet, as the case of the Barrys illustrates, even the most piercing and dismantling personal crises can in time be transformed into constructive and reformist endeavors.

Physical illness, especially when it is of a severe and life-threatenng nature, ordinarily brings in its wake intense feelings of helplessness, remorse, dread, and rage. The fears of physical pain and deterioration as well as the specter of death can precipitate a vast range of negative emotions. At their worst, these emotions may cause a person to become hopelessly nihilistic and misanthropic.

Medical Reform

A forty-year-old nurse, Ms. E., was hospitalized with the onset of acute diabetic symptoms. The symptoms were so severe that at the time of her hospitalization she and her doctors thought she might die. As a result of her hospital care, which included the administration of insulin, she soon recovered and improved so substantially that for a short time she did not require insulin. During a four-month "honeymoon" phase she felt extremely well and was insulin-free. Consequently, she began to hold high hopes for a rapid and complete recovery from diabetes.

When she suddenly relapsed and her diabetic symptoms returned, she experienced intense feelings of disillusionment and rage. Because her brief remission had falsely led her to believe that she was no longer diabetic, she initially found it extremely difficult to accept the reality of the illness.

As a nurse herself, Ms. E. was extremely attuned to the need for precise and thorough medical information and care during her stay in the hospital. To her dismay, however, she often found the hospital nursing staff remiss in their supervision of her illness. For example, because some of the nurses inordinately feared that she would suffer an insulin reaction and become comatose, they regularly plied her with orange juice, which only served to elevate her blood sugar levels and aggravate her symptoms. Because she was maintained on an improper diet during her hospitalization, she found it very difficult to adjust to a more normal diet when she returned home.

As a nurse and a diabetic, Ms. E. had become extremely knowledge-able about the monitoring and control of her illness. Thus, she had an excellent vantage point from which to evaluate her hospital's diabetic treatment program. In her view, this program required an extensive updating and reorganization. Because of her special insights relative to the care of diabetes, she was appointed the hospital's diabetic resource person.

In time, Ms. E. realized that diabetic patients related more openly and candidly with her than with most other nurses. Discovering that she too was a diabetic, the diabetic patients turned to her for her heightened sense of awareness and empathy regarding their condition. She did not disappoint them. As the hospital's diabetic resource person, she played a major role in coordinating the care of many patients.

As a result of her extensive personal and professional experiences with diabetes, Ms. E. became dedicated to the comprehensive treatment of this illness. Recognizing that no formal organization of diabetics existed in her county, she joined the American Diabetes Association (ADA) and then helped to found a local affiliation of the ADA. In rec-ognition of her knowledge and dedication, Ms. E. was elected the local chapter's education chairperson. In this capacity, she organized educa-tional meetings, health fairs, and general education programs for dia-betic patients.

Ms. E. acknowledges that at first she had a defeatist attitude as a consequence of her illness. With guilt and anger, she felt that "I was leaving my children with a terrible legacy." At times, for example, her family resented and resisted her attempts to change their diet. Her hus-band, understandably overcome with worry and anxiety, was some-times overprotective, causing Ms. E. to feel a degree of resentment to-ward him.

Despite the harrowing complexities of dealing with diabetes, Ms. E. indicates without reservation that her illness has had major positive effects upon her life. Prior to her illness, she had considered herself to be a diffident, retiring individual. Since she has been involved in or-ganizing services for the diabetic, Ms. E. has become more outgoing and assertive. She has discovered within herself leadership capabilities that flowered when she undertook organizational work. Furthermore, as a result of her illness, Ms. E.'s family has achieved a greater degree of solidarity. For example, her husband served as the president of the local ADA chapter.

Although, according to Ms. E. there are days when "I feel like chucking it," her illness has given her life new meaning. She takes deep pride in the services she renders to the diabetic community and appreciates the respect and admiration she receives in return. By controlling her own diabetes and devotedly assisting other diabetics, she has become an esteemed model for those afflicted with this disease. She is certainly an example of an individual who has transformed a serious personal setback and highly negative emotions into positive, socially beneficial behavior.

Many persons who, as children, have been repeatedly traumatized, develop serious emotional conflicts and sadistic personality traits as a result. Others, for reasons that are not always explainable, come to terms with such experiences and use them as guideposts or springboards for ordering and improving their lives. At times people will develop a special set of interests or even a career based upon certain negative experiences that were encountered during their childhood.

Vocational Fulfillment

Mr. L., a retired fire department officer and personal acquaintance of mine, was eight years old when his father died in an accident resulting from his attempts to fight a church fire. Apparently some oily rags that had been left in an attic by painters had ignited the conflagration. Mr. L.'s father crossed a section of the roof of the church the underside of which had been burned away. Thus, the ceiling collapsed beneath his weight, causing him to fall many feet below. He landed upon a church organ and also struck a fellow officer whose back was broken by the force of the blow. He was rushed to the hospital where he died of internal injuries three days later.

Mr. L., now a man of fifty-nine, states that he hardly remembers his father. Recently he recalled thinking of his father while on a drive in the Napa Valley of California. His memories of his father were bestirred by the sweet, licoricelike scent of the anise plant. He recalls smelling that plant when his father took the family on outings to the wine country during his childhood.

The death of Mr. L.'s father naturally wrought hardships upon his family. For a short time, his grandmother came to live with them in order to assist with the care of the children. The family received a pension of only $100 a month from the fire department, thus requiring his mother, who was a nurse, to undertake full-time employment. To help out, Mr. L. held many jobs as a youth, including that of house painter and delivery boy.

Mr. L. does not recall his emotions at the time of his father's death. Yet, he does recall missing his father quite acutely at times. Soon after his father's death, a discussion about World War I had taken place in one of his classes. He remembers thinking, "I think I'll go home and ask my father about those events. Since he served in the armed forces in that war, he'll know a lot about them. Then I remembered, reluctantly, that he was dead." Mr. L. also recalls that upon his father's death he was informed by his family that he was no longer Joey; rather, as the new "head of the family," he was now to be respectfully called Joe.

Soon after his discharge from the navy at the age of twenty-four, Mr. L. took a job with a large urban fire department (the same one in which his father had once served). In response to my question about the motives behind his decision to pursue his father's line of work, Mr. L. stated that he never attempted to closely investigate them. Somehow he always knew that he would be a fireman. I inquired about the possibility that one motive might be the vengeful desire to fight the enemy (fire) that had destroyed his father. Mr. L. indicated that he had never before given that thought serious consideration, but conceded that it was a possibility. He did state, however, that he had always considered fighting fires a great intellectual and emotional challenge.

When he entered the fire department at the age of twenty-four, Mr. L. met many men who had known and worked with his father many years before. Their uniformly laudatory comments about his father were a source of deep pride and inspiration to him.

For over a decade, Mr. L. served as a firefighter. He enjoyed the work immensely, regarding each aspect of his job as an exciting opportunity to learn new and important fire fighting concepts and techniques. By excelling in departmental examinations, Mr. L. continually rose through the professional ranks, becoming, respectively, a lieutenant, captain, battalion chief, and, finally, attaining the highest promotional position in the fire department, assistant chief. As well, he received an award for bravery for rescuing a man who had succumbed to toxic vapors in the storage tank of an ocean vessel.

In returning to the subject of his father, Mr. L. indicated that a day does not go by when he does not think of him. Each week when he attends church, he says a prayer for his father. In many respects, he regards his many years of dedicated service in the fire department to be an exquisite monument to his father. He feels that practically every good thing he has done with his life has been achieved with the purpose of making his father proud of him. Mr. L. also has a son who is a fireman. The fact that his is a three-generation fire fighting family fills him with enormous and justifiable pride.

When Mr. L. visited Ireland (his father's birthplace) several years ago, he met for the first time some of his father's relatives there. To his amazement, several of them commented upon the fact that he was the son of the man who had died "saving the church" approximately fifty years before. Unbeknownst to Mr. L., his father had become something of a legend in the locale of his birth.

Mr. L. attributes much of his personal strength and resilience to his faith in God. Despite the untimely and tragic loss of a parent during early childhood, he believes that one must not allow such things to deter or defeat a person. With evident sincerity and depth of feeling, he credits, along with his religious faith, his mother and his wife for their compassion in helping him weather the emotional storms of his life. He is a fine example of a person who has transformed a deeply painful and negative experience of the past into a life filled with positive achievement and reward.

The courage to transform adversity and emotionally traumatic experiences into positive, beneficial, and rewarding forms of behavior depends upon a strength of character that does not exist in all persons to the same degree. The following example may serve as an inspiration to those persons who find it exceptionally difficult to overcome or conquer the emotionally traumatic experiences of their own pasts.

Pursuing an Ideal and a Cause

Ricky, also a personal acquaintance of the author, is twenty-five years of age and a paraplegic. When he was six years old, Ricky was playing on roller skates in front of his house with a group of friends. An altercation between two neighbors took place nearby. One of the men returned to his house to get a handgun. When he returned to the street brandishing the gun, the children immediately scattered. Ricky, in his haste to get away, fell down. The man at whom the gun was aimed desperately picked Ricky up in his arms and held him aloft in front of himself as a body shield. The gun wielder, undaunted, and perhaps even enraged by this subterfuge, fired a bullet that passed through Ricky's chest and lodged in his spine. From that moment on Ricky never walked again.

Two days after this tragic event, Ricky's father, a drug addict, died from heroin overdose. In a hospital bed Ricky was informed of his father's death at the same time that he learned of his paraplegia. Although no one knew with certainty that a connection existed between his father's lethal drug episode and Ricky's recent shooting, the suspicion of a causal relationship entered many minds.

When Ricky first discovered his disability, he felt unbearably alone, deserted, living but dead, a zombie without feelings. He couldn't feel emotional pain, couldn't cry, though he very much wanted to. To further complicate matters, he couldn't fathom why he had been shot. Evidently, the actual circumstances and motives for the shooting had not been adequately explained to him. Consequently, Ricky erroneously assumed that he had been shot because he had somehow offended or antagonized his assailant. Based on this false assumption, he deluded himself into believing that this man (who had in the meantime been arrested and later convicted of the crime) would come back and "finish the job."

His undying fear of his attacker caused him daily turmoil. On Halloween, Ricky's mother came to visit him in the hospital, comically dressed as a man. Ricky, thinking she was his dreaded assailant, was terrified by her presence in his room.

After a brief period of emotional quiescence, Ricky's rage and resentment over his traumatic experience surfaced volcanically. He became angry with everyone and everything. Once, in an uncontrollable rage, he stabbed his brother and broke every window in his house. He resented and resisted anyone who treated him as a disabled individual. To prove he was tough, he sometimes smashed his head against cement pavements.

Although he initially was inclined to be highly dependent, Ricky gradually began to seek greater personal independence and maturity. At the age of twelve, he approached his mother about the possibility of operating a paper route. Thinking that such an undertaking was physically too arduous for her disabled son, she denied his request. When Ricky persisted, his mother finally relented, giving him permission to try it. With enthusiasm and energy, Ricky perambulated about the neighborhood in his wheelchair delivering newspapers. Quite soon, he was winning awards for his superlative ability to sell new subscriptions.

In many other respects Ricky attempted to conquer his disability and live as normally as possible. He eschewed the access ramps of public buildings, instead learning to navigate his wheelchair up and down stairways. When the school authorities decided to enroll Ricky in a special "alternative" school for exceptional children, he and his mother, believing that he would be seriously stigmatized and impeded by enrollment in such a program, bravely fought the decision. Ricky and his mother won out and he was eventually "mainstreamed" into the school system's regular classes. When he became old enough to drive, Ricky was advised to purchase a van specially designed for the physically disabled. Instead, he bought a car equipped with hand controls that he operated quite competently.

Ricky enjoyed athletics and avidly participated in wheelchair basketball. He played on a state championship team that went to a tournament held in Hawaii. While playing on this team he was noticed by a representative of one of the major fast-food chains, who hired Ricky to act in one of their film commercials. His appearance in the TV commercial soon led to additional work in numerous films that were screened for both the movie theaters and television. Having become well established as a screen actor, Ricky joined the Screen Actors Guild and hired an agent.

Because of his courage and perseverance, Ricky was widely recognized in his community as a civic leader as well as an outstanding spearhead and role model in behalf of the physically disabled. For his active leadership, Ricky has received many civic awards, including the local Black Man of the Year Award.

Recently, Ricky was hired by a large private organization to serve as an advisor. In this capacity, Ricky will teach other persons, the disabled and nondisabled alike, about conquering disabilities. Part of his assignment will entail going into schools in order to teach instructors and students about the nature of particular disabilities.

In looking retrospectively at his life, Ricky has taken the following philosophical position: "You must do as much as you can to lead an active, productive life. No matter what your tragedy or disability, you can't allow yourself to vegetate or use you disability to gain sympathy. When I was a young kid I came across a biblical proverb that read, 'Where there is no vision, the people perish.' This proverb gave me consolation, direction, and courage. It taught me that a person must have a goal or target to which he or she can aspire. I often keep this proverb in mind for inspiration."

As the dramatic events and achievements of Ricky's life clearly testify, even those who suffer severe personal tragedy and loss have the potential to transform such experiences into constructive, valuable, and exemplary deeds and, consequently, into a life of worth and true meaning.

It is one of the verities of human psychology that angry emotions can be expressed through either constructive or destructive forms of behavior. In this chapter I have described how certain individuals have overcome serious personal tragedies and adversities by transforming their grief, anger, and resentment into positive, purposeful behavior.

Guidelines

At this point I would like to offer the reader some guidelines for effecting such transformations in your own emotional life. To begin with, there are two general principles to keep in mind: 1) Almost all personal experiences, no matter how dismantling and tragic, hold the potential for intellectual, spiritual, and emotional learning and growth, and 2) All human emotions, including the most virulently negative and sadistic ones, can be transformed and utilized in the pursuit of constructive social and personal goals.

At any time when you are overcome with serious adversity you will at first probably find it quite difficult, if not impossible, to spot even the slightest "silver lining" anywhere in your craggy emotional terrain. However, once the worst of your pain and desolation have subsided, you can begin the process of recovery by asking yourself the following questions. Does this experience, despite the awful, disintegrating pain it has caused me, contain any elements or characteristics from which I can learn something important about myself and thereby grow from it emotionally? Does this setback symbolically contain and convey valuable information about the way I think, feel, and behave? If so, what specifically is the experience trying to tell me about my life? Does it in any respect suggest that I need to modify the ways I have heretofore lived my life in order to be happier and more fulfilled?

In short, try, if you can, to look upon even your most grueling personal setbacks as teachers or mentors that can be enlisted to educate you about yourself and provide you with essential knowledge as to how to improve the quality of your life.

Now let us turn to the matter of utilizing negative emotions for constructive purposes. Attempt, as much as possible, to look upon your angry feelings not as menacing aliens or intruders to be fought and banished, but as potential allies to be embraced in the pursuit of creative understanding and positive fulfillment. Admittedly, this is not an easy emotional feat since it is likely that you have been taught quite the opposite set of values since you were a tot.

Nevertheless, if you can allow your imagination a bit of leeway, it should not be awfully difficult to conceive of an infinite number of ways in which you can channel your anger and resentment into positive tasks and achievement. To assist your imagination, first consider those activities, vocational and avocational, for which you have an aptitude and liking. For example, take gardening. If you are an avid gardener, you have a ready-made outlet and repository for many of your negative (and of course positive) emotions. Angry feelings can be channeled into and, to some extent neutralized by, such aggressive acts as digging in the soil, killing insects with pesticides, mowing grass, and pruning trees and bushes. Thus, gardening not only can fulfill aesthetic needs but helps to canalize aggressive and sadistic emotions as well.

Sports are a natural and common outlet for aggressive and hostile emotions. Thus, you may find it beneficial for both your physical and emotional health to take up a sport if you have not already done so. This does not necessarily mean that you must engage in a violent sport such as football or boxing in order to inflict bodily harm upon others. Nevertheless, sports in general are an excellent vehicle for expressing negative emotions through socially acceptable modes of behavior. Even the highly cerebral sport of chess often involves quite aggressive and sadistic emotions. Bobby Fisher, the renowned chess master, affirmed this point when he discussed his exhilaration over mentally dominating and destroying his opponents.

Therefore, even if you regard yourself as an effete and unathletic individual, try to find a sport to your liking and pursue it with a reasonable degree of dedication. You will probably find that it will enable you to release and resolve some of your hostile, angry emotions.

Many persons of a solitary nature find it especially difficult to overcome or utilize negative emotions because they have few social outlets in their everyday lives. Despite a lack of social involvement, it is quite possible for the solitary individual to creatively utilize negative emotions in a wide variety of ways. For example, many reclusive individuals will keep a daily diary of their troublesome thoughts and experiences, written accounts that provide solace and perspective in response to negative emotions.

Those of you who possess literary talent or ambition will perhaps find it extremely fulfilling to express your angry emotions through your writings. If you are annoyed and disgruntled by, for example, the political and social events of our times, you might utilize your negative emotions to study and write about those events. In connection with this point, I'm reminded of a comment made by the late, wonderful songwriter, Malvina Reynolds, when she was asked at a concert how often she wrote her songs of social protest. She said, with a mischievous twinkle in her eyes, "I write a song whenever I get angry about the troubles and problems in our society. I guess I write a song just about every day."

If you feel discouraged because you do not write well enough to be published, don't allow that to dampen your desire to write about those things that disturb and anger you. If you really would like to see your angry thoughts and opinions in print, send a well formulated letter to the editors of your local newspaper and request that they print it. They probably will, eventually.

If you feel particularly angry over the various ways in which our ecological environment has been neglected and spoliated, an excellent outlet and resource for your righteous indignation might be one of the many organizations dedicated to the conservation of our planet. You will perhaps find it very inspiring to have your like-minded organizational peers validate and support your moral outrage over vital issues. As you would probably agree, this certainly beats sitting around and impotently stewing over such things in the privacy of your home.

Most people seem to be rather cynical and despairing about the workings of our political system. Their attitudes are especially dubious, it seems, toward the politicians who represent us in the legislatures; so much so, that the very term "politician" seems to have acquired the connotations of corruption ad ineptitude. Yet, most people seem to express their political objections and resentments only by stepping into a polling booth and flipping levers (or sticking pins into computerized cards). Although your periodic vote is definitely important, it obviously hardly expresses the many ways in which you feel angry about a wide range of social and political issues.

Whatever your ideological persuasion, there are many creative and important ways to express your political disgruntlement aside from your occasional vote. Do you feel strongly about a regional or national issue? Why not write to your senator or congressperson? Better yet, contact the staff members of your legislators, make an appointment to go see them and directly let them know what you think. I believe you will find many of them quite receptive to talking with you, especially if you are part of a sizeable contingent of individuals with common concerns.

If you feel strongly about a particular bill that is due to come before your state legislature, study the bill well, volunteer to serve as an expert witness, and testify for or against it. Wouldn't it give you a great emotional boost if you were to eventually discover that your testimony helped to shepherd a bill into law?

Naturally, as I suggested earlier, a person's vocation or profession can serve as an ideal medium for the expression and resolution of negative emotions. As a matter of fact, there is considerable evidence suggesting that a person's voluntary choice of a particular profession is often heavily based upon conscious and unconscious desires to resolve long-standing emotional conflicts. For example, some studies suggest that during their childhood physicians generally suffered from above-average concerns and preoccupations with illness and death. It has also been remarked, with a fair degree of validity, in my estimation, that psychotherapists choose their profession in order to vicariously and symbolically treat their own (imperfect) parents. The motivation to resolve fundamental emotional conflicts through specialized work can be observed, for example, in the disproportionately high number of drug and alcoholic abusers who eventually become drug and alcohol counselors.

Thus, if you are currently in the process of choosing a career, one of the factors you might take into consideration is the potential of your future profession to help you overcome and resolve your most central personal concerns, about yourself and the world around you. By doing so, you will probably appreciably raise your chances of experiencing job satisfaction as well as overall personal fulfillment.

If you are presently in a job or profession that bores and angers you because, let's say, it is unchallenging, stagnating, and demeaning, closely identify those areas of your work that are especially rankling you. Then determine how much you can either avoid or modify those work assignments. If they can be avoided or modified without jeopardizing your job, strongly consider taking such a course of action. If they cannot be avoided or modified, however, without serious personal risk, seek to find other areas of your work that will yield greater personal reward. If somehow you have exhausted all of these possibilities to no avail, then consider changing jobs or careers rather than seething miserably over your work situation, day in and day out.

If, due to fear, lack of occupational skills, or training, you cannot leave a dreary and maddening job, then reluctantly accept that fact and begin to generate other, more fulfilling, activities and pursuits in your non-working hours. You probably would also find it highly beneficial to regularly meet with other individuals who have job dissatisfactions in order to collectively bitch and grieve about your daily travail.

Many persons have been able to leave obnoxious work by gradually converting avocational interests into full-fledged businesses. For example, a former colleague of mine, a part-time nurse who was frustrated with her career, began baking pies and cakes to serve on social occasions. The general acclaim she received from her friends for her delicious goodies encouraged her to begin selling them to commercial stores and bakeries. As her reputation grew, so did her income. Eventually, she established her own specialty bakery, which has become a booming success.

Finally, I'd like to make a pitch for altruism. Too often we forget the inestimable value of helping others who are less fortunate than ourselves. Yet, many angry and unhappy people discover that by assisting others who are in need they accomplish two significant goals: 1) They become less self-preoccupied by and immersed in the morass of their own angry and depressed feelings, and 2) They receive the exquisite and inimitable gratification of knowing that they have genuinely bene-fited another human being.

Therefore, if you are in the doldrums, consider the vast number of opportunities that exist in the society around you for altruistic service. Agencies such as Big Brothers, Big Sisters, hospitals, clinics, recreation departments, libraries, schools and colleges, and Suicide Prevention, to name just a few, are constantly on the lookout for volunteers. Consider joining one of them. I'm quite sure than many of you will find that your own acts of humanity and altruism will convert and release your angry energy to benefit others and yourself.

Chapter 5

Negative Emotions and Humor

Sigmund Freud pointed out in his trenchant study of humor, *Jokes and Their Relation to the Unconscious*, that jokes are often used in the service of a hostile purpose. He wrote, "Though as children we are still endowed with a powerful inherited disposition to hostility, we are later taught by a higher personal civilization that it is an unworthy thing to use abusive language; and even where fighting has in itself remained permissible, the number of things which may not be employed as methods of fighting has extraordinarily increased. Since we have been obliged to renounce the expression of hostility by deeds—held back by the passionless third person, in whose interest it is that personal security shall be preserved—we have, just as in the case of sexual aggressiveness, developed a new technique of invective, which aims at enlisting this third person against our enemy. By making our enemy small, inferior, despicable or comic, we achieve in a roundabout way the enjoyment of overcoming him—to which the third person, who has made no efforts, bears witness by his laughter. A joke will allow us to exploit something ridiculous in our enemy which we could not, on account of obstacles in the way, bring forward openly or consciously."

The civilizing effect of humor in blunting hostility has also been recognized by a contemporary psychiatric writer, G. Vaillant, who identifies humor as a "mature" defense mechanism used by healthy individuals to cope with emotional stress and conflict.

There is considerable evidence that jokes and humor emanate largely from painful and, in some cases, even tragic events. When former president Reagan was shot, for example, he was reported to have said to the attending physicians, "I hope you're all Republicans." The likely purpose of this somewhat macabre joke was to defuse the acute anxiety he and others must have felt over his precarious condition.

In a great many respects, humor enables us to overcome much of the gravity and absurdity in our lives. It severs the bonds with those forces that drag us downward and restores balance and perspective. It can offer psychological relief and release from grief, remorse, and rage when these emotions appear to be overwhelming and inescapable. Even in the direst, most unlikely circumstances, humor can play a vital, salutary role.

For example, in his book, *Man's Search for Meaning*, Victor Frankl describes how, even living within the horrific circumstances of a Nazi concentration camp, a person can maintain his or her sanity through humor. He points out, "Humor was another of the soul's weapons in the fights for self-preservation. It is well known that humor, more than anything else in the human makeup, can afford an aloofness and an ability to rise above any situation, even if only for a few seconds."

Frankl goes on to describe how he emotionally fortified himself against the ravages of the camp by training a fellow inmate to develop a sense of humor. Each day he and this man would invent and exchange an amusing story about an imaginary incident that could happen one day after their liberation. Many men were so hungry for psychological deliverance from the oppressiveness of the camp that they would sometimes even miss their daily ration of food in order to attend inmate assemblies at which camp life was satirized through songs and jokes.

Not surprisingly, unspeakable horrors such as the Holocaust continue to insinuate themselves into our everyday lives through satire and humor. Several years ago, some will recall, former secretary general of the United Nations, Kurt Waldheim, had been very much in the news because heretofore undisclosed documents suggested his complicity in Nazi atrocities. Mr. Waldheim's conveniently faulty memory and caginess regarding his military role during the Second World War left many persons, including myself, with suspicions that he had something incriminating to hide.

Mr. Waldheim's cryptic and evasive behavior produced the following joke. Do you know what Waldheimer's disease is? It's when you get so old, you forget you're a Nazi. This obviously is a joke that has evolved from feelings of skepticism and rage. It makes use of a widespread and highly dreaded disease that impairs the memory (Alzheimer's) in order to spuriously explain why Waldheim had not been more forthright in discussing his wartime activities on behalf of the Third Reich. The rage and skepticism underlying this joke is revealed by the play on words that implies that Mr. Waldheim is not really suffering from an organic disorder or genuine forgetfulness but rather is craftily protecting himself from the recriminations and political repercussions he would have to endure if he told the entire truth.

I think it might be helpful to point out at this juncture that in this chapter numerous jokes will be related purely to illustrate the role of negative emotions in producing humor with no deliberate intention to amuse the reader. Naturally, no individual joke will amuse everyone. Most likely, certain readers will find some of the jokes in this chapter to be funny while others will perhaps consider some of them to be tasteless or offensive. In any case, I think readers will find this chapter more instructive if they keep the primary intention of the jokes in mind: to illustrate their dynamic meaning and purpose.

The fact that humor is born of suffering, pain, and alienation was well substantiated by psychologist Samuel Janus who himself was once a stand-up comic. He found at the time of his study that, although less than 3 percent of the U.S. population was Jewish, 80 percent of the nation's professional comedians were Jewish. (Janus reported his findings in 1978. It is likely that these percentages have changed somewhat, especially in view of the burgeoning numbers of black comedians who have entered the professional ranks in recent years.) The disproportionately large numbers of Jews and blacks in professional comedy is, of course, no coincidence: the historical persecution of these two ethnic groups has been, like the irritating sand in an oyster's maw, the social catalyst for great pearls of wit and humor.

Janus interviewed and psychologically tested many of the top Jewish comedians throughout the country. He found that most were ambivalent about their Jewishness (90 percent had anglicized their names) and sought refuge in humor as a means of dealing with depression, pain, and insecurity. It was even suggested by one of his interviewees that comedians must practice their comedy in order to avoid destroying themselves.

Janus discovered that almost all of the comedians in his survey had suffered major childhood traumas such as the untimely death of a parent or sibling. Many of these men and women had an overweening drive for acceptance and, like Rodney Dangerfield, felt they never had enough respect. Their use of humor, according to Janus, had a special function of serving as a "ritual exorcism" for emotional conflicts. What makes them funny, Janus explains, "is their pain."

The ebullient comedienne, Joan Rivers, in her book entitled *Enter Talking*, discusses her emotional pain throughout a childhood in which she felt starved for affection. Her father, who was a physician, worked long hours away from home, leaving Joan plagued with intense feelings of abandonment and a bottomless craving for love, admiration, and attention. Also, her parents' "pathological" preoccupations with the threat of poverty led to ugly, internecine battles between them. Joan often considered herself the inadvertent but very definite victim of her parents' conflicts. Self-conscious, chubby, and convinced of her personal unattractiveness, she eventually dealt with her emotional trials through humor.

Given the emotional storms of her childhood, it is small wonder that Joan Rivers regards humor as a weapon second in its formidability only to a gun. The feelings of anxiety and distrust that prompt and color her humor are revealed in her warning, "Never trust an audience. Never think they are truly your friends." The anguish and insecurity of her past unremittingly lingers and still expresses itself in her many self-derisive jokes about her alleged physical homeliness.

It is interesting to note how the underlying motives of hostility and aggression in humor suffuse the language we use to graphically describe humorous performances. When a comic titillates an audience with humor we say he or she has scored big, killed them, knocked them for a loop, hit them over the head, et cetera. Conversely, when comics muff their lines and disenchant their audiences, we say they have bombed or died on stage. I have been told that some comedians even refer to their dressing rooms as the tomb; in other words, the dressing room is considered a place in which they are interred right after they have "died" on stage. Obviously, it is no psychological accident that we usually refer to the denouement of a joke as the "punch" line, as if, by telling our joke, we are delivering a walloping blow or *coup de grace*.

Quite predictably, global and potentially cataclysmic events will give birth to a plethora of jokes and witticisms. For example, the Soviet plant disaster at Chernobyl raised both the meteorological and emotional thermometer worldwide. Initially, given the paucity of information about this major accident, millions of people everywhere felt a sense of helpless panic. The painful uncertainty over the effects of atmospheric contamination caused someone to invent the following two jokes. What has feathers and glows? Answer: Chicken Kiev. What is the weather forecast in Chernobyl? Answer: Clear, with temperatures in the three thousands.

As we can see, the horror and dismay aroused by this nuclear accident have been directed and transformed into a form of levity and humor. The fact that one invents such jokes about such a disaster does not, in my view, suggest that the catastrophe had been taken lightly. On the contrary, the humor in these jokes, if one can consider them humorous, bespeaks the profound dread and terror experienced by millions of persons everywhere as a result of this nuclear disaster.

On January 28, 1986, millions of people witnessed on television with shock and horror the destruction of the space shuttle *Challenger*. As the craft exploded in a brilliant fireball and fatally descended to earth with seven doomed astronauts aboard, millions of television viewers watched in helpless and horrified silence. For many days afterward the nation went into collective mourning as the causes and circumstances of this tragedy were investigated and unraveled.

Although all of the facts surrounding this disaster may never be disclosed (including, for example, whether the White House had exerted pressure on the National Aeronautics and Space Administration to launch the *Challenger*), the general impression was left that NASA had been inept and malfeasant in its administration of the project. As a result, a considerable amount of public anger had been directed at this governmental agency. The loss, perhaps needless, of human lives in this case had caused many to think that NASA regards its astronauts to be nothing more than sacrificial lambs to be slaughtered in the pursuit of extraterrestrial conquests.

The sorrow and anger generated by the tragedy of the *Challenger* produced the following joke only a few months after the public was benumbed by this horrible event. Question: Do you know what the acronym NASA stands for? Answer: Need another seven astronauts. This joke rather transparently reveals feelings of rage and resentment for those who are considered to be officially responsible for the loss of seven human beings as well as the psychological trauma inflicted upon millions of people. It is a rather typical example of how great tragedies will eventually yield humor that is used as a means for healing great emotional wounds.

As indicated, national tragedies have a way of spawning a great variety of jokes. Even the assassination of such a beloved and revered person as Abraham Lincoln has given rise to a joke that has had widespread currency. So, how did you enjoy the play, Mrs. Lincoln? Most likely, such a joke would have caused considerable consternation and disgust had it been told in the immediate wake of Lincoln's assassination. However, with the passage of over a century, there are those who can now extract some humor from a tragedy of such cosmic proportions.

In the 1970s there was a spate of so-called hate jokes that swiftly flowed back and forth across the country. Question: "Daddy, why do I keep walking in circles? Answer: Shut up or I'll nail your other foot to the floor." "Daddy, I'm tired and want to go to sleep. Answer: Just shut up and keep dealing." It is not altogether clear why such jokes emerged in the '70s, although one theory connects them to the general rage and disillusionment engendered by the Vietnam War. In certain respects, perhaps, one cannot help but view such vicious jokes as pure and simple outlets for human sadism. Yet a single theory usually cannot explain such complicated social phenomena as "hate" jokes. Perhaps the telling of sadistic jokes is considered a socially acceptable means by which people can express or neutralize their own hostile wishes and fantasies. In other words, by telling a sadistic joke one need not commit a sadistic act.

It is quite common for famous persons to arouse both the envy and admiration of the public. When such persons sully their own names and reputations by committing acts of crime or, as in the recent case of President Clinton, folly, they frequently become the butts of public ridicule and mockery. One such person is the felonious president Nixon who, as a result of his involvement in the Watergate cover-up, became an ideal target of many derogatory jokes. For example: Did you hear that President Nixon once hired a sculptor to add his likeness to Mount Rushmore? But the sculptor told him there wasn't room for two more faces. Question: "What's the caption beneath a picture of Jerry Ford, Jimmy Carter, and Richard Nixon?" Answer: Hear no evil, see no evil, and evil.

When I had read that public opinion polls indicated that large segments of the population were rehabilitating Richard Nixon by forgiving him for his political crimes, I could not resist pillorying him with an aphorism of my own: He who tampers with a Watergate shall forever be dammed.

Humor and jokes tend to reflect our innermost concerns, insecurities, and anxieties. Since our primary concerns and anxieties will shift and change throughout our lifetime, we discover that jokes about children and young persons will naturally have quite different themes than those about middle-aged and elderly persons. For example, young children worry a great deal about losing their rightful places within their families to their siblings. Consequently, they are generally highly curious about pregnancies that, in their view, often represent the vague threat of personal displacement and loss. The following joke points to this theme: A small child is walking along the sidewalk when she comes upon a woman who is quite visibly "expecting." She walks up to the woman and, pointing to her large belly, timidly inquires, "Excuse me, what's that?" The woman, charmed by the child's innocence, lightly answers, "Oh, that, that's my baby." The child, not quite satisfied with this reply, asked the woman, "Do you love your baby?" The woman delightedly responds, "Oh, yes, very much." The child, puzzled by this reply, asks, "If you love your baby, then why did you eat it?"

Sibling rivalry is a fact of life in all families with more than one child. Heated and belligerent rivalries can be the source of considerable anxiety for children and parents alike. For this reason, there are many jokes about the strife between children. A mother says to her son, "Howard, get your little sister's hat out of that puddle." Howard replies: "I can't, Mom, she's got it strapped too tight under her chin." The humor behind this joke of course relates to the casualness with which little Howard regards his sister's underwater misadventure, thereby revealing his disregard and contempt for her.

The hostile exploitation of a family's younger siblings is a frequent theme of humor and jokes. For example, a mother says to her son, "No, Eddie, you must not be selfish. You must let your little brother have the sled half the time." Eddie replies: "But, Mom, I do. I have it going down the hill and he has it coming up."

As the other end of the chronological spectrum we all face the inevitable prospect of bodily deterioration and, ultimately, death. The increasing physical decrepitude that ordinarily accompanies the aging process arouses in most people feelings of regret, discomfort, resentment and, at their worst, profound grief and humiliation. It is these very negative emotions that give rise to many jokes.

One such joke is about an eighty-three-year-old man who applies to be a donor at a sperm bank. Based on this man's age, the clinic staff are quite skeptical of his potency and his suitability as a donor. However, he assures them, "Never mind, I can do it. Just give me a chance." The man is given a covered jar and instructed to retire to a restroom at the end of the hall where he is to deposit his sperm in the glass container. An hour passes and the man isn't heard from. A second hour passes without any sign of the determined octogenarian. A third hour goes by, but no donor. Finally, after the passage of four hours, the worried staff go in search of their aged benefactor. Rather frantically, they knock at the door and inquire about his progress. He, with great annoyance, yells through the door that he is quite well but needs more time. A moment later he emerges from the restroom carrying an empty jar. "What's the problem, they anxiously inquire. He replies, "Look, I'm an old man. I need a bit of time for these sorts of things. But I'll tell you what's happened. For two hours, I tried with my left hand. And for two hours, I tried with my right hand. And I still couldn't open the goddamned jar."

The humor of this joke basically stems from the recognition of a sad dilemma that commonly afflicts the aged: sexual impotency. In the joke, however, the poor man is so physically weak that he cannot even open the jar, let alone demonstrate that he is sexually potent. His evident physical limitations, although undoubtedly a nasty burden for him to carry, are used in this joke as sources of humor with which we may ourselves face the adversities of old age.

The physical and sexual decline that commonly accompanies the aging process also appears as a theme in the following joke. A husband and wife in their early nineties are lying side by side in bed. The husband nestles close to his wife and squeezes her hand. She looks at him lovingly and returns the hand squeeze. Then, quite satisfied by this brief, cuddlesome exchange, they both fall fast asleep. The following evening the husband again reaches over in bed to squeeze his wife's hand. In response, she affectionately squeezes his hand and, without further ado, both fall into a deep repose. Each successive evening for over a week the same amatory ritual is repeated: the husband squeezes his wife's hand, the wife squeezes his hand, then the elderly couple quickly go to sleep. In the ninth day, however, when the husband reaches over and attempts to squeeze his wife's hand, she looks back forlornly and, refusing to reciprocate the gesture, says, "Not tonight, honey, I've got a headache."

We can see how this joke plays upon the theme of the physical decline and limitations that are the inevitable partners to the aging process. The couple, evidently unable to accomplish sexual intercourse, has adjusted to their plight by replacing one sexual pleasure with another. Yet, even this tiny effort becomes tiresome and unpleasant if repeated too often. Thus, the wife thwarts her husband's affectionate overtures by having or feigning a headache.

The following joke reflects still another aspect of the physical decline that accompanies the process of aging. A golfer with erratic skills requests that the manager of his golf club provide him with an assistant who could find the balls he expects to hit off the fairway. "You see," he tells the manager, "my eyes are not so good, so I'll need some help finding my golf balls." The manager reassures him, "I've got just the man for you, old Horace Grisby." When they leave the clubhouse and Horace Grisby is pointed out to him, the golfer is horrified to discover that his assistant is a man well over ninety.

The golfer testily inquires of Mr. Grisby, "Are you sure you can see well enough to find my errant golf balls?" "Of course," Mr. Grisby angrily replies. "I've got the eyes of a hawk." Taking Mr. Grisby at his word, the golfer places his ball on the tee, faces the fairway leading to the first hole, and swings his club in an uncoordinated arc. As one might expect, the ball is shanked far to the right and lands in a clump of bushes.

As they approach the area where the ball has landed, the golfer asks Mr. Grisby if he has determined the exact location of the ball. Mr. Grisby, quite annoyed, reminds the golfer, "Look, I already told you, I may be ninety-seven, but I have the eyes of a hawk. Of course I know where the danged ball landed." Plucked up by Mr. Grisby's convincing statement, the golfer asks, "Great, well, then, where is it?" Mr. Grisby suddenly stops walking and, with a blank expression upon his face, replies, "Um, I forgot."

The humor of this joke stems from an awareness that, as we grow older, some of our faculties fail at varying and distressing rates. In the case of the willful Mr. Grisby, he had apparently retained his hawklike eyesight, but, alas, had episodic losses of memory. As we have seen, his pitiable confusion provides humor to those of us who dread the impairing consequences of dementia.

As we know, elderly persons do not always or completely succumb to the loss of sexual or physical prowess. The gallant quest of one elderly gentleman to keep up his sexual potency is the theme of the following joke. There was an elderly man who had recently lost his fourth wife. He met a twenty-year-old woman and wanted to marry her. This man, who happened to be Jewish, was advised by his friends to consult a rabbi about his matrimonial plans.

He went to the rabbi who acknowledged that the situation was a bit unusual. He advised, with a wink, "Why don't you also take in a boarder?" The man agreed. Several months later he encountered the rabbi on the street. "How is it going?" asked the rabbi. "Excellently," Rabbi." "And your wife, how is she?" "She's pregnant, Rabbi." "Oh," exclaimed the rabbi. "And how's the boarder?" "She's pregnant too," he replied.

We see in this joke how the aged gentleman literally followed the rabbi's instructions, but in reality defied the rabbi's intentions by bringing into his home a female boarder whom he impregnated along with his wife. The elderly man simply would not accept the rabbi's judgment that he was incapable of satisfying his wife's sexual desires or providing her with children. In retaliation for the rabbi's well intentioned but misguided advice, he became the rascally impregnator of not one but two women.

The years between childhood and old age are ordinarily filled with the emotional pleasures and pressures of selecting and maintaining love relationships. Because the quality of one's love relationships will usually strongly determine a person's level of happiness and self-fulfillment, most people understandably invest a great deal of energy and anxiety in their most personal relationships. This anxiety unendingly finds it way into much of the humor we encounter in our everyday lives.

The making and breaking of love relationships is a regular source of concern and anxiety for a great many people. As a result, many unrealistic expectations and fantasies are conjured up by the experience of forming a love relationship, some of which, unfortunately, are bound to be disappointed. In recognition of this fact, Dorothy Parker has written the following, rather funny and cynical, verse.

Unfortunate Coincidence

By the time you swear you're his,
Shivering and sighing,
And he vows his passion is
Infinite, undying --
Lady, make a note of this:
One of you is lying.

Ms. Parker alludes in this verse to the tendency of passionate lovers to make overblown promises to one another and to assume a dangerously unquestioning attitude toward those unrealistic vows.

One of the primary sources of irreconcilable differences between love partners is the passionate conviction with which they believe in the moral superiority of their own positions. A delightful Jewish folkloric tale portrays this problem in a humorous vein. A couple could no longer tolerate living with each other and, therefore, sought counsel from their rabbi. The wife entered the rabbi's chambers first where she proceeded to hotly criticize her husband. "Rabbi, the man is no good. He's lazy, self-centered, and slovenly. He never has a kind word for anyone. He never helps around the house and as a breadwinner he's a total failure. Besides, he has a terrible temper and, no matter how hard I try, I can't reason with him."

The rabbi listened patiently to the wife's complaints. When she at last completed her angry comments, he leaned forward and quietly stated, "You know, you're right." With that, the wife, obviously satisfied with the rabbi's favorable assessment of the matter, left the house and returned home.

Next, the husband entered the rabbi's chambers. He wasted no time in lambasting his wife. "Rabbi, the woman has no positive qualities whatsoever. She doesn't know how to cook or clean house. And she's unkempt. Besides, she can't control her temper, going around shouting like a madwoman most of the time. You simply can't reason with such a person." Once again, the rabbi listened with patience and forbearance. Following the husband's peroration, he leaned forward and quietly stated, "You know, you're right." The husband, feeling vindicated by the rabbi's pronouncement, confidently left.

As soon as he left, the rabbi's wife entered the chambers. She went to her husband and demanded an explanation. "You know, I heard what went on in here. First the wife came in and accused her husband of being a louse. She blamed all their marital problems on him. You listened to what she said and then declared that she was right. Then the husband came in and he made his wife out to be a shrew and a crazy woman, blaming all their troubles on her. You listened to what he said and then reassured him that he was right. You know, they both can't be right."

The rabbi carefully contemplated his wife's remarks for a few moments and then replied, "You know, you're right."

With wit and wisdom the rabbi in this folkloric tale has exposed and addressed the essence of many of the conflicts that take place in human relationships; that is, the tendency of each person to believe and declare that he or she has a monopoly on the truth. The rabbi, a relativist in such matters, believes there is some truth in what each person believes and furthermore thinks it advisable to openly acknowledge that fact.

I related this tale to a mother and daughter who had entered therapy because each could not in the least acknowledge the validity of the other's viewpoint. During the therapy they each attempted to elicit from me an alliance with their own opinions as a means of invalidating the viewpoints of the other. When I refused to collude with either of them, they directed their anger at me. It was then that I related the story about the wise rabbi. Since the story, in their estimation, clearly contradicted their undying and humorless faith in their own beliefs, to the exclusion of all others, they were remarkably uninterested in and unmoved by my story.

As indicated earlier, calamitous and tragic events have a way of finding expression in wit and humor. Since death is one of life's great and awesome mysteries, it is a subject that arouses in most people a sense of dread and anxiety. Thus, it is also a subject that has produced an abundance of jokes and witticisms. One such joke has to do with a man who visits his dying wife in the hospital. She says to him, "You know, Alfred, you haven't acted very generously toward me during the many years of our marriage. Now that I am dying, I want to ask one small favor of you."

Alfred, who had been listening rather inattentively, inquires, "Yeh, what's that?" "Well," she says, "at my funeral there will of course be a procession of cars. Presumably, you will be driving immediately behind the limousine transporting my coffin. As a final favor, I would like you to allow my mother to drive with you in your car. Since she would consider this a great act of respect for her, I would appreciate it if you would grant me this last wish. Will you do it for me?"

Alfred scratches his chin thoughtfully and then remarks, "Well, all right, but it's going to spoil my whole day."

The husband's wisecrack reveals not only his dislike for his mother-in-law but also signifies his complete lack of concern and love for his wife. With this sarcasm, he is letting her know that on the day of her funeral he would be enjoying himself were it not for the intrusive presence of his mother-in-law.

Death ordinarily brings with it profound fears of the unknown. For this reason, thoughts of dying often stir up fantasies of either heavenly or hellish afterworlds. The following joke reflects and pokes fun at some of these postexistence fears. One day Wally had a serious heart attack and died. His wife, Bessie, was grief stricken and for many months went into mournful seclusion. Her thoughts harked wistfully back to her many enjoyable years with her husband, Wally. She wished more than anything else to speak with him and to find out how he was making out in the world of the hereafter.

One day Bessie learned of a medium who could in a single séance bring relatives in touch with their deceased loved ones. Bessie went to the medium and in a matter of only a few minutes she was speaking with Wally. "Wally, is that you?" "Yes, Bessie dear, it's me." "Oh, Wally, how are you? How is it there?" "Bessie, it's wonderful. Let me tell you about it. In the morning I wake up, have a little salad, then, forgive me Bessie, I next have some sex and then I take a short nap. When I wake up, I have a little salad for lunch, then a little more sex and then I rest for awhile. In the early evening I get up, eat a little more salad, have sex again and then go to bed for the night. And, Bessie, every day is exactly the same; just as I've described it to you."

Bessie, overcome by Wally's idyllic descriptions, exclaims, "Oh, Wally, it must simply be wonderful there in heaven. I can't wait to join you." "Heaven?" responds Wally. "I'm not in heaven. I'm a jackrabbit living in Colorado."

This joke deals with the dread we experience in facing death, the king of terrors, by depicting life after death as a hedonic, carefree existence. Gary Larson, the brilliantly funny cartoonist, has used another kind of fantasy, the fear of an eternal postexistence in hell, in order to create some of his humorous cartoons. For example, one of his cartoons shows a distinguished maestro who has been consigned to hell being led into a room where a rock band is going to give him his comeuppance by everlastingly playing their ear splitting music for his "enjoyment." Another type of hell, this one for dogs, depicts several bipedal mutts walking about hell delivering the mail and sweeping up dog crap. In yet another of Larson's cartoons, two men are seated on a bench surrounded by the roaring fires of hell while the devil's minions drive their slaves with pitchforks. One man turns to the other and mutters under his breath, "I hate this place."

We can see from the above examples how the terrors and anxieties engendered by death and dying can be the catalysts for much of the humor we encounter in our daily lives. Undoubtedly, this humor provides, however briefly, some emotional assuagement and consolation in dealing with the dread fact of human mortality.

Let us now turn to the hostilities, anxieties, and conflicts that are sometimes aroused in relation to the professions. George Bernard Shaw, through a character in one of his plays, expresses the cynical point of view that all professions are conspiracies against the laity. There are many jokes that reflect the animosity that customers, clients, and patients sometimes feel for the various professions—and vice versa. Inevitably, many of these jokes deal with individuals in my own profession: the profession of psychotherapy.

One such joke involves a man who sees a psychotherapist in an acute panic. "Doctor," he says, "you must help me." The therapist calmly inquires, "Well, what's the problem?" "You see, doctor, sometimes I think I'm a tent and sometimes I think I'm a wigwam. Then I think I'm a tent and then I think I'm a wigwam. Doctor, is it possible that I'm crazy?" The doctor sagely thinks this one over and replies, "No, I don't think you're crazy. I just think you're two tents." Said aloud, this comment sounds like too tense.

This joke reflects not only the intense anxiety and wariness with which many persons enter psychotherapy, but also indicates the resentment that is sometimes aroused by insensitive or callous psychotherapists. To even the score against such psychotherapists, so to speak, many jokes are told which depict them in an unseemly or disadvantageous light.

A joke with a similar underlying theme tells of a man, Mr. Stone, who went to see a psychoanalyst. The analyst was a rigidly traditional man who spoke only sparingly. Mr. Stone took his place on the couch, said nothing, and waited as the minutes silently ticked by. For fifty minutes neither man said a word. When the session reached its conclusion, the analyst said quietly, "We must stop for the day, Mr. Stone. That will be ninety dollars."

Mr. Stone reached into his wallet, took out ninety dollars and paid the analyst. He left the session without saying a word. He returned the following week, went directly to the couch and, for fifty minutes, neither he nor the analyst spoke a single word. Again, at the end of the session, the analyst broke the silence by saying, "We must stop now, Mr. Stone. That will be ninety dollars." Mr. Stone opened his wallet, pulled out the money and, without having uttered a single word, left the consultation room.

Each week the same experience was repeated. For seven consecutive weeks Mr. Stone and the analyst spent fifty minutes together without speaking to one another. At the end of each session the analyst would verbalize only his wish to be paid his fee and Mr. Stone would wordlessly comply.

Finally, toward the end of the eighth session, Mr. Stone lifted his head a bit and parted his lips. The analyst, perceiving this change, perked up, thinking to himself that at last they were making progress: Mr. Stone was going to say something at last. Mr. Stone turned toward the analyst, paused for a moment, and then inquired, "Do you need a partner?"

This joke primarily makes an angry statement about psychotherapists who are overly taciturn (suggesting that such therapists are not working very hard and therefore do not earn their fees) and, worse, are venal to the point of caring only about getting paid by their patients. By requesting a partnership with the analyst, the patient in this joke seeks to equalize their relationship, a relationship that he considers unfair, exploitative and, from the patient's point of view, quite enviable.

Of course, there are many jokes about physicians that reveal resentment and hostility for the medical profession. One such joke involves a woman, Ms. Carlton, who agrees to see a gynecologist for the first time in her seventy-eight years. She was led into the examination room by a nurse who introduced her to Dr. Philbert. "Ms. Carlton, would you please step behind the curtain and undress." "You want me to take off all my clothes?" she asked incredulously. "Yes, please." "Listen, Doctor, does your mother know you earn a living from doing this sort of thing?"

The underlying theme of this joke is the suspicion held by many persons that some male doctors take voyeuristic pleasure in observing and examining their nude female patients. Furthermore, the joke expresses resentment over the fact that some men actually earn a living from work that provides them with such sensual pleasures.

In addition to psychotherapists and doctors, lawyers are often the butt of jokes directed at the professions. One such joke describes what happened when a fence between heaven and hell broke down. St. Peter appeared at the broken section and called out to the Devil: "Hey, Satan, since all the engineers are over in your place, how about getting them to fix this fence?" Sorry, replied Satan. "My men are all too busy to go about fixing measly fences." Well, then," replied St. Peter, "I'll have to sue you if you don't." "Oh, yeah," countered the Devil, " and where are you doing to get a lawyer?"

This joke actually takes a nasty swipe at two professional groups, lawyers and engineers, by suggesting that their erstwhile unprofessional or unethical conduct on earth will commit them to an eternal hell.

In a similar vein, a joke tells about a lawyer's client who proclaims: "I know the evidence is strongly against my innocence, but I have $50,000 to fight the case." The lawyer replies, "As your attorney, I assure you that you'll never go to prison with that amount of money." And he didn't: he went there broke.

This joke obviously is an expression of sarcastic anger toward those attorneys who bilk their clients of their entire financial resources without properly representing them.

The many working persons who serve the public must unavoidably incur its wrath through jokes and witticisms. For example, a man went to his barber and gave him instructions as to how he wished to have his hair cut. "I'd like you to take the hair on the left side and have it stick far out. Then take the hair on the right side and have it stick far out. Then, just behind the hair above my forehead I'd like you to cut a large bald spot." Horrified, the barber, replied, "I'm sorry, sir, but I simply can't do that." "Why not," asked the man, "you did it that way the last time I was here?"

The humor of this joke is of course based upon the unhappy experience of some people who have considered themselves badly butchered at a barbershop and, as a result, harbor a grudge against the barber.

Probably the most common sources of humor are the everyday mishaps and misadventures of the human race. Blunders, mishaps, mistakes, oversights, gaffes, and faux pas are often the causes of embarrassment, humiliation, and grief. In order to psychologically recover from such experiences, we must manufacture humor as a means of removing from them their wounding power and emotional sting.

I once observed in a social situation the power of an embarrassing faux pas to produce great hilarity. In a social group was a man who had launched into a very lengthy tale about his experience serving on a jury. He told his story in a very detailed but rather interesting manner and, by and large, quite enthralled his audience. After uninterruptedly relating his experience for perhaps ten or fifteen minutes, he paused, seemingly having run out of things to say. A woman in the group then leaned forward and pleasantly inquired, "Have you finished?"

An icy silence descended upon the group who presumed that the woman was inquiring about whether the man had actually concluded his lengthy remarks. If this were truly the case, she would have been guilty of suggesting that he had spoken too long and boringly and her inquiry, therefore, would be considered rude and insulting. The silence remained unbroken until someone who knew this woman well spoke up and pointed out, quite correctly, that she was merely asking if the ex-juror had finished serving jury duty. The woman, not realizing that her question had been interpreted differently, immediately confirmed her friend's interpretation. With that, the entire group erupted in a loud and very tension-relieving roar of laughter.

The following joke illustrates a monumental blunder that leads to personal disaster. A man sees a surgeon and requests that he be castrated. The surgeon, realizing the dire consequences of such a procedure, at first denies the request. However, after the man repeatedly importunes the surgeon and reassures him that he knows exactly what he is doing, the reluctant doctor caves in and performs the operation.

Hours later, the patient leaves the operating room and is being wheeled along a hospital corridor when he encounters an old friend. "Hey, Bob," he calls over to his friend, "how are you?" "Fine," answers the friend. "Well, Bob, what are you doing here." "Oh," answers Bob, "I've come in to be circumcised. "Damn," the patient exasperatedly replies, "*that* was the word I was looking for."

Another medical misadventure is the theme of the following joke. Mr. Newman sees his proctologist about a problem with his rear end. The doctor examines his patient and extracts from his behind a long-stemmed rose. Amazed, he reaches in and finds another rose that he also removes. He continues searching and eventually he has extracted ten long-stemmed roses from Mr. Newman's anus. He then turns to his patient and inquires, "Mr. Newman, I've just removed ten long-stemmed roses from your behind. Do you have any idea how they got there?" Mr. Newman thinks for a moment and then replies, "No, was there a card?"

In this joke a bizarre medical disorder is considered funny because the patient, rather than being frightened by his condition, as one might expect, considered it with the lighthearted curiosity one might display toward an ordinary floral gift.

The following example involves a preposterous mishap that once occurred in my clinical practice and was previously cited in an earlier book of mine, *A Guide to Psychotherapy*. Several years ago I worked in a psychotherapy clinic that had an elaborate and inefficient system of billing its patients. This outmoded system was finally revamped and computerized. To each patient's name was affixed a seven-digit code number that was registered in the files of the clinic. The method of treatment, which of course was psychotherapy, was also given a seven-digit code number, based upon its listing in a medical formulary. Each psychotherapist would assume responsibility for billing each of his or her patients by filling out billing forms with these code numbers. The forms were then transmitted to a local bank that, in a completely confidential manner, processed them through computers and then sent the bills directly to the patients.

Around this time a twenty-two-year-old woman, a graduate student at a school of nursing, entered psychotherapy at the clinic. The patient was extremely depressed and inhibited. Her manner was so tentative that she seemed to wince whenever she spoke. Her mood was one of uninterrupted gloom. Toward the end of the patient's second month of therapy, while preparing one of the weekly billing forms, I inadvertently reversed the code numbers that designated the patient's name with those of the treatment services she was receiving at the clinic. In other words, the services described on the bill, covering a one-week period, would be determined by the code number incorrectly attached to the patient's name (as listed in the formulary), rather than by the code number of the actual services she received.

As a result, the patient soon received a bill that read as follows: First week, Psychotherapy, second week, Psychotherapy, third week, Psychotherapy. Services for the fourth week read quite differently, however. The patient was charged for, as inconceivable as it may seem, the following service: Scrotectomy (an excision of part of the scrotum). When I saw the copy of the bill that was returned to the clinic describing the delivery of such an unorthodox procedure, I was at first aghast. If my memory served me correctly, I was certain that I had not performed this delicate operation upon my patient. I then began to fear that she would regard this mistake as either a very tasteless joke or as an indication of some blundering stupidity on my part (which it was). Before too long, however, I began to view this farfetched mix-up as a rather hilarious comedy of errors. I hoped that the patient would also see the ridiculous humor of my charging her for an operation upon her phantom scrotum. Perhaps our sharing this absurdity together would lead to greater rapport between us and help to jar loose some of her depression.

No such luck. The next time I saw the patient she made no reference to the strange item on her bill. I began to think that for some reason she hadn't received or seen the bill. Finally, being unable to quell my curiosity any longer, I asked her if she had gotten her bill. Hesitantly, she said she had, without elaborating. "Did you notice the peculiar item on the bill?" I asked, with a chuckle. Flatly, and with some annoyance, she said it had caught her eye. "What's your reaction to it?" "Well," she went on to say blandly, "I just assumed that someone made a mistake."

She then abruptly changed the subject and I thought it best not to pursue it any further at that time. Certainly, the absurd humor of this incident had no therapeutic value to this depressed patient.

This example illustrates the point that a therapist, even if he or she regards a remark to be immensely amusing, cannot always consider this a golden opportunity to begin joking with the patient. The therapist must carefully consider several factors, including the patient's own particular brand of humor, the manner and timing of the humor and, perhaps most importantly, the patient's receptiveness to being treated with humor, to the extent that this can be determined from what the therapist knows about the patient's current emotional state.

Many jokes unreservedly exploit highly tragic misadventures. The following joke is an example. A deaf and blind man was assigned to ring a bell each day in a very high tower that overlooked a small village. Since he could not see the bell or hear its peal, he decided to make sure that he hit it by running at it full force and slamming his head against it. One day he ran at the bell and missed it. After passing it at high speed, he hurdled through an opening in the tower and a few seconds later was killed by the fall. The villagers gathered around and inspected the body. "Does anybody know this man," asked one of them." "I think I know him," said one of them. "His face rings a bell."

The poor man's brother, who also happened to be deaf and blind, replaced him as the village's bell ringer. Regrettably, he used the same method for ringing the bell that his brother used. One day he too missed the bell, fell off the tower, and was killed. A crowd gathered and inspected the body. "Does anyone know this man," inquired one of the crowd. A man stepped forward and indicated that he thought he knew him. "I could swear I know him. Oh, sure, I do know him, he's a dead ringer for his brother."

We can see from the anecdotes and jokes included in this chapter that a good deal of humor derives from emotional pain. At times we laugh or become jocular because we may actually feel like crying or even fighting instead. The painful setbacks and mishaps we encounter in our daily lives may cause us considerable grief and anger, but humor always remains an indispensable means for coping with our many adversities.

I originally composed the following limericks for a cookbook that was sold as a fund raiser for a youth orchestra. I am including them in this chapter because they illustrate the role of calamity, misfortune, and emotional hardship in humor.

Composers and Delectable Compositions

Mr. Ferde Grofé
Prepared his favorite soufflé
Which he bent over to survey.
To his dismay,
In fell his toupee.
Tasting it, he liked it better that way,
Which saved the day.

The Mormon Tabernacle Choir
Cooked a giant fryer.
They turned up the fire,
Higher and higher.
Then to bed they did retire.
When they came back they found a nasty pyre.

Mrs. Franz Liszt
Served her husband tasteless grist.
He left home in a huff, calling it a vile mess.
Leaving Mrs. Lizst Lisztless.

The Giacomo Puccinis
Served their guest just teeny zucchinis.
To their delight,
The guest had little appetite,
Yet he thought the Puccinis
Untrustworthy meanies.

Mr. Anton Dvorák,
Cooking a very light flapjack,
Flipped it far above his head.
He looked up with a frown,
For the morsel to come down.
After five days, he ate cornflakes instead.

Tomaso Albinoni
Lunched upon an abalone.
The fish, an obvious phony, was much too bony.
So, at the advice of his musical crony,
Angelo Corelli,
He ate only the belly.

Young Arturo Toscanini
Thought the veal scallopini
Much too tough for his palate.
So, for six hours each day,
Until he became gray,
He hit it with a mallet.

Many years back
Mrs. J.B. Bach
Baked a muffin
Upon her oven.
Seeing the muffin bake,
The oven, a thief did take.
Mrs. Bach screamed in great shock,
"Bring my Offenbach."

Virtuoso Arthur Rubinstein,
Preparing to dine,
Undertook to barcarolle.
He covered it with butter,
Which makes me shudder,
To think of all that cholesterol.

Rimsky-Korsakov
Came down with the whooping cough.
The doctor prescribed broth,
His wife gave him chowder,
Which only made poor Rimsky Kov
Even louder.

Moe and Bea together made a birthday cake.
Moe would decorate, Bea would bake.
The cake turned into an ugly tart.
Perhaps it was Bea's oven, or Moe's art.

Mrs. Rachmaninoff
Served her husband beef stroganoff
With very little relish.
She left off the sauce,
Which caused him remorse.
So he asked her to please embellish.

Mr. Gustav Mahler
Left the ice cream parlor
Quite hot under his collar.
With one dollar he tried to pay
For a delicious sundae.
The sundae cost a dollar and a penny,
Just one penny too many,
Causing poor Gustav great woes
Over the debt he Berlioz.

The following story was written shortly after I had returned from a somewhat untoward trip to the state of Illinois. Readers who travel by plane will no doubt find the travails described in this tale rather familiar and, I hope, rather comical. This story exemplifies how one can, if one chooses, convert misfortune into comedy.

DON'T LEAVE HOME WITHOUT . . . ON SECOND THOUGHT, DON'T LEAVE HOME, PERIOD

When, about thirteen years ago, I became a diabetic, I needed no medical explanation. I knew in my heart of hearts exactly what had happened. It was then that my pancreas, which had always been an inveterate blabbermouth anyway, declared, in a most surly, mutinous tone of voice, "Jerry, I've had it with you. I quit. Since the time of your early childhood you've been sending ice cream sundaes, sugary sodas, pastries, chocolate bars and sweet candies by the carboy down to see me for processing. How much, do you think, a poor human organ like myself can bear? You think, maybe, insulin grows on trees? Get yourself another patsy. I'm taking an early retirement. By the way, since we're on the subject, you should know that I'll be filing a workman's compensation claim against you. You'll be hearing from my lawyer in the morning."

Having been heartlessly abandoned by this lifelong helpmate, I was naturally forced to turn to other sources for compassion and guidance. With Johnny-on-the-spot enthusiasm, family, friends, doctors, nurses, dieticians, and fellow diabetics all pitched in with sage advice and pampering kindness. Practically every day, I was deluged with information, both scientific and occult, about how I was to transform my life in order to adjust to the daily vicissitudes of diabetes.

I learned that there were several major variables that would govern my blood sugar level and ultimately determine the general state of my health: insulin dosages, exercise, the quality and quantity of my food intake, other illnesses such as the common cold and, fascinatingly, the ever-varying level of my emotional equilibrium. It was this last variable that I found especially challenging because ever since my pancreas took the law into its own hands, I had found it rather difficult to remain my usual level-headed self. After all, as you will of course concede, it is a bit unnerving to discover that an essential part of one's anatomy has suddenly committed a shameless act of treason. I wondered: is there such a being as a calm, easygoing diabetic? Or is such a concept inherently oxymoronic, or, more to the point, just simply moronic?

Since the onset of my diabetes, I have kept a watchful eye on blood sugar levels, aiming, religiously, to stay "in control." I have been generally aided in my endeavors by ample and pleasurable exercise and, thank goodness, by a constitutionally tranquil nature. Therefore, it is with deep shame and embarrassment that I must confess in these pages that both my constitution and my tranquility are mysteriously eviscerated whenever I undergo the experience of long-distance travel. I would now like to share such an experience with you.

In recent years I have been invited to a fairly large number of college campuses to do some speechifying about students who are disruptive. In April of this year (1994), I received such an invitation from two colleges in Illinois, one in Chicago and another in the southern part of the state.

I left my own college at about 11:30 in the morning to catch a plane that was due to depart about 1:00 in the afternoon. The college is ordinarily about fifteen minutes from the San Francisco Airport, so I assumed that by leaving at 11:30 I had adequately buffered myself against all possible scheduling mishaps. As I leisurely approached the exit to Highway 101, the road that leads directly to the airport, I espied in the distance some barricades that had been installed at the exit along with a sign instructing oncoming vehicles to detour to the north. Since the nearest airport to the north that flew planes to Chicago was in Portland, Oregon, I was not in the least amused by this thoughtless whim of the California Highway Authority. Having no choice, however, I wound the car to the north and exited from the highway at the next turnoff. I found myself in an unfamiliar part of the city with no idea how to retrace my way back to the southbound side of the highway that would take me to the airport. But, by blending and averaging out the nearly unintelligible directions of the three street pedestrians I had stopped, all of whom looked hopelessly lost themselves, I managed to extricate myself from the city streets and was once again confidently beelining my way to the airport.

I arrived at the airport at about 12:15, certain that I had ample time to catch the 1 o'clock flight, since the normal walking time from the parking lot to the gate is no more than ten or fifteen minutes. As I was soon to realize, however, normalcy on this trip refused to be the norm. There was not, alas, a single vacant stall in the entire parking lot adjacent to the terminal from which my plane would leave. Thus, I was forced to park my car in a lot that required a walk of about twenty-five minutes. Walking briskly, arms akimbo with heavy luggage, I was, gratefully, able to capture my day's quota of exercise quite nicely, while working up a nice, even profusion of sweat about equal to that of a full vigorous morning on the tennis court.

I arrived at the gate with, I thought, about ten minutes to spare. But as luck (if that is the correct word for such a quirk of fate) would have it, the plane's new departure time was listed as two o'clock. According to one airline official, the plane had been delayed an hour in Singapore. No further explanation was forthcoming and, as far as I was concerned, none was necessary. I could easily supply my own. Considering the plane's point of origin, and using my Sherlockian powers of deduction, I immediately grasped the fact that several passengers must have vandalized the airport in Singapore and were being held up in that dippy island-state for a good caning. I figured it would take just about an hour, give or take a few minutes, for the Singaporean authorities properly to soak the rattan canes in brine, administer a few good lashings and, just to complete their auto-da-fé on a high note, bid the bloodied tourists a hearty fare-thee-well.

The plane arrived shortly before two and, to my surprise, everyone deplaned seemingly unscarred and in fine fettle. The flight to Chicago was uneventful, although, as usual, the peanuts were a lot tastier and more plentiful than the ersatz dinner that was served. In Chicago, a shuttle bus took me to a rental car agency several miles from the airport. On our way, the driver sideswiped a pickup truck in which two men were riding. If memory serves me correctly, I was quite sure I had recognized them to be two of the hillbillies who appeared in the movie *Deliverance,* though, of course, I could be mistaken. The driver of the truck, greatly irked by the carelessness of my bus driver, followed our bus for about two miles, shaking his fist at him every now and then. Until they finally left us as we approached the agency, I was quite certain that they would cut us off, board the bus with antique Winchesters, and force me to commit unnatural acts that are practiced only by denizens of the Appalachian backcountry.

When we finally reached the rental car agency, I rented a large, fancy Lincoln, which my travel agent had managed to secure at discounted prices. With a map in hand and afire with a renewed sense of adventure, I headed into the city of Chicago. As soon as my car and I entered the streets of the city, I recognized the obvious: I was lost.

Again. After circling around for about thirty minutes, I came within a few blocks of my destination, but, because so many of the nearby streets were one way, I never quite hit the mark.

Finally, I decided to pull into a gas station where I asked a cab driver for directions. In an accent that I, born with an amazing acuity for such linguistic distinctions, immediately identified as native to Tolbuklin, a small city in northeastern Bulgaria, he told me to go to the end of the street, make a right, and then another right. That would, he was certain, get me to my intended destination. I understood from this man's authoritative manner and bearing that he knew the streets and byways of the city like the back of his hand. Then I looked at the back of his hand and observed, to my horror, that it was nothing more than an ugly mass of skinless bones and ganglia, all quite revolting and indecipherable. I jumped back into the car and sped away, just in the nick of time, for he was about to shake my hand in a gesture of international friendship.

I drove to the corner, just as I was instructed to do by the Bulgarian cab driver and made a right turn. A moment later I was wondering why the city of Chicago was celebrating my arrival by setting off bright flashing lights about me. I was, however, quickly disabused of this self-centered notion when I realized that the flashing lights were coming from a revolving bubble atop a police car that was right behind me. Thinking the police car might be in some distress, I pulled over to offer help.

An officer hopped out of his car and came forward. He leaned toward my window and, as he did, I noticed with, I must grudgingly admit, a good degree of aesthetic appreciation, that his neck resembled in its thickness, coloration, and texture, a redwood tree I had once driven my car through in northern California.

The police officer asked for my license. After giving it a quick once-over, he asked if I could spell my name for him. Since I have been quite capable, from the time I was a four-year-old, of spelling my name for anyone who might ask me to carry out this simple task, I granted his request. At first, thinking he might be engaging me in a curbside spelling bee, I was tempted to ask him if he could spell *his* name for *me*. Then, glancing at his redwood neck, I allowed valor to take an excellent walloping from discretion, and squelched the temptation.

The officer explained that I had made an illegal right turn at the corner. Did I not see several signs at the corner indicating that a right turn was prohibited? I told the officer that it was dark at the corner, I was a stranger to the city and therefore unfamiliar with the area, and furthermore, I was just advised by a cab driver to turn there. Unimpressed by my petition for mercy, he asked me if I had in my possession an AAA card. I wondered why. Did he actually need *my* card in order to have one of the city vehicles towed? Reluctantly, I handed over my AAA card, which, I later learned, was kept as collateral in case I ultimately decided to vamoose and refuse to pay my fine. Taking my plight into account, he told me that he would mercifully issue me a minor citation, which, I later came to discover, reduced my life's savings by seventy-five dollars. The card was later returned to me by mail a few weeks after I had paid my fine.

I finally arrived at the college dormitory where I was to spend the evening. My old college pal, Paul, whom I had not seen in several years and who had been waiting there for about three hours, greeted me with a warm smile and hearty handshake, topped by a heart-rending welcome of unexpected ardor: "What the hell took you so long, Jerry?" Touched by the fierce fraternal affection underlying this query, I explained about the canings in Singapore and how I was delayed by Chicago's finest in order to help, in my own small and modest way, with their towing service and budgetary deficits.

Paul and I went upstairs to my room where I took an insulin injection. He had reassured me that there was a pizza restaurant in the neighborhood that was open until quite late. I reassured him that the very last thing I wanted to eat at that late hour was pizza. He reassured me that the restaurant served a variety of other dishes as well. Not altogether reassured by all these assurances, I reluctantly allowed him to shepherd me to this gourmet's Valhalla. We opened the menu and, to my pleasant surprise, the restaurant did indeed serve a nice assortment of dishes other than pizza. Then the waiter came over to inform us that, as of ten minutes ago (10:00 p.m.) the restaurant was serving only pizza.

Paul and I traversed the neighborhood in search of other, more desirable, eateries. It was definitely heartening to discover that there were quite a few respectable looking restaurants in the immediate environs. Undoubtedly, it would have been even more uplifting had any of these worthy places remained open after ten o'clock. So Paul and I wended our way back to the pizza parlor, while I began to wonder how my insulin was holding up with all this vigorous hiking about. At this point, I was humbly beginning to consider pizza, not as a late night indigestible, but rather as a genuine lifeline to my future on this planet. Never before, in my memory, had I held such a deeply appreciative attitude toward any food. I eagerly ate the pizza along with, I might add, a good side order of humble pie. The pizza was barely edible, but evidently plentiful enough to satisfy my hyperactive insulin.

After a long nostalgic chat with Paul and a good night's sleep, despite a few seismographic rumblings from my stomach, I was ready for breakfast. I knew of a breakfast place near the college where I was to speak, so I collected my luggage, checked out of my room, and headed over there. Just before leaving the room I took an insulin injection. When I was within one block of the restaurant, I realized that I had left the insulin in the room, so I hoofed my way back to the dormitory, where a security guard helped me retrieve it. I was able to be pretty philosophical and self-forgiving about this oversight since I know that whenever I travel I tend to feel a bit harried and become forgetful.

After the breakfast and the speech, I was on my way to Charleston, in southern Illinois, to visit another campus. On my drive through the city streets I lost my way only once, which elated me, since it was so far below my usual average when I travel great distances from home. Finally I found my way to the highway that would, in about three hours, take me to Charleston. With each successive mile the traffic grew sparser and pretty soon I was able to put the Lincoln on cruise control and relax to some wonderful classical music broadcasted by a college radio station in Urbana.

After about an hour on the road I noticed a slight but disquieting meteorologic change was taking place. As if some heavenly rheostat had been gradually turned down, the sky, which had been overcast and zinc gray most of the day, was now becoming lower and darker. Within a few minutes, a few strands of eiderdown were landing on my windshield. Not knowing much about this area of the country, I assumed it must be duck hunting season, but could not understand why hunters would be shooting these birds so near a highway. The thought was discomfiting, to say the least.

The light, papery fuzz soon began to increase in size and volume and it was only then that I, in a moment of penetrating insight, realized that the "eiderdown" was really snow. But this was impossible. It was already April and supposedly I was in central Illinois. Panic overtook me in its viselike grip. I realized that I must have made a horrible mistake. I feared that instead of heading south to Charleston when I left Chicago, I had instead somehow turned to the north and was now in upper Ontario, Canada, brainlessly making my way, like a migratory bird, toward the Arctic Circle. All about me were fields completely blanketed with snow, stretching illimitably into the distance like endless white wafers.

Lost and disoriented, I gave thought to stopping at a nearby farmhouse or even a local igloo to ask directions. One thing was certain: I was not dressed for this weather and, what's more, when I gave even a moment's consideration to the possibility that I might have to subsist in the coming days on a diet of caribou and seal meat, I began to look back upon the previous night's odious pizza dinner with a peculiar sense of wistfulness.

I turned on a cowl light and pushed a button. A doohickey made in Detroit silently told the outdoor temperature: twenty-eight degrees Fahrenheit. This was weather in which Farley Mowat could frolic about fully naked. But I, newly arrived from sunny California, was surely out of my element.

Eureka! (which, along with myself, can also be found in California most of the year), I passed a sign that indicated that Memphis, Tennessee, was several hundred miles to the south. I was heading in the right direction after all and, with any luck, I might actually reach Charleston in the foreseeable future.

I pulled into Charleston around four o'clock and checked into a small motel where I had made a reservation. As you will soon see, I arranged to have many more reservations about this motel over the next two days. The manager, a pale young man with blond hair and a quaint cowlick that I would think no respectable cow would ever deign to put her tongue to, and who most likely was a local college student (and who most likely was also flunking most of his courses), was on the phone with a woman who, I surmised, was suffering from some serious malady that allowed her to be his faithful girlfriend. Since I was only a paying guest at the motel, he ignored me for several minutes while negotiating a date for that evening.

When he had finally concluded his amatory transaction, he brushed back his cowlick and asked what I wanted. For some inexplicable reason, it seemed to come as a great surprise to him that I wanted, of all things, a room in his motel. I signed the register and then asked him if he could help me with a small favor. I needed to have my insulin placed in the refrigerator and my freezable containers placed in the freezer. He looked at me with a blank stare, almost as if I had just asked him to perform a prodigious task of abstract calculus, and then repeated my request in reverse: "So, let me get this straight. You'd like me to put your insulin in the freezer and the containers in the refrigerator. Did I get it right?"

"Well, almost, nit. I mean, no, son. No, just the reverse. This is very important, so please attend to what I'm about to tell you. Do not, I repeat, do not, freeze my insulin." Then I slowly and clearly repeated the instructions as he carried away the insulin bottles and containers to another room. I heard him open and then close a refrigerator door there and for the next several hours I wondered if it was ever a medically sound practice to use defrosted insulin. As I left the lobby, cowlick wished me a good stay and I, wishing to be friendly, had given a moment's thought to ask him his name. However, I realized that if he mumbled anything that remotely sounded like N. Bates I would not be able to shower during my entire stay in that motel.

The next morning I went to retrieve the insulin. When I arrived in the motel lobby a man who was standing behind the counter with a bath towel wrapped around his waist was shouting in a foreign language at a woman I took to be his hapless wife. When he saw me, he smiled beatifically and then retreated to another room. Another man emerged from that room. A wraithlike individual with a starkly ghoulish appearance, he carried about him faint but hideous echoes of the grave.

"Good morning," he said.

"Good morning," I obediently replied. I was pleased to see that we were off to such an excellent start. "I'm checking out and I'd like to have my insulin and containers returned. They're in the refrigerator."

He replied by saying something that sounded like, "Omgas rumbeck sooly mutton." I understood the mutton part, but not one for eating ovine animals in the morning, I demurred.

"No thanks. I'll just take my insulin and containers and leave."

"Pulbas loomis ab swim."

The part about a swim puzzled me since I had not noticed a pool at the motel and it had just stopped snowing. Was he, perhaps, in some snide, subtle way, telling me to go take a jump in the lake? I kept repeating my request. He, in evident exasperation and perplexity, took out the guest registry and showed it to me. I guess he thought I was looking for another guest. Finally, after I had pointed many times to the other room and repeated the word "refrigerator" every few seconds, he turned his zombie eyes away and followed them into the back room. He returned with the insulin and containers, which, to my relief, had somehow been placed in their proper refrigerator compartments. I then grabbed my luggage and raced out of the godforsaken place just as I noticed him staring thirstily at the veins in my neck.

I was advised to drive back to Chicago's O'Hare Airport via a highway that bypassed the city itself. All went well as I approached the airport. Just to be on the safe side, however, I asked a toll collector the distance to the airport. He told me twenty-one miles. As I approached the twenty-first mile I kept a sharp eye out for an airport exit. There was none. As a matter of fact, I never did see an airport exit, although I saw in the sky many planes making their descent to what presumably was O'Hare.

Then, necessity forced me to look at the matter with cold logic. Why, I asked myself, should one of the largest airports in the world bother with erecting highway signs that directed drivers to its terminals? Why can't it simply and justifiably rely upon its fame as a major transportation hub and assume that everyone, including befuddled out-of-staters like myself, will eventually find the place on their own? Good thinking, what?

At the twenty-fourth mile I asked another toll collector for directions to the airport. He told me to get off the highway at the first exit and drive back about five miles. I did just that and after about four miles I asked a fellow driver for directions to the rental car agencies. She gave me clear, explicit directions and when I arrived in the vicinity of the agencies I discovered that there was one, and, mind you, only one, agency that was located about three miles away from all the others. Should I, dear reader, state the obvious? Yes, it was the agency from which I had rented the Lincoln.

When I finally checked into the agency, I left the car in the lot near a crossbar. A few minutes later a young lady with an annoyingly officious and huffy manner asked which car I had returned. When I told her, she said, "Yes, Mr. Amada, I thought so. It has a dent in the front."

"What! I had no accidents with that car. I hadn't looked it over when I took it out, but I know it was not damaged while I was driving it."

"We'll see about that, sir," was all she said.

Just at that moment, a supervisor, who noticed that I was beginning to writhe and froth at the mouth, no doubt the incipient signs of an apoplectic seizure, took matters into his own hands. Calmly and with great sympathy for my enfeebled state, he said, "Mr. Amada, please. Just go take your luggage and leave. It's O.K. I'll take care of this matter for you."

It was so kind of him. Hesitating for a moment because I thought he was about to take time to direct me, by now a certifiable valetudinarian, to the nearest nursing home, I did as he instructed. I arrived at the airport, miraculously, two hours before the time of departure. I was told by a guard that, if I didn't mind a walk of about fifteen minutes, I could get a bite to eat in a restaurant located in a distant terminal. After a walk of about ten minutes, I accosted a woman wearing a spiffy, commanding uniform—a personage of obvious authority and vast knowledge anent airports —and asked how I could get to the restaurant.

She said, "Oh, I'm sorry, sir. You're walking in the wrong direction. You'll have to turn around and go back in the other direction."

Dismayed by this untoward news, I said, "But, a guard told me the restaurant was in this direction. Are you sure?"

She then looked nonplussed and began lifting and revolving her head ceilingward, apparently in search of some architectural clues up there as to our present whereabouts. Then, with flustered embarrassment, she said, "Oh, you're right. You're going in the right direction. Keep going another five minutes and you'll be there. You know, in all my years working here, I've never before made that mistake. Bon appetit."

I didn't say this to her, but I had no difficulty whatsoever believing that I was the first person throughout her entire professional career that she had ever victimized with such deplorable misinformation.

On the return flight to San Francisco I relaxed and used the aerial confinement to regain my composure. There was a brief moment, I must admit, when I thought I saw on the wing of the airplane the creature from Rod Serling's *Twilight Zone*, but then realized that it was merely the reflection in the window of the man in the business suit sitting next to me. When I looked over at him, I noticed with horror that he did, indeed, bear a remarkable resemblance to Serling's ghoul. Then I thought, quite quixotically of course, that a wing might detach itself from the plane, causing us to crash. And then I realized that whether we crashed or not was really only a matter of a pinion. Finally, while musing about the possibility of my imminent demise, and thinking that, by means of some extraordinary celestial mix-up, I might actually spend my perpetuity among the angels, I realized that I had, alas, left my harp in San Francisco.

When I finally arrived home I made a fervent promise to myself. I have long acknowledged that travel is broadening and good for the soul, but from now on I think I'll manacle myself to my bed, crawl under the covers, and let my mind do all the wandering.

I will conclude this chapter with an article that I originally published in the now defunct magazine, *Bay Views*, in March, 1978. I think it illustrates how fine a line exists between psychological pain and humor. By the way, I have never been able to precisely determine to what extent my article contributed to the ultimate demise of the magazine in which it appeared.

Here's Mud in Your Ear

On a rare childless day in the latter part of a rapidly waning summer, my wife and I shuffled a few schemes for turning out a bit of unusual fun. Not being natural hedonists, dozens of ideas were alternately submitted and discarded as too trite or too childish. After having planned so many days of our adult lives with the purpose of placating noisy and ungrateful kids, it was inanely difficult to plan an outing that combined the proper amount of pleasure with mature, practical considerations.

My wife suddenly flashed, "How about a visit to a Calistoga (California) health spa? The mud baths would be novel fun and *therapeutic*, especially since your tennis back has been acting up again."

"Marvelous," I said.

We quickly learned from friends that reservations were not necessary, so immediately set out on an inspired hour-and-a-half drive north to Calistoga. Calistoga is a small, sleepy, one-street town in northern California whose seeming tranquility is heatedly belied by an abundance of boiling, ever-spuming underground springs. The geysers in this part of the country give ample and perpetual support to several health spas that each year attract thousands of stiff and rickety tourists in search of eternal relief and well-being.

We were grimly oriented to the offerings of the health spa by a smile-proof receptionist who handed us a brochure and proceeded to repeat, word for word, the jumbo benefits described in the brochure. I had the distinct impression that she suffered moral disgust from visions of countless frumpy, sweaty bodies traipsing through her baths, all in varying stages of crude disrepair. We were told that ten dollars (the price has since gone up considerably) would cover the costs of the whole treatment: mud bath, mineral water bath, steam room, blanket wrap, showers, and massage. The price was reasonable, so we handed over our personal belongings and, following our first instructions, turned in opposite directions to enter segregated facilities.

My first salient sensations were largely olfactory. As a matter of fact, the long corridor leading to the baths smelled very much like an old factory. For a moment I wondered why the premises hadn't been fumigated since rodents must be scavenging for the rotten eggs left about. I then realized that the offending stench was the sulfur from the erupting springs that are continually piped into the bathhouse.

As I turned a corner a friendly, disembodied voice greeted me with an invitation to enter a cubicle, undress, and await further instructions. The attendant turned out to be a pleasant young man who wore a towel draped about his waist; not from modesty, I thought, but perhaps in deference to an environment in which wearing a towel is a bit like donning a suit and tie when the neighbors drop over for a barbecue. It's just a matter of occasionally wanting to be a bit dressier than your company.

Just as I finished undressing, the attendant returned (I learned that punctuality is central to the bathhouse operation, for reasons that will become clear later). I was brought to a shower stall, given a sliver of soap, and told to clean up. Was there a jeering presumption that I would ever go anyplace where I had to undress, be it a bathhouse or a doctor's office, without having taken a shower at home first? My mother always insisted that I brush my teeth extra carefully on the day they were to be cleaned by the dentist. In any case, the shower was strong and temperate and left no hard feelings.

The attendant then guided me to an area of the bathhouse where several rectangular concrete tubs were situated in a single row. The tubs were filled with a dark, oozy mass into which hot water was being piped. "Is that the mud?" I queried. "Yes, sir, now if you'll lie on your back with your head upon the board, I'll cover you."

I gingerly climbed onto the mud and found, to my surprise, that I became only partially submerged. The mud's dense consistency kept me afloat. The mud was warm and cushiony and actually felt clean, if you can accept the oxymoronic notion of clean dirt. The attendant then began to gently push my legs and arms beneath the mud, at the same time scooping large clods that he spread over me from toe to Adam's apple.

The attendant volunteered, "This is volcanic mud heated to about 105 degrees." I knowledgeably replied, "Oh." I didn't really understand how volcanic mud differed from the *schmutz* my kids drag through the kitchen on a rainy day. The mud bath was to last ten minutes. The first few minutes were sheer primeval delight. I found myself possessed with a perverse envy of the hippo or even the pig, despite the latter's bacon-destiny. Entering approximately the fifth minute in the tub, however, two disquieting developments began to take place.

Most importantly, my head began to slide off the board and mud began to enter one of my ears. I began to wonder what it would do to me to have large quantities of volcanic mud inside my head. Would it change my personality? Would I become more irritable, more eruptive? The attendant had been returning every minute or so with a cool washcloth which he used to wipe the sweat from my forehead. I knew he was due to return soon, so I felt reluctant to scream out in protest of my gradual interment. I was beginning to think of myself as a trapped, persecuted character in a macabre Poe tale.

The attendant made a timely return. "How're we doing?" he asked with fraternal interest. "Our head is slipping into the mud," I observed. He apologized and tilted the board back to its proper position beneath my head. At this point I realized that I was becoming moderately uncomfortable. I noticed that rivulets of water were rushing about my head and chest, a contingency for which I momentarily had no explanation. My guess was that an extra water pipe had been installed deep into the tub, in the vicinity of my chest. I, of course, was eventually forced to realize that the gushing about me was my own perspiration which, because of the impacted mud, had begun coursing up and down, rather than off, my body. In another minute I wanted out. The mud was well over one hundred degrees and I was every bit as warm as the mud. I would have a seizure and suffer irreversible brain damage! In a few moments I would dehydrate into an igneous mush! My pores were now delivering hot Niagaras all over my body. I could almost hear them crying out patriotically for their master, "Give me liberty and give me breath."

At just the right moment a bell chimed which signaled the salvational return of the attendant. Because of the considerable weight of the mud and my state of complete exhaustion, it was necessary for the attendant to push me out of the ooze from behind. I then took another shower from which I made my way to a bathtub filled with hot mineral water in which I soaked myself into further oblivion. In ten minutes the attendant beckoned me to follow him into the sauna. The sauna was probably heated to about 115 degrees. Since I had barely recuperated from the hot mud and hot mineral bath, the rigors of the sauna took effect immediately. I panted for fresh air and began to feel faint. There was a small aperture in the door which was angled in such a way, I noticed, as to enable an outsider to conveniently observe the occupant after he has swooned onto the floor.

After a few minutes the attendant inquired if I might wish to come out. Spartanlike, I refused. As he turned the corner, barely out of view, I furtively stepped out of the sauna, took a few gulps of cool air and reentered my earthly inferno. I had had my meager revenge upon my tormentor/attendant.

I finally left the sauna of my own accord. The attendant walked briskly ahead of me into my original cubicle and I slavishly dragged myself after him. Here he swathed my entire body with sheets and a heavy army blanket. Room temperature was probably about eighty degrees, yet amazingly, I felt cool in my tight cocoon. The attendant brought me a cup of sulfur with a straw that was initially quite refreshing. A second sip, however, brought home the vile taste of the sulfurous drink, and although I was parched and dehydrated, I used the rest of the water to pour over my inflamed head. In a few minutes the blanketing began to show its treachery. The insulation raised my anatomical thermostat and soon I was gushing and gasping again. Finally, I was rescued by the masseur who greeted me with, "Are you ready to go to work?" I was grateful for the deliverance and we decamped for his room.

The masseur was an elderly, taciturn, and extremely powerful man who pounded, pushed, rubbed, and stretched me with great thoroughness and care. He began his work by giving each toe a firm, independent tug and then proceeded to mightily trespass up my corrugated spine. Finally, his hands found the base of my skull into which he dug his fingers vigorously. What form of skullduggery was this, I wondered. During this time I bravely tried to carry on a tasteful conversation, but even my vocal cords seemed to have succumbed to heat prostration so that the best I could manage was an occasional grunt. Where does mental hygiene end and masochism begin, my psychologically minded mind pondered.

In twenty minutes I was released to return to my cell where I dressed. Then I languidly returned to the waiting room which my wife entered from the women's quarters at almost the exact same moment.

"How did you like it, Jerry?"

"Great. How about you?"

"Fantastic. Let's come back sometime soon, okay?"

"Fine. It's so relaxing and healthful."

The next day at home the weather was clear and in the eighties. My wife asked me to remove some rubbish from the backyard. I barked at her, "You don't expect me to get myself filthy in this heat, do you?"

Chapter 6

Negative Emotions and Creativity

In this chapter we will consider the potential of the negative emotions to inspire imagination and creativity.

Charles Dickens

Clearly, one of the greatest and most imaginative of all writers was Charles Dickens. Throughout much of his childhood Dickens's family lived in straitened circumstances. Due to his father's financial carelessness, Dickens and his family were forced for a time to live in a debtor's prison. These experiences were stamped bitterly and indelibly upon Dickens's character.

In his autobiography Dickens writes, "The deep remembrance of the sense I had of being utterly neglected and hopeless; of the shame I felt in my position; of the misery it was to my young heart to believe that, day by day, what I had learned, and thought, and delighted in, raised my fancy and my emulation up by, was passing away from me, never to be brought back anymore; cannot be written. My whole nature was so penetrated with the grief and humiliation of such considerations, that even now, famous and caressed and happy, I often forget in my dreams

---

I wish to thank Merle Miller for her assistance with this chapter.

that I have a dear wife and children; even that I am a man; and wander desolately back to that time of my life."

The neglect and humiliation he suffered as a child, anguishing and undermining as it was to him, ultimately served as a central theme and propelling force in all of Dickens's novels. The plight of the impoverished and bereft Oliver Twist, for example, was certainly a dire circumstance of life with which Dickens could strongly identify. In many of Dickens's novels there is a childhood fantasy that is played out, at times, as is the case with most fantasies, quite implausibly.

The fantasy begins with a child who, like Dickens himself, is born and raised in squalor but who is destined, through a series of fortuitous events, to acquire social eminence and affluence. For instance, Oliver is miraculously rescued from a den of thieves and orphanhood whence he is restored to his proper genealogy in order to live a life of comfort and opulence. Even Tiny Tim, Bob Cratchit's crippled son in the *Christmas Carol*, who throughout most of this novel appears to be an absolute goner, providentially survives and prospers as the just beneficiary of the penitential Ebenezer Scrooge.

Dickens of course never completely overcame the despair, bitterness, and rage he experienced as a result of his childhood hardships and privations. This rage is cyclonically unleashed at one of his characters, Miss Havisham, who, in *Great Expectations*, slyly pretends to yet another orphan, Pip, that she is this young man's benefactress. For her deceit toward the defenseless Pip, Dickens sets fire to Miss Havisham at her own living room hearth and the despicable dowager dies horribly from the conflagration for, as Dickens's clever play on words seems to suggest, having her sham.

Dickens uses his novels to take revenge upon others who have exploited or abused children. The evil Fagan, who has entrapped and misused Oliver, dies by hanging, that "hideous apparatus of death."

Dickens was shocked and outraged by the monstrous neglect of education in nineteenth-century England and by the woeful disregard of the schools by the state. In particular, he was infuriated by the notable unfitness and cruelty of many schoolmasters who, without examination or qualification, opened and administered schools throughout England. Dickens angrily declaimed, "But, what of the hundreds of thousands of minds that have been deformed forever by the incapable pettifoggers who have pretended to form them!"

In *Nicholas Nickleby* Dickens introduces the noxious schoolmaster, Squeers, who repeatedly tyrannizes and terrorizes his charges. Through Nicholas, Dickens tells Squeers, "I have a long series of insults to avenge and my indignation is aggravated by the dastardly cruelties practiced on helpless infancy in this foul den." With that, Nicholas sprang upon Squeers and "beat the ruffian until he roared for mercy." In this passage, Dickens takes symbolic and passionate revenge upon all the schoolmasters of England who have maltreated him and other children.

When Dickens was appalled and disgusted by the enormously costly litigation that proceeded glacially through the courts of England, he again wrote a brilliant novel: *Bleak House.* In this novel, which describes a drawn-out lawsuit tried within a moribund legal system, Dickens levels a scathing indictment against venal attorneys and antiquated courts.

As we can see, Charles Dickens used to great creative advantage his rage and indignation over the oppressive social conditions that had played such a central role during his own unhappy childhood.

W. Somerset Maugham

Another writer who has derived enormous creative energy from the adverse circumstances of his own life is W. Somerset Maugham, whose masterpiece, *Of Human Bondage,* is transparently autobiographical. The principal character of this novel, Philip Carey, like Maugham himself, was born with a clubfoot that not only limited his motility, but was also a source of savage and humiliating ridicule from his peers. In once especially poignant episode, Philip is physically bullied by his schoolmates into exposing his clubfoot, the ugliness of which they poke at and comment upon with morbid curiosity and repugnance.

Philip Carey, already painfully shy and self-conscious, was tormented by his classmates as he limped about the school. Like Maugham, he was orphaned as a youth and placed in the care of his aunt and uncle, the latter of whom was a stern, self-indulgent clergyman.

With power and poignancy, Maugham has written a novel that describes the excruciating psychological pain he had suffered as a youth. As a means of coming to terms with the emotionally traumatic experiences of his childhood, he wrote masterfully about his own past through the fictional character of Philip Carey.

Franz Kafka

Another writer whose personal torment appears pervasively throughout his novels and short stories is Franz Kafka. In his *Letter to His Father*, Kafka reveals the manifold events of his childhood that shaped and permeated his later personality. He readily acknowledges at the outset of this letter that he is afraid of his father. His earliest direct memory was when as a small child he kept on whimpering for a drink of water, partly to amuse himself. After several threats had failed to have any effect, his father removed him from his bed and placed him outside a shut door on a balcony where he was to remain alone in the darkness.

Kafka states that his father's method of disciplining him in this instance was typical of the man and that it did him, Franz, inner harm, despite its desired effect of rendering him more obedient. Then, referring to a theme that frequently recurs throughout his writings, Kafka states that he is often dominated by a sense of nothingness that he attributes directly to his father's influence.

Kafka goes on to reveal how he felt both physically and intellectually dominated by his father who ruled the world from his armchair. His father considered his own opinions correct, all others were mad and perverse. Kafka then points out that his father took on "the enigmatic quality that all tyrants have whose rights are based on their person and not on reason." As one might expect, the perception of authority figures as remote, enigmatic, and irrational is repeated as a central theme in all of Kafka's writings.

The impotent rage, guilt, and disillusionment that he feels over the disparity of power and prerogatives between himself and his father is powerfully voiced in the following passage: "You, the man who was so tremendously the measure of all things for me, yourself did not keep the commandments you imposed upon me. Hence the world was for me divided into three parts: into one in which I, the slave, lived under laws that had been invented only for me and which I could, I did not know why, never completely comply with; then into a second world, which was infinitely remote from mine, in which you lived, concerned with government, with the issuing of orders and with annoyance about their not being obeyed; and finally into a third world where everybody else lived happily and free from order and having to obey. I was continually in disgrace, either I obeyed your orders, and that was a disgrace, for they applied, after all, only to me, or I was defiant, and that was a disgrace too, for how could I presume to defy you, or I could not obey because, for instance, I had not your strength, your appetite, your skill, in spite of which you expected it of me as a matter of course; this was the greatest disgrace of all."

The enigmatic and capricious power of higher authority is brought forth as a central existential theme in Kafka's symbolic classic, *The Trial*. In this novel an industrious bank clerk, Mr. K. (Kafka uses this initial to undisguisedly identify himself as the main character of the novel) is suddenly arrested one morning. When he asks why he is arrested, he is told, "We are not authorized to tell you that." Throughout

the remainder of *The Trial* Mr. K. impotently defends himself against
unspecified charges and is finally disposed of by having a knife thrust
into his heart. Like the young Kafka who agonized over his relationship
to his father, Mr. K. suffers shame, disgrace and, ultimately, annihila-
tion at the hands of an enigmatic and unappeasable authority.

In another novel, *The Castle*, Mr. K., a land surveyor, attempts to
gain access to a castle in order to be confirmed in his appointment.
However, he encounters a series of obstacles and a recalcitrant official-
dom that prevent him from having contact with the castle. Although
Kafka never completed this novel, we know that he informed his
friends that Mr. K. dies of exhaustion without ever reaching the castle.
Again, we see in this novel Kafka's perception of his father resurrected
in the form of yet another remote, unapproachable, and unintelligible
authority figure (the castle).

Finally, in his extraordinary and terrifying short story, *The Meta-
morphosis*, Kafka's principal character, Gregor Samsa, awakes one
morning from a fitful sleep to discover that he has been transformed in
his bed into a gigantic insect. Gregor suffers insults and degradations at
the hands of his family who neglect, abuse, and betray him at every
turn. As his family unites against him, Gregor, the filthy and discarded
insect, spiritually and physically breaks down until he dies a squalid
and undignified death.

The existential horror and desolation described in this story clearly
mirror the world that Kafka lived in as a child, the world which he described to his father as dominated by a sense of nothingness and filled
with disgrace. We can see from Kafka's anguish-ridden writings how
much his brilliant creative work was the product of a bleak childhood
and deep personal conflicts.

Evelyn Waugh

Another writer who has brilliantly fictionalized his own personal
experience of torment is the British novelist Evelyn Waugh. In his
novel, *The Ordeal of Gilbert Pinfold*, Waugh describes the tribulations
of Gilbert Pinfold who embarks on a recuperative voyage to Ceylon.
Three years prior to writing this novel, Waugh himself suffered a brief
bout of hallucination that closely resembles the disorientating setbacks
of the beleaguered hero of his novel, Mr. Pinfold. Mr. Waugh's own
hallucinatory episode, which no doubt confused and alarmed him, became the grist for a novel which is both touching and amusing.

The plot of this novel begins when Mr. Pinfold—who, like Waugh
himself, is a prominent and prolific writer—sees his doctor about a
severe attack of the "aches." His physician, Dr. Drak, advocates a

warm climate and some new and "pretty powerful" pills. Soon after boarding the *Caliban*, Mr. Pinfold is beset by a variety of auditory hallucinations, including barking dogs, seductresses who offer protection from vague and ominous threats, blaring jazz bands, and strange revival meetings.

In the end, Mr. Pinfold recovers nicely from his illness that seemed to be a reaction to the overuse of chloral. Dr. Drake acknowledges that lots of people hear voices and that the voices are nearly always offensive. Although he regards Pinfold's illness as a simple case of chemical poisoning, Pinfold himself seems to express Waugh's own point of view regarding the crisis he had just weathered.

Following the medical consultation, Pinfold "knew, and the others did not know—not even his wife, least of all his medical adviser—that he had endured a great ordeal and, unaided, had emerged the victor. There was a triumph to be celebrated, even if a mocking slave stood always beside him in his chariot reminding him of mortality."

This novel seems to have given Waugh the opportunity to put his emotionally turbulent experience at sea into proper perspective. With wit and pride he has written a novel that fundamentally tells about his own journey into the realm of unreason and his triumphant return from and conquest of the ordeal.

Richard Wright

A writer who has certainly given an eloquent portrayal of his own ill-fated childhood is the gifted black novelist, Richard Wright. In his novel, *Black Boy,* Wright writes with unsparing power about the poverty, hunger, and violence in which he grew up. With stark candor he reveals, "I was a drunkard in my sixth year, before I had begun school. With a gang of children, I roamed the streets, begging pennies from passersby, haunting the doors of saloons, wandering farther and farther away from home each day. I saw more than I could understand and heard more than I could remember. The point of life became for me the times when I could beg drinks. My mother was in despair. She beat me; then she prayed and wept over me, imploring me to be good, telling me that she had to work, all of which carried no weight to my wayward mind. Finally she placed me and my brother in the keeping of an old black woman who watched me every moment to keep me from running to the doors of the saloons to beg for whisky. The craving for alcohol finally left me and I forgot the taste of it."

Wright's early childhood was one in which hunger was a constant companion. "Hunger stole upon me so slowly that at first I was not aware of what hunger really meant. Hunger had always been more or less at my elbow when I played, but now I began to wake up at night to find hunger standing at my bedside, staring me gauntly. The hunger I had known before this had been no grim, hostile stranger; it had been a normal hunger that had made me beg constantly for bread, and when I ate a crust or two I was satisfied. But this new hunger baffled me, scared me, made me angry and insistent. Whenever I begged for food now my mother would pour me a cup of tea which would still the clamor in my stomach for a moment or two; but a little later I would feel hunger nudging my ribs, twisting my empty guts until they ached. I would grow dizzy and my vision would dim. I became less active in my play, and for the first time in my life I had to pause and think of what was happening to me."

Trapped between the white world that treated him with indifference, contempt, and cruelty, and the black world that largely resented his attempts to better himself, Wright not only discovered new ideas and visions with which to master his existence, but also wrote an unforgettable autobiographical novel that tells with great pathos of the emotional trials of his youth.

Fyodor Dostoevsky

Like W. Somerset Maugham, Fyodor Dostoevsky suffered from a physical disability. His frequent attacks of epilepsy contributed to a lifetime of suffering that left him a crushed and embittered man. Because he suffered from this particular handicap he was able to describe an epileptic seizure with stark and compelling realism in his outstanding novel, *The Idiot.*

In the following passage the principal character of this novel, Prince Myshkin, is overcome with an epileptic seizure that is described with a gripping sense of horror by Dostoevsky, who knew about such things firsthand. "Then suddenly something seemed torn asunder before him; his soul was flooded with intense *inner* light. The moment lasted perhaps half a second, yet he clearly and consciously remembered the beginning, the first sound of the fearful scream which broke of itself from his breast and which he could not have checked by any effort. Then his consciousness was instantly extinguished and complete darkness followed.

"It was an epileptic fit, the first he had had for a long time. It is well known that epileptic fits come on quite suddenly. At the moment the face is horribly distorted, especially the eyes. The whole body and the features of the face work with convulsive jerks and contortions. A terrible, indescribable scream that is unlike anything else breaks from the sufferer. In that scream everything human seems obliterated and it is impossible, or very difficult, for an observer to realize and admit that it is the man himself screaming. It seems indeed as though it were someone else screaming from within the man. That is how many people at least have described their impression. The sight of a man in an epileptic fit fills many people with positive and unbearable horror, in which there is a certain element of the uncanny."

With powerful vividness and insight, Dostoevsky has in *The Idiot* basically described his own lifelong experience with epilepsy. His literary genius enabled him to artistically incorporate his own chronic emotional torment over epilepsy into this novel, presumably meeting a long-unmet and understandable psychological need to share his personal anguish with many others.

Jack London

Jack London was another author who in his youth had encountered severe personal adversities and disadvantages. Through courage, perseverance, and intensive self-education, London overcame and transcended the social and economic constraints with which he had battled as a youth. He wrote about these struggles in his autobiographical novel, *Martin Eden.*

Like his creator, Jack London, the fictional character, Martin Eden, struggled throughout his life to support his family. As youths, both London and Eden had been relatively uneducated and uncouth. Both had become sailors at an early age and both possessed an unquenchable drive to study and write. Tragically, both author and character died deeply disappointed and alienated men, despite their considerable literary attainments.

The following passage from *Martin Eden* undoubtedly describes the pathetic self-consciousness and uncouthness of London's own personality as a young man. "He [Martin Eden] talked only when he had to, and then his speech was like his walk to the table, filled with jerks and halts as he groped in his polyglot vocabulary for words, debating over words he knew were fit but which he feared he could not pronounce, rejecting other words he knew would not be understood or would be raw and harsh. But all the time he was oppressed by the consciousness that this carefulness of diction was making a booby of him, preventing him from expressing what he had in him. Also, his love of freedom chafed against the restriction in much the same way his neck chafed against the starched fetter of a collar. Besides, he was confident that he could not keep it up. He was by nature powerful of thought and sensibility, and the creative spirit was restive and urgent. He was swiftly mastered by the concept or sensation in him that struggled in birth-throes to receive expression and form, and then he forgot himself and where he was, and the old words—the tools of speech he knew— slipped out."

London further writes about his own unlettered youth when he describes Martin Eden's foray into a local library. "From every side the books seemed to press upon him and crush him. He had never dreamed that the fund of human knowledge bulked so big. He was frightened. How could his brain ever master it all? Later, he remembered that there were other men, many men, who had mastered it; and he breathed a great oath, passionately, under his breath, swearing that his brain could do what theirs had done."

With stout resoluteness coupled with an insatiable thirst for knowledge and reading, London's brain indeed "could do what theirs had done." In the process, he creatively used the chaos and struggles of his own past to serve as the foundation for the plot and central character of his eloquently written novel, *Martin Eden*.

Samuel Pisar

Naturally, not all writers choose to fictionalize the accounts of their past tribulations. In a moving saga of his own struggle for personal freedom entitled *Of Blood and Hope*, Samuel Pisar, today a world-renowned international lawyer, tells how he miraculously survived a Nazi death camp and a brief period of postinternment lawlessness that resulted in imprisonment, to eventually rise to the summits of American political and corporate life.

Pisar explains his reasons for writing this stirring autobiography in the following words. "The gratuitous retelling of the gruesome events of my youth has never appealed to me. Neither do I believe in the value of personal memoirs as a guide for others. But when I think back to the days during which a combination of slogans and bombs tore apart my happy childhood, when I see mankind heading once again toward some hideous collective folly, I feel that I must either lapse into total silence or broadcast to the world my urgent sense of the horrors that threaten to destroy our own and our children's future.

"This is why I decided to decipher and transmit some of the lessons that lay concealed in the torrents of blood and hope that had flooded my life. I wanted to convey to as many as I could how, not so long ago, a proud civilization had collapsed physically and morally, before my very eyes—the eyes of a child—and had left behind only cruelty, suffering, and destruction. I wanted to tell it in the raw, which was the way I had lived it and felt it and thought about it; to convey everything that came to preoccupy me later, as reality upon reality imprinted itself on my flesh and on my mind, and made me what I am, and what I think and feel today, and what I see ahead.

"I had to stop and think and tell—tell our story to whoever would listen, like a beggar with an outstretched bowl, asking for the coin of attention under an impassive sky. I had to tell it, not worrying about what it exposed or how well it fit into the scheme of my current life, hoping that when my tale was done it would mean something to the lives of those who read it. Hoping also that it would clear up, for me, some truths which I needed to absorb more fully, if the miracle of my salvation was to continue to ripen within me."

In *Of Blood and Hope* Pisar relives the bloody, dark chapters of his early life and thereby bestows upon his readers an eloquent legacy from which they may gain hope and meaning. In this respect he has amply lived up to his self-imposed duty to convey special insights regarding one of the darkest periods in human history.

Clifford Beers

The psychiatric literature is of course replete with important documents regarding the nightmarish psychological struggles and recoveries of mentally ill patients. One of the most telling of such accounts is the autobiography of Clifford Beers, *A Mind that Found Itself*, written in the early part of the twentieth century.

Beers describes in this volume the shockingly inhumane treatment he received in various psychiatric institutions following his abortive suicide attempt. Suffering from ungovernable thoughts and hallucinations, Beers, once placed in psychiatric custody, received little more from the supervising physicians than physical restraint and intellectual deprivation. "The assistant physician, instead of making it easy for me to rid myself of an excess of energy along literary and artistic lines, balked me at every turn, and seemed to delight in displaying as little interest as possible in my newly awakened ambitions. When everything should have been done to calm my abnormally active mind, a studied indifference and failure to protect my interests kept me in a state of exasperation.

"But circumstances now arose which brought about the untimely stifling—I might better say strangulation—of my artistic impulses. The doctors were led—unwisely, I believe—to decide that absolute seclusion was the only thing that would calm my over-active brain. In consequence, all writing and drawing materials and all books were taken from me."

Beers suffered from the incompetence, abuse, and injustice meted out by his institutional caretakers throughout the three years of his institutionalization. Using a ruse to mislead the psychiatric staff into believing that he had just made a suicide attempt, he then informed them, "You probably think I've just tried to kill myself. It was simply a ruse to make you give me some attention. When I make threats and tell you that my one object in life is to live long enough to regain my freedom and lay bare the abuses which abound in places like this, you simply laugh at me, don't you? But the fact is, that's my ambition, and if you knew anything at all, you'd know that abuse won't drive me to suicide. You can continue to abuse me and deprive me of my rights, and keep me in exile from relatives and friends, but the time will come when I'll make you sweat for all this. I'll put you in prison where you belong. Or if I fail to do that, I can at least bring about your discharge from this institution. What's more, I will."

Although Beers eventually lost his ambition to put these men in prison since, as he put it, "were they not victims of the same vicious system of treatment to which I was subjected?" Upon his discharge from the hospital, Beers fulfilled his promise to "lay bare the abuses which abounded" in psychiatric institutions. Upon his recovery from mental illness in 1904, Beers returned to a career in business. However, in 1909 he helped to breach the barriers of shame, ignorance, and stigma by founding the National Committee for Mental Hygiene. Later, in 1928, in order to deal with the recurring shortage of funds for mental health facilities, he also established the American Foundation for Mental Hygiene.

Beers devoted much of his life to improving the institutional care of the mentally ill. He died on July 9, 1943, after serving as the principal pioneer of the mental health movement for over three decades. By dint of his boundless energy and courageous willingness to bare his soul in *A Mind that Found Itself*, Beers contributed permanently and immeasurably to the welfare of mental health recipients and practitioners alike.

The creative expression of psychological conflicts and negative emotions take place of course in all spheres of the artistic world. Great musical composers, for example, have exquisitely expressed their profoundest emotions, both negative and positive, through their compositions.

Gustav Mahler

Gustav Mahler once remarked, "Whoever listens to my music intelligently will see my life transparently revealed." Mahler, who, according to his principal biographer, de La Grange, at age five replied to the question regarding what he wanted to be when he grew up with the terse answer, "A martyr," was an example of a great composer whose life was deeply marked from birth with profound personal tragedy. He considered his parents severely ill-matched, looked upon his mother as a martyr and his father as a temperamental and brutal man. Of the twelve children born into the Mahler family, eight brothers died in succession, one from suicide at the age of twenty-five.

In his childhood Mahler escaped into a dreamworld in order to isolate himself from family feuds. At the age of eleven he witnessed a brutal rape which, according to one authoritative writer, may account for why in his creative mind sensuality and human suffering were closely linked. Thus, those familiar with Mahler's works will hear and feel in his music haunting melodies and themes that reflect and revivify the suffering of his childhood.

At the age of fifty, one year before his death, Mahler consulted Sigmund Freud about his concern with impotency and marital dissatisfaction. In one of the briefest treatments in the recorded history of psychoanalysis (a four-hour stroll through the town of Leyden) these two titanic figures explored the origins of Mahler's psychological distress. In their discussion Freud alluded to certain parallels between Mahler's relationships with his wife and with his mother, the latter of whom played a very dominating part in Mahler's life. Mahler was very impressed with Freud's efforts and apparently their analytic chat bore fruit, since Mahler quickly recovered his potency and connubial gratification.

In the course of their discussion Mahler revealed to Freud that when he was a young boy he had witnessed a particularly painful scene between his mother and father that became unendurable to him, driving him from the house. At that moment, however, a hurdy-gurdy was playing the popular Viennese folk song, "Ach, Du Lieber Augustin."

Mahler regarded this incident to be of pivotal psychological importance to his creative powers. Henceforth, whenever he felt carried to great emotional heights a street song would involuntarily make itself heard with piercing clarity. The folk airs that eventually became such an integral part of his art, although they deeply shocked many of his contemporaries, are now considered one of the more daring and innovative aspects of his work. It is remarkable to think, as de La Grange points out, that a profoundly painful and barely remembered childhood memory "opened a new chapter in musical history."

Because Beethoven, Schubert, and Bruckner had all died after composing their ninth symphonies, Mahler dreaded the ominous number nine in connection with symphonies. Also, at the time he wrote his ninth symphony Mahler was suffering from heart disease, a fact which has led some interpreters of this work to believe that it reflects his feelings about his impending death. Some have even speculated that the variations in the first movement were unconsciously placed there to simulate the irregularities of his own heartbeat. In any case, there is in the second movement of this piece the definite atmosphere of a dance of death and at the conclusion of the symphony one is left with the unmistakable impression of release from earthly things, as if a farewell and transfiguration were taking place. Barely two years after he had written this symphony Mahler succumbed to heart disease.

Sergei Rachmaninov

A number of great composers have written outstanding musical compositions in response to a severe personal crisis. Sergei Rachmaninov, perhaps the most popular Russian composer of the twentieth century, began life in an aristocratic and landowning family. However, when he was nine, the family's entire fortune was lost due to his father's risky financial ventures. The family estate was sold and Sergei's father soon deserted his wife and children. The instability and turmoil of his childhood seems to have left Rachmaninov especially prone to recurrent moods of incertitude and depression.

Following the unsuccessful performance of his Symphony No. 1 in D Minor in 1897, Rachmaninov fell into a particularly deep depression. Although Rachmaninov realized that this symphony had been ineptly conducted under the baton of Glazunov, he considered the composition itself to be wanting. As he described it, "Its defects were revealed to me with a terrible distinctness .. something within me snapped and all my self-confidence collapsed. When the indescribable torture of the performance finally ended, I was a different man."

Although he briefly recovered from this psychological blow, he soon suffered a relapse, drank heavily, and was unable to undertake creative work. Alarmed by his condition, his fiancée induced him to seek the services of a psychiatrist, a Dr. Nikolai Dahl, who specialized in autosuggestion. For three months in 1900 Rachmaninov underwent treatment with Dr. Dahl in order to restore his self-confidence. Each day he repeated the hypnotic formula: "You will begin to write your concerto .. you will work with great facility .. the concerto will be of excellent quality." Rachmaninov's assessment of his experience was summarized in the following words: "It was always the same, without interruption. Although it may sound incredible, this cure really helped me. Already at the beginning of the summer I began again to compose."

The upshot of his collaborative work with Dr. Dahl was Rachmaninov's Piano Concerto No. 2 in C Minor. This composition, which is marked by its directness, simplicity, and robustness, is gratefully dedicated to "Monsieur N. Dahl."

Wolfgang Amadeus Mozart

Wolfgang Amadeus Mozart, whose music is cherished throughout the world, was a child prodigy who received determined assistance for his extraordinary musicianship from his father. After a lifetime of composing and performing successfully for the general public as well as royalty, Mozart's last years were marked by impecuniousness and distress.

At the age of thirty-five, fatally ill and despondent, Mozart's serious illness led some people to believe that he had been poisoned. However, later medical research indicated that Mozart's heart had been irreparably damaged by youthful attacks of rheumatic fever and by his many years of unremitting work and financial anxieties.

In July, 1771, an ominous-looking stranger called upon Mozart and ordered from him a requiem mass for an unidentified patron. Mozart was awed and frightened by this unheralded event which he construed as a portent of disaster. In actuality, the stranger who called upon Mozart was the steward of Count Franz von Walsegg who was attempting to have Mozart compose a piece of recognized worth for which the count himself could take credit. Mozart accepted the commission and spent the remaining weeks of his life quite obsessed with his work on the *Requiem Mass.*

The *Requiem Mass* contains throughout its entirety Mozart's chilling awareness of his own impending death. The grandeur, sublimity, and other-worldly beauty of this composition leave no doubt that Mozart was herein writing his own requiem. The *Requiem Mass* contains a prayer for the dead as well as a depiction of the turmoil of the sinner in the presence of the final judgment. In the *Confutatis* Mozart makes us aware of the terrible fate of sinners. In the *Lacrymosa*, on the other hand, the music is imbued with the mood of grief. Finally, in the *Agnus Dei*, the soul has found peace at last and the *Mass* soon after ends in a quiet integration.

While at work on the *Lacrymosa*, Mozart was smitten by a partial paralysis. A priest was summoned to administer extreme unction. Mozart's friends gathered around his deathbed to sing through the *Requiem Mass* with him. When they reached the first bars of the *Lacrymosa* Mozart began to weep bitterly and put the score aside. When he died the next morning the last thing he tried to do was mouth the sound of the timpani in his *Requiem.* Ultimately, his pupil Franz Xavier Sussmayr completed the work, although we will never know exactly what share of the score can be validly attributed to Sussmayr's efforts.

Frederic Chopin

Another renowned composer whose work was sometimes marked by suffering, sorrow, and grief is Frederic Chopin. As a matter of fact, Chopin's chief sources of inspiration were his own personal tragedies as well as the historical tragedies of his native Poland. Chopin's childhood happiness was stained by the death of his tubercular sister, Emilia, and by his own delicate constitution.

As the age of twenty-six Chopin fell in love with Maria Wodzinski, the daughter of old friends. Maria and Frederic planned to marry, pending parental consent. To Chopin's deep disappointment, the matrimonial plans were called off due to the Wodzinskis' fright over Chopin's reputed ill health.

Disconsolate, Chopin escaped to England on a sight seeing trip whence he returned to Paris where he encountered the free-spirited novelist George Sand. Sand fell in love with Chopin and offered herself as his mistress. Overcoming his moral scruples and under the pretext of poor health, Chopin set off to winter on the island of Majorca with George Sand and her two children. For a short time Chopin and Sand were blissfully happy on Majorca, however, when the weather broke, Chopin's health seriously deteriorated. Suffering from the cold, damp weather and malnutrition, Chopin was generally suspected of having tuberculosis and as a result driven from the villa he and Sand occupied by its owner. The lovers were compelled to spend the remainder of their stay on Majorca in a deserted, windswept Carthusian monastery.

George Sand, describing Chopin's condition at this time wrote, "None could be less constant in his moods, of a cloudier and more delirious imagination, of a more impossible touchiness and exigence. But one could not reproach him for all this; the fault lay solely with his sickness. Chopin's spirit was roasted alive: the fold of a rose leaf or the shadow of a fly would drain the life blood from his veins. Apart from me and my children, he found everything under the Spanish sky distasteful and revolting. Impatience for his departure nearly killed him; he felt the delay even more cruelly than the inconvenience of his enforced stay." Reduced to critical weakness, Chopin abruptly returned to Marseilles where medical care helped save his life.

The crisis in Majorca, for all its gloomy and harrowing adversities, was the emotional crucible in which Chopin was to conceive several dramatic musical compositions, including the Sonata in B-flat Minor, Opus 35. This sonata, which is considered one of the great achievements of the piano, is one of the most vigorous of Chopin's longer compositions. The Sonata is basically a poem of death, the four movements being the four cantos. The composition begins with melodies and rhythms that suggest a mood of terror. In the Sherzo there is the effect of terrifying pursuit and headlong flight. Death is on the prowl and victorious over the multitudes. In the third section of the drama, death is triumphant as depicted by the magnificent Funeral March, a musical score that has become popular throughout the entire world. The finale of the Sonata is characterized by a running passage that reveals the brute force of death as it destroys all things.

It is interesting to note that Chopin, when he performed the Sonata in Manchester, was beset by a strange set of emotions. He had played the first movement and the Scherzo when he suddenly rose from his chair and departed. He then quickly reappeared and completed the composition. He explains his actions in the following letter to a friend.

"A strange adventure befell me while I was playing my Sonata in B-flat Minor before some English friends. I had played the Allegro and the Scherzo more or less correctly. I was about to attack the [Funeral] March, when suddenly I saw arising from the body of my piano those cursed creatures which had appeared to me one lugubrious night at the Chartreus [Majorca]. I had to leave for one instant to pull myself together, after which I continued without saying anything." Evidently, Chopin had received during this performance a visitation from the specter of his disastrous experience with George Sand on the island of Majorca. Yet it was this very experience which had been the creative wellspring for one of his greatest musical compositions.

Robert Schumann

Robert Schumann, one of the leading German composers of the early nineteenth century, was as a young man both a composer and a playwright of some literary merit. After a brief stint in law school, Schumann devoted himself exclusively to performing and composing music. Following an accident to one of the fingers of his right hand, he gave up hopes of becoming a virtuoso and confined himself to composition.

Following a brief love affair with a sixteen-year-old named Clara Wieck (broken off by her father), Schumann went into seclusion, expressing his anger and sorrow by drinking heavily, publishing a lampoon on Clara in a journal, and by writing the Fantasy in C Major for piano. After publicly vilifying Schumann, Clara Wieck's' father could not produce in a court of law proof of Schumann's alleged drunkenness and the couple were eventually allowed to reconcile and marry.

Clara Schumann was herself a fine concert pianist who placed pressure upon her husband to attain even greater musical heights through writing symphonies, which he undertook with considerable success. However, because Robert needed silence for composing, she found it difficult to practice in the home. For his part, Robert did not take well to accompanying his wife on her concert tours during which her fame and talent eclipsed his own.

Following his return from one of Clara's tours of Russia, Robert began to suffer from symptoms of a psychological breakdown, including auditory hallucinations. Several years later, after taking over the post of director of music in Dusseldorf, Schumann's competence became seriously impaired by mental decline. He became completely introverted and at times was even unaware of his surroundings.

By 1854, his forty-fourth year, Schumann's health failed altogether. Assailed by incessant aural noises and the imagined ministrations of angels and demons, he was indeed a very tormented man. At times he believed that the dead masters were dictating melodies to him. In February, 1854, Schumann threw himself into the Rhine River, from which he was rescued. He was taken to a private asylum at the town of Endenich. Visits from Brahms and the young violinist Joseph Joachim disturbed him greatly and Clara was kept from him until shortly before his death. Although he seemed to have recognized her, he could not speak intelligibly. After a period of two-and-a-half years in the asylum, Schumann died, on July 29, 1856.

It is remarkable that Schumann, although he had begun to show signs of mental illness as early as 1844, continued to compose such remarkably fine works in his later years as the Second and Third Symphonies, the Cello Concerto in A Minor, and the Faust music.

Bedrich Smetana

Another composer, Bedrich Smetana, the "father" of Czech music, manifested his musical talent early, but his father's prejudice against music as a profession discouraged formal instruction. Despite his lack of formal training, Smetana made rapid progress as a composer. However, tragedy struck him quite early in life. After marrying a woman with whom he had fallen in love when he was only nineteen, Smetana and his wife had four daughters of whom only one survived. Following the death of his first daughter, he composed the elegiac Trio in G Minor, in which he expressed his profound grief.

In 1874 Smetana began to suffer from severe headaches which were soon followed by deafness. At first he complained of an uninterrupted whistling in his ears "like the A-flat major chord in the first inversion in the high treble." Then he heard buzzing and roaring sounds "as though I were standing under a waterfall." Then: "I hear absolutely nothing, not even my own voice. Concentration with me is impossible. I hear my own piano only in fancy, not in reality. I cannot hear the playing of anybody else, not even the performance of a full orchestra in opera or in concert. I do not think it is possible for me to improve. I have no pain in the ear, and my physicians agree that my disease is none of the familiar ear troubles, but something else, perhaps a paralysis of the nerves and the labyrinth and so I am wholly determined to endure my sad fate in a calm and manly way as long as I live."

Smetana remained deaf for the rest of his life but his disability did not limit his musical activities. As a matter of fact, on the very first day on which he became deaf he conceived the central theme of the first of the tone poems which are collectively entitled *Ma Vlast*, perhaps Smetana's greatest orchestral monument to nationalism.

Smetana's last opera was one of his greatest disappointments. The *Devil's Wall* was performed before small audiences and Smetana was humiliated by the paltry earnings that resulted. He declared, "I shall write no more."

In 1875, at the age of fifty-two, Smetana wrote two autobiographical quartets. Both were written when he was completely deaf. The first and more celebrated quartet betokens his deafness through a high E in the first violin that is heard over tremolos in the other three strings. "I permitted myself this little joke, such as it is, because it was so disastrous to me. There is a little ray of hope in a passing improvement, but remembering all the promise of my early career, there comes a feeling of painful regret."

Smetena's deafness was only a prelude to a complete mental collapse. In 1882, defying the orders of his physicians, he worked on his not yet completed Second String Quartet. Extremely disturbed and depressed at this time, it is not surprising that Smetana's Second String Quartet is a work of deep melancholy.

By 1883, Smetana had become completely mad. He was consigned to an insane asylum in Prague, where he died on May 12, 1884.

We have thus far been examining the role of negative experiences and negative emotions in the creative work of writers and composers. Now let us turn our attention to the lives and works of several noted painters as they reflect their range of negative experiences and negative emotions.

Rembrandt Harmenszoon van Rijn

Born on July 15, 1606, the Dutch painter Rembrandt Harmenszoon van Rijn is considered among the greatest of painters from all countries and periods. His deep concern for humanity has made his work universally understandable and appreciated. His ability to depict human expressions, movements, and gestures was unsurpassed.

Because he had evidently shown promise at an early age Rembrandt was the only one of nine children who was prepared by his family for a university education. Although he matriculated at the Leiden University in order to prepare for city administration, his "natural emotion" was for painting. Thus, his parents sent him to a painter, a Mr. Jacob van Swanenburch, in order to learn the fundamentals of art. This Rembrandt did, of course, remarkably well.

By 1627 Rembrandt had mastered the fundamentals of painting, drawing, and etching and was developing his own distinctive style. Throughout his life Rembrandt executed numerous studies of himself. As a matter of fact, it might be rightly said that he was his own favorite subject. These self-portraits, with their wonderful play of light, reflected and penetrated his many moods and emotions.

In 1634, at the age of twenty-seven, Rembrandt married Saskia van Uylenburgh, the daughter of the former mayor of Leeuwarden. Rembrandt made many moving sketches of his homelife with Saskia, including a drawing of Saskia in bed that depicts her as a woman who is suffering from the shock of tragedy. Small wonder that Rembrandt portrayed his wife with such poignancy; the Rembrandts had three children who died in infancy and a fourth, Titus, who lived only twenty-seven years. Saska, herself, died only a few months after the birth of their only surviving child, on June 14, 1642.

Shortly after his wife's death, Rembrandt employed Geertghe Dircx, a widow, to serve in his household as Titus's nurse. Within a short time Geertghe became Rembrandt's common-law wife. However, by 1649 Rembrandt had taken into his affections Hendrickje Stoffels, who apparently also began as his household employee. Thus, Geertghe left Rembrandt and then immediately sued him for breach of promise. Rembrandt later brought charges against Geertghe for breaking an agreement with him that prevented her from selling jewelry that she had willed to Titus. She was sentenced to prison but freed through the intercession of friends.

His wife's death, the tumultuous conflicts with Geertghe, and a financial bankruptcy seemed responsible for certain stylistic changes in Rembrandt's work. His paintings of the 1640s became more introspective, quiet, and structured. His subdued self-portraits of this period are highly contrastable with the more buoyant studies of himself that he painted only a few years before.

By 1649 Hendrickje Stoffels had fully replaced Geertghe Dircx as Rembrandt's mistress, a situation which only became more complicated when Hendrickje became pregnant. Hendrickje and Rembrandt were summoned to appear before the Council of the Reformed Church of Amsterdam and accused of having illicit relations. After ignoring the Council's first two calls, Hendrickje finally appeared and admitted that she had engaged in "concubinage" with Rembrandt, a confession for which she was "severely reprimanded." When at the end of October, 1649, Hendrickje gave birth to Cornelia, the child was duly baptized by the Reformed Church, suggesting that their illicit relationship was either officially forgiven or forgotten.

Despite financial bankruptcy in 1656 and Hendrickje's death in 1663, Rembrandt did not, as the popular media have since suggested, become a pitiful recluse in his final years. On the contrary, as he grew older his creative powers seemed to reach even greater heights. Rembrandt continued to paint self-portraits until the year of his death (1669). Although he is shown with a somewhat roguish smile in one of these portraits, for the most part these later self-studies reflect the somber and contemplative mood of an elderly man who has aggrievedly experienced the loss of four children and two wives and is looking morosely toward the ending of his own life. Rembrandt died on October 4, 1669, and was interred in the same church as his only son, Titus, who had died only eleven months earlier.

Francisco José de Goya y Lucientes

Francisco José de Goya y Lucientes, the great Spanish painter, was born on March 30, 1746, at Fuendetodos, near Saragossa. Goya was considered the foremost painter in Spain during his own lifetime, noted for his melancholy images in oils and his revolutionary spirit in behalf of the Spanish people in their struggle against oppression. For fifty-three of his eighty-two years Goya was a servant of the Spanish crown. Therefore, by far the majority of his paintings are the result of official commissions.

Although little is known of Goya's earliest years, it is evident in his paintings that he held a rather defiant and contemptuous attitude toward his patrons, that is, the members of the royal and aristocratic families. His contempt and scorn for the aristocracy was at times displayed by the flippant (and somewhat dangerous) liberties he took to include himself in their portraits. As well, Goya in his paintings of royal and aristocratic families highlighted the ugliness and vulgarity of these personages to the point of caricature. In one instance he actually scrawled his signature backward at the base of such a painting in order to suggest that he was impertinently turning his back to his despised subject when he affixed his signature to the painting. When Goya painted a portrait of the Duchess of Alba, on whose estate he had resided after her husband's death, he stiffly painted this woman, famous for her beauty, as if she were a painted, porcelain doll.

During a visit to Andalusia in 1792, Goya was afflicted with a serious illness that caused temporary paralysis, partial blindness, and left him permanently deaf, so that he could only communicate by sign language or writing. He wrote about his painful experience in a letter that accompanied eleven small paintings to Bernardo de Iriarte: "In order to occupy an imagination mortified by the contemplation of my sufferings and to recover part of the very great expense they have occasioned, I devoted myself to painting a group of cabinet pictures in which I have succeeded in making observations for which there is normally no opportunity in commissioned works, which give no scope for fantasy and invention."

In 1818, Goya suffered from another serious illness. In commemoration of his recovery he one year later painted a self-portrait with his doctor in which Goya, depicted in the agonizing throes of physical suffering, is supported in the arms of his physician. After this illness Goya became quite reclusive and devoted himself to the famous "black paintings" with which he decorated his home. Their subjects are invariably sinister, horrific, and mysterious, no doubt emblematic of the mood of cynicism, pessimism, and despair by which the ill and aging Goya was overcome. Despite old age and infirmity, Goya continued to record the world around him in paintings, drawings, and in the new technique of lithography. In the view of many art critics, it is the work of Goya's old age —melancholy, somber, and violent—that established him as the greatest master of his age and the first of the moderns. On April 16, 1828, at the age of eighty-two, Goya suffered a paralytic stroke and died.

Edvard Munch

Perhaps nowhere in the history of painting does the expression of agony, tragedy, and horror appear more graphically than in the paintings of Edvard Munch, a Norwegian painter who developed a highly personal art form that was the forerunner of twentieth century Expressionism. In his self-defense, Munch once declared, "I shall paint living people who breathe, feel, suffer and love. The sacredness of this will be understood and people will take off their hats as though they were in church."

Born in 1863 into a family respected for its political and cultural contributions to Norway, Munch was one of five children. His mother died of tuberculosis when he was five; ten years later a sister died of the same disease. Another sister became mentally ill. Munch's father and brother also died when he was quite young. Thus, sickness and death would preoccupy Munch throughout his entire life and become the leitmotifs of much of his artistic work. The very titles of some of his paintings reflect his macabre childhood impressions: *The Sick Child* (1886), *The Death Chamber* (1892), *By the Death Bed* (1895), and *The Dead Mother* (1899).

For a short time Munch attended art school in Christiana (Oslo). At this time Christiana was a provincial town, ruled by a conventional and narrow-minded gentility. Among his friends were Ibsen and Strindberg and together these men challenged and breached the social conventions of their culture. An exhibition of Munch's works in Berlin in 1892 created a public scandal due to the emotionalism and unconventionality of their imagery. Munch's unique form of expressionism, however, was soon accepted and he became a European celebrity as a result.

The sixteen years following the "Munch Affair" were his most productive. It was during this phase that Munch suffered a nervous breakdown perhaps as a result of the ferocious compulsiveness with which he drove himself. The spiritual anguish that tormented him and which he considered universal is exemplified in his most famous painting, *The Cry*. Perhaps more than any of his other paintings, *The Cry* bespeaks the misery and anxiety of human existence as subjectively perceived by Munch.

It was not until a few years after he had recovered from his nervous breakdown that Munch ceased to paint themes and images of human beings beset by ruthless passions and went on to produce paintings of brighter color that reflected a more positive frame of mind. During this period, his most noteworthy works were the murals he painted for the festival hall of Oslo University. Munch spent his last years in seclusion at his Norwegian farm near Oslo where he continued to paint with perseverance until his death on January 23, 1944, one month after his eightieth birthday.

Vincent van Gogh

Perhaps more than any other painter Vincent van Gogh is associated in the mind of the public with mental torment and emotional instability. Van Gogh is generally considered the greatest of the Dutch painters after Rembrandt. Significantly, much of his reputation is based upon the works of his last three years, a period of great psychological turbulence that ended in suicide at the age of only thirty-seven.

Vincent van Gogh was born in 1853, the eldest of six children of a Protestant pastor. Although his earliest years were largely unproblematic, as a young man he encountered a series of emotional crises and disappointments. From 1873 to 1875 van Gogh worked as an art dealer in London. While in that city he fell in love with a woman who rejected his affections, causing van Gogh to retreat into solitude.

Van Gogh disliked art dealing and, thwarted in love, he eventually went to work as a missionary in a coal mining district of southwest Belgium. There, in a moment of spiritual passion, he gave away all his worldly possessions and was soon dismissed for a too literal interpretation of Christian doctrine.

Impoverished and disillusioned, van Gogh went into seclusion and devoted himself to his true vocation, painting. His artistic career was extremely short, lasting only from 1880 to 1890. At first, van Gogh found it difficult to work without formal training; therefore, he sought out the society and guidance of other talented painters. Thus extending his technical knowledge, he painted peasant life with a freshness and insight that was only appreciated after his death.

From 1886 to 1888 van Gogh lived in Paris. However, he tired of city life and in February, 1888, left Paris and assumed residence in Arles. The following months were among van Gogh's most productive. It was a period in which he used his vast energy and imagination to paint the many subjects he came upon in Arles, including the fruit trees, the town and its surroundings, and the townsfolk themselves. Van Gogh at this time had hopes of forming a working community of impressionists and as part of this endeavor he induced Gauguin to join and work with him. Temperamentally incompatible, the two men conflicted and could not sustain their working relationship beyond two months.

Under the strain of these conflicts, van Gogh emotionally collapsed and, in a bout of insane fury, cut off part of his left ear. After convalescing in a hospital for about two weeks, he returned home where he resumed his work by painting *Self Portrait with Pipe and Bandaged Ear*, which depicts the painter with a bandage wrapped around his *right* ear (the mirror image from which he painted), staring forward with a patently melancholic demeanor, and smoking a pipe.

A few weeks later van Gogh was rehospitalized due to a relapse of his mental disorder. In April, 1889, in order to preserve his sanity, which he naturally regarded as essential to his work, he voluntarily entered the asylum at Saint-Remy-de-Provence where he remained for approximately a year. While in the asylum van Gogh continued to paint. Since there was a paucity of subjects for his paintings, he was required to work largely from memory, a method he staunchly resisted. Thus, he involved himself more imaginatively in the interplay of the surrounding elements and, as a result, his best works of this period are bolder and more visionary than those of Arles.

In May, 1890, van Gogh returned to Paris. Four days later he went to stay with a homeopathic doctor-artist at Auvers-sur-Oise, where he again enthusiastically used his bucolic surroundings as subjects for his paintings. For a short time he created highly expressive and visionary paintings. However, after quarreling with the doctor-artist and despairing of ever finding a cure for his depression and loneliness, he shot himself and died two days later, on July 29, 1890. Although largely unknown at the time of his death, van Gogh's reputation has justifiably grown ever since.

We have seen in this chapter how great writers, composers, and painters have been able to incorporate and transform their own personal tragedies and adversities into resounding artistic creations. The grief, rage, depression, and bitterness that sometimes disrupted, and in some cases put an end to, their lives, found bountiful creative expression in their great works that will stand forever as a monument to their courage and perseverance.

Chapter 7

Negative Emotions and Politics

I think it fair to assume that most politicians decide to enter politics, in part, out of a genuine sense of idealism and altruism. The desire to reform and transform the political conditions of a nation can be a very powerful motivating force for many political aspirants. Keen observers of the personalities of political figures have also noted, however, a tendency on their part to use their prominent societal positions to acquire and exercise personal prestige, stature, and power.

I myself have also hypothesized that a major source of inspiration to those who seek political prominence is the need, both conscious and unconscious, to overcome negative experiences and negative emotions. I have speculated that politicians, during both their childhood and adulthood years, have experienced their share of major disappointments, setbacks, and misadventures. I have also speculated that the personal traumas they have experienced have played an instrumental role in goading these men and women to enter and remain in politics where they can constructively and creatively "work through" (to use a psychoanalytic term) their past hurts.

In order to test my hypotheses, I have conducted interviews with some rather well-known political figures: Mayor Kenneth Gibson, Senator John Stennis, Senator Barbara Boxer, Senator George McGovern, Senator S. I. Hayakawa, Congresswoman Elizabeth Holtzman, and Congressman Barney Frank. I attempted, with some degree of success, I believe, to interview a group of politicians who were diverse in terms of geography, gender, political ideology, ethnicity and, in the case of

Congressman Frank, sexual orientation. I interviewed Senators Boxer and Hayakawa in person. My interviews with Mayor Gibson, Senator McGovern, Congresswoman Holtzman, Senator Stennis, and Congressman Frank were conducted on the telephone. The interviews were of decidedly different lengths due, in large measure, to the particular exigencies of the respective interviewees' work schedules. To each of the persons interviewed for this chapter I wish to extend my gratitude and appreciation for their generosity and kindness in taking time out from their busy assignments to share their personal thoughts with me.

Kenneth Allen Gibson

Birth date: May 5, 1932

Mayor of Newark, N.J. 1970-86

Mayor Gibson was elected as one of the first black mayors of a major American city. I naturally assumed that, as a black politician, he would have witnessed firsthand many of the deplorable conditions in this country that undermine and oppress ethnic minority groups. Perhaps, I reckoned, his anger and outrage over these conditions had inspired him to seek public office.

Mayor Gibson at first downplayed his negative emotions concerning the ills of our society, stating that he rarely got angry. He acknowledged, however, that he had entered politics because he had first been involved in civil rights struggles after graduating college. He had found that there were problem areas such as inadequate housing and educational services that were not being properly delivered, especially to inner city minority groups.

As a member of a group of civil rights activists and a newcomer to the group, Mayor Gibson was chosen in 1966 as a "sacrificial lamb" in a losing cause to seek election as Newark's mayor. He campaigned well and, although he lost, he was encouraged enough by his relative success to run for the same office in 1970. He entered politics by winning the 1970 mayoral election.

Mayor Gibson emphasized in our interview that he wanted to do something about the fact that blacks and Puerto Ricans in Newark did not have as much political strength as they should have had. Because they had too little political power, they received inappreciable attention from legislators, he stated.

I queried the mayor about the obstacles and frustrations he had encountered in effecting the kinds of changes for which he had electioneered. He listed several sources of frustration. Gibson discovered very early on that it takes a lot longer to accomplish things in the public sector than he had originally thought. Because of the inherent checks and balances within the political system the mayor had to share certain powers with the city council. Also, state law supersedes and prohibits certain actions of the chief executive. In Gibson's view, the mayor must always struggle to get things done quickly against a system that is designed to slow things down.

Specifically, the mayor cited his difficulties in appointing the heads of city departments as a source of frustration. Because the city council must confirm each appointment, there were frequent delays and reversals that caused the entire appointment process to bog down. Another serious problem to which the mayor referred was the inordinately complicated problem of raising adequate funding for his beleaguered city. Since state law prohibited a city from raising monies by imposing taxes without permission from the state, a city such as Newark suffered from chronic and severe financial hardships.

I asked Mayor Gibson if he suffered any particular adverse consequences because minority groups might harbor unrealistically high expectations of a black mayor. He stated that he didn't think "the people" expected more from him than anyone else. In his view, minority groups not only do not expect miracles of a black mayor but also derive joy and pride from the knowledge that someone in city hall profoundly understands and sympathizes with their plight.

I wanted to know what most disappointed the mayor during his tenure in office. He alluded to an incident that had occurred in a local park. A Hispanic group held a festival in the park that was disrupted by some bickering among several persons who had had too much to drink. The mayor personally marched the people from the park to City Hall where he held a conference with them. The next day some agitators went out and stirred them up again. As a result of the ensuing disturbance two persons were killed. That tragedy Mayor Gibson regards as his biggest disappointment in his sixteen years in office.

I next wanted to know if Mayor Gibson had experienced anything in his childhood of an especially disturbing or traumatic nature that may have inspired him to enter politics. He assured me that his childhood was relatively problem-free. His home, although poor, was quite stable. He actually did not place particular emphasis upon material things, so the material deprivations of his family did not overly distress him.

I asked Mayor Gibson to tell me what especially troubled him about the society in which we live. He enumerated several principal concerns. He feels that there are too many people in this country who are deprived of adequate medical care because of an inability to pay. They suffer because they don't have access to the doctors or the hospitals they desperately need. He also believes that education in this country is in "very bad shape." He thinks many educational systems in this country fail to live up to their duty, even in affluent areas.

Mayor Gibson was defeated in the 1986 election. I asked him to describe his feelings about losing this election and to share any regrets or misgivings he might have concerning how he presented himself to the public during his campaign. The mayor was quite philosophical on this point. "Sometimes you win and sometimes you lose," he aphoristically replied. He states without reservation that he regretted nothing he had done in his sixteen years of office, including how he conducted his last mayoral campaign.

Returning to the subject of his childhood, the mayor depicted his earliest years in a rather reserved manner. He feels that his basic philosophy of life was formed in the crib and that he grew up very quickly. "I was an old man when I was a baby," he points out with pride. He attributes his strengths, standards, values, and respect for other people to the great influence of his family.

Now that he had been electorally removed from office, I asked him what he intended to do professionally. The mayor is actively and enjoyably running a consulting firm that deals with developers, banking and investment people in Newark all of whom are interested in improving the life of the city. In other words, although he is no longer the highest public official of the city, he is still committed to taking an active and intense interest in the betterment of the lives of Newark's citizens.

John Cornelius Stennis

Birth date: August 3, 1901

United States Senator from Mississippi, 1947-88

Date of death: April 23, 1995

Senator Stennis stated that he entered politics during the depression, following an earlier career respectively as a lawyer and a judge. He acknowledged that the depression had a deep and lingering impact upon him during those years. The prices of agricultural products like cotton had plummeted in his state. As a result, poverty was everywhere.

The senator indicated that at first he was torn between entering a career in law or medicine. An older brother, who himself was an attorney, influenced him to decide in favor of a law career. As a young man,

Senator Stennis served as a drugstore clerk in a little town where there was only one drugstore. In November, 1918, an influenza epidemic swept through that area of the country "like a September gale, taking people right and left." He was the only clerk left and he kept the drugstore open day and night, filling prescriptions. (He was not legally authorized to fill prescriptions but, considering the dire emergency, was instructed to do so anyway by the local doctors.)

Senator Stennis points out that the human devastation caused by the influenza epidemic made a lasting impression on him. Since there were no regulations regarding the sale of morphine or cocaine, people used these drugs in excess and thereby became habituated to them. Henceforth, the senator has diligently "spread the news" about the adverse effects of abusing dangerous drugs.

In 1972 Senator Stennis suffered severe injuries as a result of a mugging that took place in front of his home. I asked him to describe this traumatic experience and to explain how he had emotionally coped with it. He pointed out that it all began as a street holdup. Three men jumped him, demanding money. He had no money, so one of them stepped back and said, "Well, I'm just going to kill you."

And he almost did. That man shot the senator, causing him grievous wounds. He was unconscious for about ten days and when he awoke he was weak and seriously debilitated. In response to my question regarding the possibility that he felt great anger and resentment toward the men who perpetrated the crime, Senator Stennis stated that he did not allow those emotions to consume him. Instead he made a far-reaching decision to use his will power to get better and be useful again. He would pay whatever price was necessary to recover and, keeping in mind a sign in his office that read "Keep Ahead," he looked forward to a better future.

Not long afterward another severe adversity struck the senator; he underwent an amputation of his leg due to cancer. He had since been in a wheelchair to which he had become accustomed. Senator Stennis takes little credit for his ability to survive his surgery, instead considering his capacity to carry on largely as a tribute to his surgeons.

Taking into consideration the catastrophic medical crises with which the senator has courageously contended, I asked him to tell me if he had some guiding philosophical principle that enabled him to deal with adversity. He said he tries to avoid the "wishy and the wobbly" by maintaining an attitude of positive determination and purpose. He feels that it has been a guidepost and a tonic for him to always try to look ahead and keep moving, regardless of circumstances.

When the senator first entered the Senate he had manifested a strong interest in the cause of world peace through the work of the United Nations. In response to my question regarding this subject, he stated that he had long been conscious of the need to settle international disagreements by means other than war. For this reason he supported the concept of a world court that could settle matters between nations. He regrets that the United Nations did not mature or develop fast enough to prevent the Korean and Vietnam wars; however, he acknowledges that the U.N. has provided a uniquely positive and valuable forum for nations to air and resolve their differences.

Senator Stennis has served in the United States Senate longer than anyone else in American history other than Senator Carl Hayden. I asked him to what he attributed this senatorial longevity. He states that he had never had any far-reaching political machine. In his view, his constituents were generous enough with him to accept his promises on faith. He feels they displayed confidence in him because they understood his word was good. In sum, he attributes his legislative successes to those personal qualities that reflect and coincide with the wishes of the people he has represented.

Barbara Boxer

Birth date: November 11, 1940

United States Congresswoman from California 1983-93

United States Senator from California 1993-Present

I began our interview by asking Senator Boxer to tell me if there were any particularly difficult or adverse personal experiences that may have inspired her to enter politics. She began by mentioning the fact that the Holocaust had made a deep and lasting impression on her and her family. As a young child she had heard stories about how many people were lost, relatives and friends of relatives, the young and the old. Being Jewish herself, it outraged her to think that this could happen to any people.

As a little girl, Congresswoman Boxer read the *Diary of Anne Frank*. She cried over a sense of tragic awareness that people could inflict this kind of pain on each other. It was these childhood experiences that engendered in her the sense of outrage she now feels over such violations of human rights as the apartheid that took place in South Africa.

There were other profound tragedies that pushed Senator Boxer in a positive direction: the assassinations of John Kennedy, Martin Luther King, and Bob Kennedy. The murders of these exceptional men caused her to seriously question the world in which her children would grow up. She decided that she couldn't just be a young mother, playing tennis, doing the things that "my generation was taught we were supposed to do."

Shortly after the assassinations of Bob Kennedy and Martin Luther King, Ms. Boxer organized a group called the Education Core, in Marin County, California. This group went into low-income areas in the county and helped high school dropouts, mostly women. They helped these people find careers. The organization set up a school, provided job training, and made contacts with prospective employers.

The Vietnam War also instilled in Senator Boxer the intense desire to effect positive change. Therefore, in 1972 she decided to run for political office. Although she was defeated, she began working for members of Congress and became involved in senatorial elections.

Senator Boxer explained that, in her view, the things that inspired her to pursue positive goals were initially the many negative things that were happening in the world. She supposes that if everything were going great in the world, she'd be on the outs somewhere enjoying life. The serious problems of the world cause her to ask herself, "Hey, are you here to make a difference? Or, are you here to just let it happen?"

I asked Senator Boxer why Robert Kennedy's assassination was especially pivotal to her. She said that the deaths of Martin Luther King and Robert Kennedy suddenly made her feel that there might be a new, malignant pattern developing in American politics. She had barely begun to put all the negative feelings about John Kennedy's death behind her when suddenly his brother's assassination brought on the horrible feeling of déjà vu. The killing of Robert Kennedy was the third assassination of one of Ms. Boxer's heroes and it was then that she vowed, partially in behalf of her two children, that "I had better get off my butt and do something about the state of the world."

I naturally wanted to know if there were any especially difficult or painful experiences in her personal background that may have played a part in her eventual involvement in politics. Senator Boxer readily alluded to being blessed with loving parents who provided her with a happy and very secure homelife. The one "traumatic" experience she recalls occurred at summer camp, when Senator Boxer was a teenager. One summer she decided to invite a good friend to join her at camp. When they arrived in camp she introduced her friend to her other pals. By being catty and plotting, her friend "stole" her pals from her that summer.

She cried bitterly to her mother about this misadventure and asked permission to come home. Then a counselor took her aside and pointed out that since she could not change the situation she might do better to stop wasting her time with people who didn't care about her. Perhaps it might be preferable, he said, to give other, more caring, people a chance to know her. She took the counselor's advice and made friends with another group of campers. One of these friendships became life-long. "I also wound up winning the All-Around Camper Award that year," she added with justifiable pride.

This painful experience, according to Senator Boxer, caused her to understand for the first time what it was like to be alone and really isolated, not part of the group. It was particularly distressing because it happened with someone she really liked and trusted. She states that she drew an important moral lesson from this unfortunate experience. The lesson, in her view, is to avoid sinking into such an experience until you are completely defeated by it. Instead, it is essential to reach out from a negative experience and turn it into something positive, with people around you who can help.

Senator Boxer went on to apply this moral lesson to her involvement in politics. She believes that if a person is too consumed by the desire to be a member of an in-group that person may wind up feeling a loss of dignity and self-respect. However, if a person stands up for her dignity and her principles, she will be far better able to live with herself. For example, when she served on the Marin County Board of Supervisors she was usually in the 3-2 minority. But she always spoke out on the issues and kept her dignity. Senator Boxer is especially proud of her outspoken and consistent opposition to the military build-up and to the "Star Wars" program that took place during the Reagan administration. Her dynamic and dedicated sponsorship of environmental and feminist legislation is also a great source of pride and gratification to her. And, considering her electoral successes, to her constituents as well.

Now, as a member of the Senate, she continues to apply these self-same principles to her legislative work. She states that even her philosophical "archenemies" in Congress respect her courage. She sums up her position by saying, "I think we all at some point must grow up and realize that we have to step out from the crowd even though it's sometimes hurtful."

George Stanley McGovern

Birth date: July 19, 1922

United States Senator from South Dakota, 1963-81

Presidential Candidate, Democratic Party, 1972

I first asked Senator McGovern to discuss those social or political problems that particularly aroused his anger or concern during his tenure in the Senate. He alluded immediately to the Vietnam War. He considers the Vietnam War to be the major, transcendent issue that angered and challenged him during his years in the Senate. Attempting to lead the fight in the Senate against the war was of immediate and central importance to him.

In response to my inquiry as to why the Vietnam War had affected him so deeply, Senator McGovern listed several factors. For one, he considered this war to be flagrantly wrong. Thus, he viewed it with a sense of political outrage. He believed the United States was completely destroying another nation for no legitimate purpose. There was the defoliation of forests and agriculture, the tragic disruption of human life, the needless, senseless killing of innocent men, women, and children.

To make matters worse, the senator adds, there were never any legal procedures nor a full-scale statement of purpose upon which the Vietnam War could be legitimately predicated. In his estimation, the closest we came to that was the Gulf of Tonkin Resolution, but there was really no discernible constitutional basis for carrying out such a military action.

I asked the senator if there were other issues that also aroused his political interest and indignation. He replied that earlier in his political career he had studied and written about the problem of widespread hunger. It was painful to him to see such universal hunger, considering the vast surpluses of food that were available to starving peoples. Because of the senator's deep concerns over this issue, President Kennedy called upon him to administer Food for Peace. In this capacity he was able to develop new policies for subsidizing special programs for

feeding the hungry. He states that, most definitely, the companion issues of hunger and war contributed to his sense of anger and outrage.

Because I knew Senator McGovern had written about the problems
of labor, I asked him to comment on that subject. He acknowledged
that he felt indignation over the repressive working conditions of many
laborers, including the early Colorado miners. The miners were subjected to many indignities, including lockouts. Senator McGovern believes that by writing about these conditions he could channel his anger
as well as his compassion for the workers into intellectual activity that
provided him with considerable literary and academic satisfaction.

I next queried the senator about the 1972 election and about Watergate. He stated that he did his best to get the country to focus on the
problem of Watergate during the 1972 election. He tried to expose it,
but, as he admits, his efforts had little effect. He revealed that it is
sometimes difficult to live with this realization, especially knowing, as
he does, that if the election were held again, with Watergate out in the
open, he would win.

Senator McGovern spontaneously referred to the "Eagleton complication." Soon after Senator McGovern chose Thomas Eagleton as his
vice-presidential running mate, it was discovered that Senator Eagleton
had a psychiatric history. This not only aroused widespread anxiety
among the general voting population about the psychological suitability
of this possible successor to the presidency, but, tragically, it also
caused doubts in the minds of many persons about Senator McGovern's
own judgment, thus costing him untold numbers of votes. Some years
ago I had the pleasure and privilege of having breakfast with Senator
McGovern. During our chat he indicated how he had been impaled on
the horns of a terrible and inextricable dilemma in 1972. Because of
the public outcry and clamor over his selection of Senator Eagleton, he
decided to consult a well-known and highly respected psychiatrist in
order to secure his opinion and advice about the Eagleton mess. The
psychiatrist had gloomy news for Senator McGovern. He said that a
third of the populace probably didn't care one way or the other about
Senator Eagleton's psychiatric history. A third of the public, however,
was probably sympathetic to persons with psychiatric problems and
would resent and defect from Senator McGovern if he dropped Senator
Eagleton from the ticket. On the other hand, another third of the population probably feared and felt prejudiced against psychiatric patients
and would, therefore, repudiate Senator McGovern if he kept Senator
Eagleton on the ticket. In other words, no matter what he did about the
"Eagleton complication," Senator McGovern stood to lose the election.

Senator McGovern believes that, without the "Eagleton complication" he would have most likely won ten to twelve states in the 1972

election. He also believes that such a credible showing would have enabled him to have gone on to become the Democratic presidential candidate in 1976. And, had he been the nominee in 1976, he is firmly convinced that he would have won that election. He sums up his feelings in the following manner: "When you think about the fact that you could perhaps have occupied the White House were it not for some of these unfortunate circumstances, you do sometimes feel a sadness when thinking about those past events."

I next encouraged Senator McGovern to discuss his childhood years. He described his growing up years as very stable and stimulating. He mentioned in passing that his father was a minister, but remarked more pointedly, in response to one of my questions, that he recalled no particularly traumatic or painful experience while growing up.

I asked the senator to describe his reactions to the political assassinations in the sixties. He said that he had felt them to be a great blow but he did not brood over them or consider them to have a great influence in terms of his own political career. His own personal reactions at the time were that he regarded the deaths of John Kennedy, Martin Luther King, and Bob Kennedy as a tremendous loss. He went on to add, "It was such a terrible waste to have these young men, at the peak of their power and influence, shot down like criminals in the street." He stated, however, that the assassinations did not cause him to dwell on the possibilities of encountering such dangers when he himself ran for the presidency.

Finally, I asked Senator McGovern if he held any guiding principle that enabled him to deal with such disappointments and setbacks as his defeat in the 1972 election. He replied by saying that he generally took time to reflect on his personal situation, then sought some worthwhile and fulfilling activity that "I could lose myself in." He pointed out that he never let a setback or a defeat throw him into idleness or depression. He instead always moved ahead to what seemed to be the next challenge. He could recall no time when he was ever immobilized by a defeat or disappointment. There were always other challenges to be met, always plenty to do, even if he were frustrated in a particular pursuit.

Samuel Ichiye Hayakawa

Birth date: July 18, 1906

Date of death: February 27, 1992

United States Senator from California, 1976-82

I asked Senator Hayakawa if he had been inspired to enter politics by any particular issues that especially angered or concerned him. He immediately referred to his life in the years 1966, 1967, and 1968. In his view, many fine universities were being destroyed by radical uproar during those years. He considered it a kind of mania that spread from university to university, until it hit his campus at San Francisco State University. He thought students were foolish enough to give up their studies, disrupt classrooms, and stop the educational process, in order to make often "unreasonable and ridiculous demands which they said were not negotiable."

In May, 1968, the president of San Francisco State resigned. His successor was appointed immediately afterward and he too resigned after six months. The trustees of the California State University system, on the suggestion of a man whom Dr. Hayakawa had never met, then selected him to run the college.

One year before his presidential appointment, Dr. Hayakawa had been vacationing with his family in Mexico. He became so highly absorbed with the "disaster" that was befalling the universities that he spent most of his vacation writing a memorandum to himself as to what needed to be done. He undertook this work without the slightest anticipation or aspiration that he would one day be called upon to become a college president.

When he was actually called upon, he accepted the position, on one condition: that he would be able to use all the law enforcement necessary to maintain order and keep the classes going. He was given the go-ahead and the following week he spent much time with the State University lawyer and the San Francisco chief of police, planning strategy. He then declared the college to be opened and classes to be resumed.

That morning certain radical students put a sound truck in front of the campus from which they urged other students to maintain the strike by boycotting classes, and exhorted teachers not to teach. This led to the famous incident in which Dr. Hayakawa climbed onto the sound truck, pulled the wires out of their loud speaker system and found himself on television that very noon and that evening and the rest of the week, suddenly having become a national and international celebrity.

Dr. Hayakawa thought of how "goddamned mad" he was at those students for disrupting what was to him almost a sacred institution, the university. A university had always been more important to him than a church because it is where the life of the mind is cultivated and cherished and nurtured. He, therefore, thought any attempt to destroy the university to be a frightful thing to do. In reference to the theme of my book, he stated, "If you're talking about negative emotions leading to positive behavior, I was mad enough to use the police where necessary, and won out. And restored the academic process so that teachers were able to teach and students were able to go to class."

After his retirement from the college in 1973 various political professionals came to Dr. Hayakawa and offered him several choices of political office, including United States senator. He states that they were in despair over the universities at the time and wanted someone who understood and could deal with the situation. After some dillydallying, he decided in 1976 to run for the Senate and so he became a senator.

I asked Dr. Hayakawa if he entirely objected to all of the purposes, objectives, and viewpoints of the radical students. He responded by acknowledging that at the heart of their demands were some "reasonable things." Except, he added, "They didn't have to burn down buildings in order to get them."

Was Vietnam an issue, I wanted to know. Dr. Hayakawa states that it never came up. Before he had become president of the college the radical students had wanted to get the ROTC off the campus as a symbol of militarism. In response to my raising the issue of the Vietnam War, Dr. Hayakawa indicated that his views and positions on international problems had nothing to do with running for the Senate.

Dr. Hayakawa said that he was happy in the Senate. If he disagreed with someone and was defeated on the floor on a measure that he liked, he wasn't filled with great heartbreak. He took it in stride. He also states that there was nothing about the legislative process that especially engaged his personal emotions or his partisanship.

We next turned to Dr. Hayakawa's personal background. He pointed out that as the eldest son he was excessively treasured by his mother. Thus, he was always sure of himself. This enabled him to ignore and withstand personal insults. If someone mistreated him, it was "their lack of character. Things bounce off me very quickly."

I invited Dr. Hayakawa to select a personal experience that might have been especially disheartening to him. He mentioned that many years ago, when he was twenty-three, he had dated a Swedish woman. After visiting her at her home, her parents banished him because he was Japanese. Dr. Hayakawa says that this falling-out troubled his girlfriend more than himself. As he puts it, "I just knew that they were ignorant people. I hated to give her up, but that was the end of that."

Dr. Hayakawa stressed that this was not a traumatic experience for him. He explained that his parents fortified him against that sort of experience long ago. They did this by inculcating in him great pride in his race, his history, and his family.

Since we were on the subject of racial prejudice, I asked Dr. Hayakawa to share his views concerning the internment of Japanese-Americans during World War II. He stated that, although he was very much concerned about the matter at the time, he regarded the internment as a military necessity. He believes that the actual landing of Japanese troops on the West Coast was a realistic possibility and the internment was a warranted precautionary measure against such a threat. He further thinks that the internment actually protected the Japanese-Americans themselves because, in his view, they might have been shot by their neighbors in the event of an invasion by Japan.

Dr. Hayakawa believes that the atomic bombing of Hiroshima and Nagasaki were also military necessities. He bases his view on his understanding of Samurai ideology, which never accepts defeat. He, therefore, has concluded that if the Americans had attacked the Japanese mainland, the Japanese would have defended themselves "to the last man, woman and child. Everyone would have gone down dead rather than suffer disgrace." In the view of Dr. Hayakawa's father, who lived in Japan at the time, if Hiroshima hadn't happened, the war would have gone on for another five or six years. In a curious way, Dr. Hayakawa speculates, the atomic bomb gave the Japanese a convenient rationale to surrender. It permitted the Japanese to surrender without disgrace, without violating the Samurai code. In sum, based on his research findings, Dr. Hayakawa did not regret or feel angry about either the internment of the Japanese or the use of the atomic bomb against Japanese cities that took place during the 1940s.

Toward the end of our interview, which was held in Dr. Hayakawa's home, a man unexpectedly entered the room. Dr. Hayakawa pointed out that the man was his thirty-eight-year-old son and a Down's syndrome child. I commented that having such a child was obviously an example of an adversity in his life and asked Dr. Hayakawa how he had dealt with his feelings about this tragedy.

Dr. Hayakawa concluded our interview by responding in the following manner: "It was a terrible blow for us to discover that we had brought a retarded child into the world. My wife and I had no previous acquaintance with the problems of retardation—not even with the words to discuss it. Only such words as imbecile, idiot, and moron came to mind. And the prevailing opinion was that such a child must be 'put away,' to live out his life in an institution. That was twenty-eight years ago. In that time, Mark has never been 'put away.' He has lived at home. Mark has contributed to our stability and serenity. His retardation has brought us grief, but we did not go on dwelling on what might have been, and we have been rewarded by finding much good in things the way they are."

Elizabeth Holtzman

Birth date: August 11, 1941

Congresswoman, 16th District New York, 1970-72

Our interview began with my question about the events and issues that inspired Ms. Holtzman to enter politics. Ms. Holtzman pointed out that it was her exposure to city government that inspired her to enter politics. She had worked for the mayor of New York City and found that working on governmental problems was intellectually challenging and emotionally rewarding because you were able to accomplish things for your community. And, she added, the work need not be corrupting.

I next asked Ms. Holtzman if there were any events in her personal background of an especially painful nature that may have inspired her to seek to change society. She responded by referring to her experience in the South during the early days of the civil rights movement. She had seen there a horrifying picture of brutality, cruelty, and the humiliation of people. Because of her work in the civil rights movement she felt very strongly about the need for change.

Ms. Holtzman elaborated by providing examples of her observations. She had seen poor, black children standing outside a swimming pool during the summertime, on an extremely hot day. There were white children swimming in the pool while the black children were not allowed to use the pool because blacks were simply not allowed to use "white" facilities. To make matters worse, the governmental authorities in the community had closed down "black" swimming pools.

During her stay in the South Ms. Holtzman also saw people beaten and arrested for their civil rights activities. It was painful for her to witness blacks who had to get off the sidewalk and walk in the middle of the street due to racist city ordinances and practices.

I next asked Ms. Holtzman if there were any particular things in her personal or family background that had played a part in her developing a sense of idealism. She remarked that her parents were immigrants. They saw that this country stood for justice, for opportunity, and for human dignity. As a result, she herself developed some of those expectations.

Congresswoman Holtzman was a very prominent figure during the Watergate investigations. Assuming that she had been outraged by the political abuses perpetrated by the Nixon administration, I asked her to tell me what especially disturbed her about this unsavory period in American history. She began by stating that, inasmuch as she had never particularly liked either Mr. Nixon or his policies, her main reactions to the scandal were ones of sadness. It saddened her to see the desecration of the presidential office, the extreme abuse of power, and the criminal scheming that went on.

I asked if Ms. Holtzman saw the root of the problem to exist in Mr. Nixon's character. She stated, quite emphatically, that she did see the problem in this light. In the hours and hours of listening to the tape recordings of the president and his top aides a clear pattern of political scheming emerged. It disturbed Ms. Holtzman that the president and his aides did not ask, "What is the *right* thing to do?" Rather it was always, "How do I cover this thing up? How do I get out of it? How do I deceive? How do we lie?"

Taking into account her comments about the desecration of the presidential office, I asked Ms. Holtzman how she felt about the pardoning of Mr. Nixon. She pointed out that she was very much opposed to the pardoning of the president. As a matter of fact, she elaborated, she was the only member of Congress to put the tough question right to President Ford about whether there was a prior "deal" that had been negotiated between the two men. When I next asked Ms. Holtzman what she thought of President Ford's answer to that "tough" question, she answered that she is still waiting for his answer.

I encouraged Ms. Holtzman to discuss what she thought should have been done with or to President Nixon. She replied by saying that there should not be two standards of justice in this country. In her view, he should have been treated as we would treat any other citizen of this country. He should have been treated with due process, not an aborted, truncated process. Certainly, not with the special hands-on treatment he did receive. Congresswoman Holtzman firmly believes there should have been no pardon and that a full criminal process should have been allowed to take place. She also thinks that a "deal" was a distinct possibility.

Ms. Holtzman is quick to point out that, as painful and traumatic as the Watergate crisis was, she believes it actually strengthened the nation. In her view, it caused people to more deeply realize how committed we were to constitutional government and democracy. In the end, we wanted a government in which the rule of law was paramount. This, in her view, was an extremely important thing to discover about us as a nation.

I asked Ms. Holtzman if that sad experience made her into a cynic. Or did it possibly inspire her to work harder? She commented that it is very hard to make her into a cynic. She would not be in government if she were a cynic. More than ever, she believes that people in government can act ethically. She feels that there is so much of importance that has to be done that a person cannot give up. The stakes are too high.

At the time of this interview Ms. Holtzman was the district attorney for Brooklyn, New York. I asked her if her job was in any way an extension of the work she had done in Congress. She explained that her current work was a very different kind of universe. Although it was not as global, it was more intense and much deeper. The day-to-day problems were not as abstract. She regards that work to be much tougher than being in Congress. Yet she feels there is still an immense opportunity in a legal system that is antiquated and archaic and overwhelmed; there is still room for improvement and innovation, for creativity, for reform.

What especially upsets her about the judicial system, I wanted to know. Ms. Holtzman referred first to the callousness of the system toward victims. There is also a widespread failure to be innovative.

What then has Ms. Holtzman done to overcome these defects in the judicial system? Since she has become the Brooklyn district attorney there has been a systematic effort to get restitution from defendants. Almost a million dollars had been collected from defendants to pay back victims of crimes. Furthermore, Ms. Holtzman was instrumental in giving victims a voice in the sentencing process. After a homicide trial the families of victims are invited to make a direct plea to the judge about the kind of sentence to be imposed by the court.

Another innovation effected by Ms. Holtzman and her staff has been to develop counseling services to provide immediate, direct help to victims who have been traumatized by crime. Also, laws have been changed to protect children who have been victims of sexual abuse by reducing their exposure to the trauma of participating in the prosecution.

With pride Ms. Holtzman points to other creative innovations such as making punishments fit the crimes. If, for example, a person commits the crime of putting graffiti on the subways, he will have to scrub it off, regardless of whether or not this was a first offense. Thousands of young criminal offenders have received sentences that involve cleaning parks, working in hospitals, helping the elderly, and working in zoos and botanical gardens.

Congresswoman Holtzman emphasized that it was the opportunity to effect such creative changes that drew her into public life. She sums up her feelings by saying, "It's a great privilege to try to help your community and your city and your country."

I requested Ms. Holtzman to share her personal philosophy about dealing with negative emotions when she has experienced a serious setback or disappointment. She replied that her basic view is an optimistic one. She feels that people can made a difference; even one person. Standing and working for what's right can make that difference, in her estimation. Finally, she deeply believes that a person has to work for a world that is just, fair, and peaceful.

Barney Frank

Birth date: March 31, 1940

Congressman, 4th District Massachusetts, 1981-Present

The interview with Congressman Frank began with a question about his childhood years. Specifically, I asked if he recalled any particular experience from his youth that may have inspired him toward a career in politics. His immediate response was to recount how, at the age of fourteen, he had read in the newspapers about a black youth of the same age, Emmet Till, who had been beaten to death for whistling at a white woman. The moral outrage he felt over this senseless act of bigotry aroused in him strong desires to resist all forms of racial discrimination and injustice.

Relatively early in his life Mr. Frank became aware of his abiding concerns regarding the suppression of free speech in American society. He learned by watching the televised hearings how McCarthyism had brutally abridged the constitutional rights of ordinary citizens. He also came to understand the plight of those Japanese-Americans whose forcible internment during the Second World War had instantaneously deprived them of their personal freedom. These political upheavals were catalysts that engendered in Mr. Frank a passion to combat all forms of unfairness and oppression.

As a gay man, Mr. Frank felt constraints, internal and social, upon his own freedom. For that reason, he did not come out of the closet until he was in his forties. When he finally exited the closet he resolved to provide support and leadership to gay causes by marching in gay parades and sponsoring gay rights legislation. When he did "go public" with his gayness, Mr. Frank initially experienced considerable apprehension over the possibility that this act of disclosure would cost him not only the respect of others but possibly even his very political career. In this regard, I asked Mr. Frank if his family was sympathetic and supportive to him during this time of crisis and he emphatically iterated that they were.

Since at the time of this writing Mr. Frank was closely involved with the impeachment proceedings, I asked him his impressions of this rather historic event. He replied that he thought it ironic that a gay man, who not many years ago would have been considered a social and sexual pariah (and in some benighted bastions of our country continues to suffer such a stigma), was now one of those overseeing a proceeding that related to the sexual behavior of a heterosexual man. When I asked Mr. Frank to hazard a guess regarding the outcome of these proceedings, he replied by stating that the House might vote the articles of impeachment but the Senate would not, in his estimation, convict.

I asked Mr. Frank if he could recall any particular pivotal moment that seemed to affect the course of his political career. Without hesitation he identified the time when Pope John Paul II promulgated Canon 285, paragraph 3, prohibiting Catholic clerics from serving in public office, thereby removing Father Drinan, Mr. Frank's predecessor, from his seat in Congress.

I asked Mr. Frank if being Jewish had in any respect shaped his political philosophy and aspirations. With some animation he stated that the combination of being gay and Jewish undoubtedly sensitized him to the discrimination that has traditionally been aimed at minority groups in our society. Although, unlike Barbara Boxer, he does not feel that the Holocaust made a powerful impact upon his life, at least not directly, he acknowledges that his Jewishness has been a major factor in fostering his liberal beliefs and his progressive political objectives.

Mr. Frank's family was not religious; however, he pointedly averred, he strongly identifies himself as a Jew. When I inquired about whether he had therefore incurred a significant degree of anti-Semitism over his lifetime, he replied by indicating that he had not in many years been victimized by this form of prejudice. He did recall, however, that in high school (Bayonne, New Jersey) Jewish students were usually not elected as class officers.

I encouraged Congressman Frank to tell me something about one of his most painful personal setbacks. He alluded to an experience he once had with a male hustler whom he hired to carry out errands, not sexual favors. When this relationship ended the hustler publicly accused Mr. Frank of betrayal, stating that he had been hired for sex. The public brouhaha that followed in the wake of this man's public accusations deeply humiliated Mr. Frank and caused him serious depression for several months. He then rebounded by successfully refuting the allegations. Regrettably, however, he was issued a public reprimand in the House of Representatives, compounding, of course, his humiliation.

My final question to Mr. Frank related to how his colleagues in the House generally treated him. Did any of them recoil from him because he was gay? In a tone of evident contempt, he remarked that one of his colleagues has assiduously kept his distance, evidently thinking that he will contract something contagious if he gets any closer. Then, with some exuberance and pugilistic fire, he said, "I'm not concerned with who stays away from me. I know who the bigots are and *I* stay away from *them*."

On a more personal note, Mr. Frank confided, in a tone of evident sorrow, that he had recently ended an eleven-year relationship with a lover.

Finally, I requested that Congressman Frank tell me if he lived by any particular guiding principle. He said that although none came to mind, he simply wanted to devote himself to redressing the conditions of discrimination and unfairness that were so prevalent in our society.

Impressions and Conclusions

The interviews described in this chapter did not appear to fully confirm all of my hopes and hypotheses, nor, I believe, did they entirely refute them. I had presupposed that one of the principal motivations underlying my interviewees' original involvement in politics concerned their need to repair and cope with some of the personal disappointments and traumas of childhood. With the sole exception of Senator Boxer, who alluded to a betrayal by a girlhood friend, none of the other interviewees disclosed especially painful or traumatic childhood experiences. Why? Did none actually exist?

There are several possible explanations for this conspicuous absence of references to early life difficulties. First, because the events themselves occurred in the distant past they perhaps with the passage of time had become obscure and, therefore, mentally irretrievable, especially during the course of only a single, brief interview. Second, the interviewees, without exception, were apparently reared in wholesome, secure family environments that instilled in them a very positive appreciation and fondness for their parents and siblings. Consequently, the highly negative events of their childhood, assuming that they must have taken place at least occasionally, may have by comparison with their positive childhood experiences paled into relative insignificance and, therefore, were not specially vivid or memorable to the interviewees.

I have considered other possibilities. Persons who feel deeply grateful and appreciative toward their parents, as did my interviewees, often feel guilty and ashamed about harboring critical attitudes toward them as well. I wondered throughout the interviews to what extent the interviewees held back, consciously or unconsciously, when they were invited to express themselves about moments of unhappiness during childhood because they felt that to even slightly complain about the quality of their upbringings would constitute a foul betrayal of their parents. Finally, to be somewhat less psychoanalytic, it seemed quite possible to me that the interviewees had simply and sensibly declined to air their family's "dirty linen" to an interviewer such as myself who was a complete stranger to them and who might, in their view, misconstrue or publicly misuse such intimate information.

The interviews rather conclusively confirmed my expectation that one major driving force in the lives of most political figures is their dissatisfaction and outrage concerning the social ills of their nation and the world. Mayor Gibson referred to the horrid state of the educational and health care systems in this country; Senator Stennis to the frightful conditions of the depression, to the destructiveness of addictive drugs, and to the ongoing inability of nations to settle their disputes peaceably; Senator Boxer to the Holocaust, political assassinations, the Vietnam War, the nuclear arms buildup, and Star Wars; Senator McGovern to the viciousness and immorality of the Vietnam War, to widespread hunger, to the repressive working conditions of miners, and to the tragedy of Watergate; Senator Hayakawa to the radical assault that had been made upon cherished educational institutions; Congresswoman Holtzman to the moral travesties of Watergate and the Nixon administration, and to the aberrations and defects within the judicial system; Congressman Frank to the conditions of discrimination that corrode American life.

To one extent or another, each of the interviewees expressed dismay, anger, or indignation over some of the appalling political and social conditions they had observed in the nation and in the world. They tapped and utilized their own desires and ideals to address and redress those social problems that most negatively affected their sensibilities. By channeling their creative energies into constructive political and legislative work they were able to transform their negative reactions to the social ills of the world into healing and positive endeavors.

What has enabled these particular individuals to surmount and transcend their own adversities and negative emotions? For one, they each, at least to this interviewer, seemed to be constitutionally strong and resilient individuals. Also, they all expressed the conviction that they had drawn great strength, perseverance and a sense of purpose from their families. Thus, Senator Hayakawa could deal with a nasty racial rebuff in his early twenties with relative equanimity. Senator McGovern, despite great disappointment over coming within a hairsbreadth of the presidency, never allowed himself to be immobilized by the experience. He continued to look forward to new challenges. Despite a near-fatal mugging and the amputation of a leg, Senator Stennis, until the time of his death, still looked forward to a productive and fulfilling life. Congressman Frank, like a courageous gladiator, engages in open combat with bigots and bigotry in asserting his rights as a gay man.

Although they represent and reflect a wide range of ideological opinion, the political figures in this sample seem to share a remarkably similar set of values when dealing with the hardships of life. Senator McGovern says there are always more challenges to be met. Senator Hayakawa says it is better not to dwell on what might have been, but rather in finding good in things the way they are. Congresswoman Holtzman stresses the importance of working for what is right and maintaining the belief that even one person can make a difference. Senator Stennis keeps a vision before him of always looking ahead, regardless of what circumstances may be. Mayor Gibson depends for his strength upon the values and standards instilled in him by his family, especially the value of respecting the integrity and rights of other people. Senator Boxer draws inspiration and courage from her steadfast belief that "We all must at some point grow up and realize that we have to step out from the crowd even though it's sometimes hurtful." Congressman Frank gives his life meaning by fighting for fairness.

What these prominent and socially dedicated individuals share is a broad set of profound convictions and ideals that serve to nurture and sustain them throughout their private and public tribulations. For the most part, these ideals and convictions are of an optimistic, visionary, and altruistic nature. Also of noteworthy importance is the fact that each of these persons has found his or her own inimitable way to philosophically view failure, defeat, and disappointment as an inherent, ineluctable part of life; a part of life, admittedly, that will often sadden, discourage, and deter an individual but need not entirely crush or vanquish the human spirit.

Chapter 8

On Handling Negative Thoughts and Emotions

Early in this century Sigmund Freud and his psychiatric cohorts found, or seemed to find, that the basic conflicts that led to neurosis were sexual in nature. Fear and repression of sexual feelings gave rise to physical and behavioral symptoms that were both persistent and debilitating.

Nowadays, psychotherapists treat patients who are faced with a rather different set of psychological circumstances and stresses. Although most individuals have not completely broken free of their Victorian sexual shackles, it is evident that great strides have been made in the realm of human sexuality since Freud's time. Many psychotherapy patients now discuss readily and openly the vast range of sexual thoughts and activities that regularly flow through and influence their lives, including how and when they have sexual intercourse, masturbate, engage in oral and anal sex, or enjoy an erotic round of cinematic or literary pornography. Although such topics still cause large numbers of people a good degree of skittishness, in contemporary American society there are certainly fewer and milder proscriptions of sexual thoughts and feelings than had been the case at the time of Freud's discoveries.

Regrettably, the progress we have made in overcoming sexual taboos has not been matched by our success in coping with the so-called negative emotions: anger, envy, hatred, resentment, defiance, and vindictiveness. For example, in my psychotherapy practice it is quite common for a patient to share with me explicitly and unabashedly the details of a recent sexual encounter. Yet this same individual might have a veritable conniption if I were to suggest that behind some of his or her actions lurked a hostile, envious, or competitive thought.

Envy

In this regard, I recall an interview with a college instructor who, without reserve or inhibition, described to me how she had freely and enjoyably given fellatio to her lover in the front seat of his car. In the same session this patient staunchly resisted my efforts to point out her feelings of envy, rage, and grief toward an older sister who had recently been blessed with an unexpected and sizeable financial windfall. Somehow, the idea that she could hate and envy her sister, even fleetingly, because of the latter's good fortune, shocked and consternated her. She regarded such thoughts as morally reprehensible and forbidden and, although her sister's recent boon was the primary emotional bombshell that had shattered the patient's self-esteem and prompted her to seek psychotherapy in the first place, she initially could not accept the notion that she could hate and envy (and still love) her more advantaged sister.

Escaping from Negative Emotions

It is quite common of course for most persons to want and seek immediate emotional relief and refuge from negative thoughts and emotions. However, in our desire and eagerness to escape our anger and grief we often miss the opportunity to learn and grow from our negative feelings and experiences. We simply and understandably want to *feel better*, now and at all costs. Consequently, if we can find some method for immediately soothing our inflamed negative emotions (e.g., tranquilizers), we glom onto it, rather than carefully sorting through and thoroughly understanding what is irking us. Clearly, it is putting the cart before the horse to expect powerful negative emotions to simply disappear of their own accord as if one could only ignore them or will them away.

Obviously, there are no clear-cut, infallible prescriptions or formulas for effectively dealing with negative emotions and thoughts. Nevertheless, I would like to set down some general principles that may serve the reader as helpful guidelines for coping with hostile feelings.

General Principles

First, it is important to recognize that there are some decided advantages to resisting the temptation to immediately disown or cast away negative emotions. Because we wish to rid ourselves of hostility and resentment as quickly as possible, we may deny that we are feeling negatively, or worse, we may attribute our own negative emotions to the villainy of others whom we then resent for being our "adversaries." Although it may at times require a huge intellectual and emotional effort, it is often extremely beneficial to regard negative emotions as a natural and intrinsic part of one's own personality.

In order to accept one's own hostile emotions in a nonjudgmental spirit, however, it is important to consider a principle that is, on moral and religious grounds, repugnant and anathematic to large numbers of people. The principle to which I am referring is as follows: There is no thought or emotion, no matter how revolting, sadistic, perverse, or disproportionate, that is *inherently* immoral, cruel, destructive, or evil. Feelings and thoughts of envy, rage, bitterness, revenge, defiance, and hatred are as human and as natural as are feelings of affection, love, sensuality, and pleasure.

Before summarily condemning this principle (or me, for propounding it), there are certain facts to be considered with respect to the negative emotions. For example, since most individuals experience hostile and even sadistic emotions and thoughts many times throughout the course of each day without ever committing serious acts of sadism, there is no reason to believe that a hostile emotion or thought will *necessarily* lead to a sadistic form of behavior. In other words, what a person thinks and feels, no matter how devious or malevolent, may be spontaneously transformed into socially acceptable behavior regardless of its sadistic origins. For example, there are many persons who, out of deep feelings of rage and envy, will devote themselves altruistically to the welfare of others, perhaps genuinely revealing their negative emotions only when they are not sufficiently appreciated or rewarded for their generosity.

It is essential, therefore, to realize that emotions and thoughts are ordinarily distinguishable from overt deeds and must be judged according to a different set of moral standards and criteria. A thought or emotion, no matter how sadistic, can be neutralized in an infinite number of ways, such as humor, activity, intellectual reflection, or work. A sadistic, murderous thought or emotion can do absolutely no harm to others or oneself unless or until it is transformed into a sadistic deed. We can of course acknowledge that hostile fantasies and emotions often cause the person who harbors them considerable distress, irrespective of whether they have been enacted and thereby harmed others. The primary reason for this, however, usually is the tendency of those who domicile hostile thoughts in their minds to involuntarily attach guilt, shame, and self-contempt to their angry feelings. Thus, I would suggest that one of the first steps in effectively dealing with negative thoughts and emotions is to regard them as wholly distinct from negative, harmful deeds and, therefore, accept them as morally neutral.

A Morally Neutral Perspective

If we can view and accept our angry emotions and thoughts in a morally neutral light, we will naturally increase our capacity to also accept full ownership of our negative feelings. Unless we realize that our own hostile feelings represent the integral, inalienable, and unexorcisable underside of our personality and our very being, our sadistic feelings will tend to dominate and control us, rather than vice versa.

A Historical Context

A second step in effectively dealing with negative thoughts and feelings is to consider the historical causes and contexts of angry emotions. That is, it may be very helpful to understand what in our own personal experiences, past or present, is making us feel and think negatively.

In this regard, I have very frequently interviewed persons in therapy who have, for understandable reasons, been mystified and demoralized by their own hostile emotions. Having come up with no adequate explanation for their hostilities and depression, they remark, "I have no reason for feeling this way. As a matter of fact, things are going pretty well in most respects. So, I should be happy. I guess there's no reason for feeling miserable. Maybe it's just that I like to be depressed and am seeking pity."

The person who suffers from such a predicament is unable to explain the causes for his or her own emotional distress, therefore, wrongly assumes there are no substantive reasons for this state of woeful unhappiness. One of the first important steps in psychotherapy, therefore, is to convince and reassure such an individual that there are *always* reasons and causes for all emotions, including hostility and depression. Perhaps the basic causes for the intensification of negative emotions and thoughts are subtle and obscure because they took place early in the patient's life and are being unconsciously reactivated by current events. As we might expect, individuals who cannot ascertain a valid cause or explanation for their own negative emotions will perhaps misattribute their hostilities to an evil and immutable force or quality within themselves. Thinking that there is no reason for their angry feelings other than a vague, lamentable deficiency in their character or personality, they will perhaps despair of ever coming to terms with their own negative emotions. In other words, if there is no known cause for one's distress, there is likely to be no known remedy either.

In considering the sources and causes of one's own negative emotions, it would be helpful to establish, if possible, a chronology or sequence of those important psychological events that brought about the intensification of hostile feelings. Although it may not be possible to pinpoint exactly when and where one became angrier and more discontented, a brief review of past personal events may provide an eye-opening insight into when and why a particular experience was psychologically derailing.

In this regard, it is helpful to keep in mind two general principles: 1) Ordinarily, some personal events are more significant and pivotal than others in generating negative emotions, therefore, it is usually best to avoid the old saw, "Oh, everything bothers me equally, so there are really no particular reasons for my anger and depression." The fact that certain causes for emotional conflicts have not yet been identified is not adequate reason for ruling out determinable causes for one's hostile emotions, and 2) Angry emotions are almost always catalyzed by tension, interpersonal disagreement, conflict, or a disruption that has taken place within an important emotional relationship. Thus, if we closely and painstakingly examine our own negative emotions, we will more than likely find that they have been aroused by, and targeted at, particular individuals who are especially emotionally important to us (e.g., a parent, lover, spouse, sibling, employer, co-worker, teacher, etc.)

The Interpersonal Catalyst

Once having determined *who* it is that has triggered off our intense hostile feelings, it should not be an awfully complicated task to uncover *why* it is that this particular person has gotten under our skin. For example, has this individual recently ignored, insulted, cheated, deceived, deserted, rebuffed, misunderstood, misled, or injured us in some respect? If so, we can next address the question of whether, considering this person's hurtful behavior, our own hostile reactions are appropriate or proportionate to the emotional injury we have incurred.

If we find that our emotional reactions are not befitting the actual encounter we have just experienced with that person, we may then need to look elsewhere for a deeper explanation for our uncalled-for hostile feelings. In doing so, it may be helpful to trace our negative emotions to the events of our more distant past, including those of our early childhood, which may have played an important part in making us especially vulnerable to the everyday slights of others. By understanding the inextricable connection between our present hostile reactions and the long-buried resentments of our own personal past, we can improve our ability to put our negative emotions into realistic perspective and, thereby, cope with them more creatively and effectively. Without being able to detect the earliest origins of our excessive, inappropriately directed emotions, we may not only inadvertently victimize others with our hostilities, but also feel quite guilty for venting anger at those who do not warrant such mistreatment from us.

Let us say, however, that our anger and resentment are appropriately and proportionately aroused by someone who has been especially cruel or inhumane toward us. What are our options in such a case? Ordinarily, there is a multitude of possible responses. If, for example, we have suffered a serious indignity or threat from someone whom we will undoubtedly never see again, such as a reckless hot rodder who has deliberately cut us off at an intersection, we may choose to accept the fact that we have good reason to be furious and then philosophically resign ourselves to the fact that we cannot redress every injustice we suffer in life.

If the person who transgresses our feelings and integrity is someone we know well and are deeply emotionally involved with, the potential responses to such an individual are more complicated and, therefore, require more considered reflection. If it is an employer or an instructor, for example—that is, someone who occupies an authoritative role in our lives and, therefore, can seriously jeopardize our economic or academic prospects—we may be inclined to use caution and diplomacy in expressing our anger. Then again, if an instructor or employer (or any other authoritative figure) engages in persistently harassing us or violating our civil rights, we may very well throw caution to the winds and justifiably take corrective or retaliatory action, such as a lawsuit, against such an individual.

It is extremely common for many persons to rationalize their inability to express anger toward their parents, lovers, spouses, and friends by stating with genuine conviction, "There is definitely no use in confronting my father (mother, teacher, friend, etc.) with my anger because he will never change. So, what's the use?" On the surface, this appears to be a plausible justification for withholding one's rage and indignation. However, when we examine such comments closely, we usually discover in them some rather serious flaws.

First of all, the purpose and value of expressing our anger toward an offending individual may not be necessarily to change that person's character, personality, or behavior. Rather, it is often of great intrinsic psychological value to express one's anger over a personal insult or injury simply in order to let the offender know where we stand; that is, to convey our sense of outrage by conveying the fact that we respect ourselves too much to tolerate shabby treatment. By expressing such a self-respecting position to someone who has undermined our self-respect we may very well augment our self-esteem.

A second factor to keep in mind when we consider expressing our angry feelings toward another individual is the potential our actions may have for actually achieving what we may least expect and most want: namely, a positive change, if not in the offender's personality, at least in how he or she behaves toward us. Of course cynical persons who are confronted with such a positive possibility will riposte, "Look, I've often tried expressing my anger and resentment in my talks with my father. But he always outtalks and outwits me and I wind up feeling worse than if I had kept my mouth shut. No, I won't try that again."

Although these individuals seemingly have good cause for harnessing their angry feelings, there are several reasons I would not accept their comments at face value. First, it is of paramount importance to know something about why their fathers repeatedly outsmart and outtalk them. Are they too timid and overawed by their fathers? Do they cry and cave in to their father's arguments too easily? Do they allow their fathers to make them feel guilty for asserting themselves with them? Are they viewing their fathers as too psychologically fragile to withstand and recover from the anger they feel for them? Do they irrationally believe that their fathers will withdraw their love for them if they become openly angry with them? In short, are there ways in which they unwittingly sabotage their own efforts to courageously express and defend their angry emotions? Until these questions are satisfactorily answered, it is probably best to be skeptical when people suggest it is entirely futile to stand up for their rights.

Another matter to consider is the extent to which the expectations of certain persons are realistic with respect to how quickly their expression of angry emotions will truly effect positive results. Many individuals unrealistically expect that if they could only once reveal to certain other persons the anger and resentment they feel toward them, no holds barred, they will immediately be understood, acknowledged, validated, and treated respectfully, forevermore. And, since such far-reaching breakthroughs rarely happen so quickly or so dramatically, the first time they meet with only partial success in asserting their angry emotions, they regard the experience as an egregious failure and resolve at all costs not to repeat it. Unfortunately, they little realize that it often requires firm, unequivocal, and *repeated* assertions of one's genuine feelings *over a period of time* before certain other individuals will regard these feelings with seriousness and respect.

Naturally, the manner and tone with which individuals share their negative emotions will have overriding importance in determining whether they will be taken seriously. Many persons complain that their concerns and gripes are never taken seriously by their friends or family. Frequently, if we listen closely to the despairing comments of such individuals, we will discover that whatever they say, including their most heartfelt laments, is couched in a language and tone that is equivocal, tentative, and unconvincing. Thus, although such persons may be conveying the content of their negative thoughts and feelings, by being indirect, ambiguous, and cautious in their expression of negative emotions, they fail to transmit the essence of what they truly feel. Not surprisingly, their feelings, consequently, tend to be ignored and negated by others.

Of course there are those individuals who one-sidedly, unvaryingly, and inexhaustibly focus upon and express their negative thoughts and emotions to anyone who will listen, with little regard for the effect their negativity may have upon others. Their unceasing overemphasis upon the dismal aspects of their lives may well have the effect of depressing and antagonizing their confidants, who for good reason are inclined to consider them self-centered bellyachers.

Frequently, when I have questioned psychotherapy patients about their inability to vocalize angry emotions to the individual who has provoked them, I have received the following exasperated reply, "What do you want me to do? Scream, shout, throw something, hit him, have a tantrum?"

I find it interesting and significant that it is the patients themselves who have conjured up fantasies of tantrums and violence in response to the idea of expressing anger. This usually suggests: 1) The patients' negative emotions are very intense and perhaps of a highly sadistic nature since it was they, not I, who spontaneously painted the image of violent thoughts and actions when discussing the prospect of expressing their anger, and 2) The patients are constricted by their anger into believing that the only effective forms of expressing anger are flagrant and violent. Since they strongly associate the expression of anger with violence, they very likely feel very guilty and anxious about their negative emotions since they believe their negative emotions will cause harm to others. Very likely, this is one of the reasons they are so reticent and inhibited about expressing angry feelings in the first place.

Such people, unfortunately, often fall into a vicious circle of their own making. Their inability to verbalize negative emotions on a piecemeal basis sometimes leads to the storing up and intensification of hostility until it reaches sadistic proportions. When people attempt to indefinitely put angry emotions in cold storage they sometimes find that they have instead placed them in a fiery cauldron where they parboil until their raging intensity becomes frightening and difficult to control. Since the angry emotions have become frighteningly intense and sadistic in nature, these people will feel they have no choice but to suppress and suffocate them all the more, thus leading to another round of even more hostile feelings and wishes.

There is a widespread myth that angry emotions are best managed by cathartically releasing them wherever and whenever they arise, irrespective of the social circumstances and probable consequences of such behavior. Common sense, however, suggests that the mere indiscriminate release of anger does not necessarily diminish the intensity of one's hostility. On the contrary, there is considerable evidence suggesting that the indiscriminate release of hostility only begets more sinister forms of hostility. In the most extreme cases, for example, such as those involving multiple murderers, the compunctionless and unbridled release of fury in the commission of a heinous crime, rather than slaking the bloodthirstiness of the killers, only whets their appetite for further mayhem. Those who have closely observed individuals who are prone to recurrent temper tantrums will readily recognize that the volatile loss of emotional control usually leads to heightened exasperation and self-hatred, thus causing even greater susceptibility to emotional rampages. Clearly, the mere release of anger and hostility coupled with disregard for social context and consequence is no panacea for psychological conflicts brought on by negative emotions and thoughts.

I myself was experientially taught this lesson many years ago. I was sitting in my office calmly reading a magazine and minding my own beeswax when I overheard loud, crackling sounds issuing from the office across the hall. The office was used by a psychotherapist who worked primarily with young children, so I assumed, evidently correctly, that the commotion was due to some form of play therapy in the works. After a few minutes, the office opened and the therapist emerged, breathing heavily and sweating profusely. "Hey, Jerry," he called over, "do me a favor, will you. Take over here."

The therapist indicated that he and his patient, a boy of about thirteen, had been engaged in whacking each other with lightweight rods made of a synthetic material which, when struck hard against human skin, gave off a loud, sharp but painless report. The purpose of using these rods, according to what I had read about them, was to enable psychotherapy patients who were fearful of expressing anger or aggression to liberate and resolve their hostile emotions by beating up on their psychotherapists in a socially acceptable and totally harmless way. Although I had long been skeptical of such psychotherapeutic techniques, I agreed to battle it out with the chubby adolescent who stood before me with a bored and deadpan expression on his face.

To my surprise, as soon as I had put on my protective goggles and had rod in hand, I was assailed by vengeful feelings. Although I felt no physical pain from his blows, I certainly didn't like the evident sadistic pleasure my adversary was deriving from his onslaught. Without plan or forethought, I jumped into the fray and began blasting him with as much force as I could muster. For five minutes we stood there, toe-to-toe, two gladiators pummeling each other.

As we began to tire and slow down, I realized an interesting fact. At the outset of this encounter I had been in a calm frame of mind and felt friendly and sympathetic toward this boy. However, soon after we began to furiously attack each other I felt intense feelings of hatred and vindictiveness toward him. By the time we concluded our battle, I had overcome most of my hostility, but when I left the office of the therapist and returned to my own, it was quite some time before I completely simmered down and overcame the irrational belligerence I felt as a result of that harmless duel.

So, paradoxical as it may seem, the direct, physical ventilation of anger, in this instance at least, only served to inflame hostile and sadistic emotions. Yet, I don't regard my own experience to be a highly singular one. It seems that most people who burst out angrily at others, without regard for the social or personal consequences of their actions, usually feel even more rage as a result, at least until they are able to reasonably talk out and sort out their negative emotions afterward.

More Guidelines

If the unfettered outburst of negative emotions is not in itself an effective means with which to deal with one's own hostility, what might we then adopt as reliable guidelines for determining when and how to express angry emotions? In addressing this problem, I would suggest that we first attempt to predict or anticipate the possible interpersonal consequences of either expressing or inhibiting angry thoughts and emotions. Second, in considering the consequences of expressing or inhibiting hostile thoughts and feelings, it is ordinarily important to determine, as realistically as possible, whether our actions will enhance or diminish our self-esteem. No matter how gratifying or exhilarating a momentary outpouring of hostility may be, if in the long run it leads to the lessening of one's self-esteem, such a catharsis obviously has no recognizable value and can only be personally detrimental.

How can we best predict the consequences of expressing our angry emotions? Of course there are many factors to be taken into consideration. One of the primary factors will naturally be our own personal history in dealing with negative emotions, including all of our long-entrenched idiosyncratic patterns of expressing anger. For example, if we repeatedly express anger indirectly, say, through sarcasm and derision of others, we are likely to discover that we estrange rather than gain rapport with people. Thus, if we truly wish to alter the quality of our social relationships, it would be well to consider expressing our negative emotions in ways other than through the abusive disparagement of other individuals.

If, on the other hand, our negative emotions are expressed almost exclusively in the form of lighthearted humor and levity, we may indeed tend to amuse and charm others, which, if to our way of thinking is a desirable objective, our efforts may have their legitimate rewards. However, the overuse of humor as a means of expressing angry emotions may be fraught with pitfalls such as the possibility that others may never take our negative emotions very seriously.

A patient who has had recurrent difficulties in expressing anger directly and candidly, remarked with pride that she tries to camouflage her anger by the use of sardonic witticisms. She then hopes that other individuals will "pick up on" her anger and take her feelings seriously. When I asked her if things usually turned out as she had hoped, that is, whether people accurately "read" and acknowledged her negative emotions, she admitted that usually they did not, but she still preferred to shroud her hostile feelings in humor so no one would think ill of her. As a result, she naturally felt unacknowledged and unappreciated a good deal of the time.

Other individuals have quite the opposite problem. They tend to express their anger and hostility too bluntly and too woundingly. As a result, although they may have just cause for being angry and for directing their hostility at certain individuals, their inability to alloy or temper their anger with compassion, humor, or tact causes them to be dismissed and despised as pitiless curmudgeons.

These examples illustrate the importance of one's *manner* and *style* in the expression of negative thoughts and emotions. Although most people wish and seek to have their angry feelings validated by others, the manner in which they repeatedly express hostility may defeat their purpose and result in an invalidation of their intent. For this reason, if certain individuals discover that they chronically encounter failure in their attempts to have their angry emotions validated, they would do well to pay close attention to their style of communicating those feelings.

A second factor to be considered when expressing angry feelings is the *person* to whom we are directing those feelings. A number of questions may come up in this regard. Is this person a genuine culprit or are we using him or her as a convenient scapegoat for our own inner conflicts. Is this person someone who at this particular time can respectfully listen to and supportively respond to our feelings? Is this person someone who occupies a role that can either seriously assist or undermine us (such as an employer, parent, instructor, etc.) if we direct our angry feelings toward him or her? What is the overall quality of our relationship with this person? What are the pros and cons, advantages and disadvantages, of revealing our angry feelings toward this person? These and a great many other questions about the person toward whom we will be directing our negative emotions will inevitably arise whenever we consider expressing feelings of hostility.

Another important factor is the *social situation* or *milieu*. There are of course many social situations that are rather conducive to expressing anger and others that strongly militate against the successful expression of anger. For example, generally speaking, expressing anger in private social situations tends to reduce the level of social embarrassment and humiliation to the participants and thereby diminishes the potential for a conflagration of tensions. This does not mean, of course, that anger must be expressed only in private situations in order for it to be properly acknowledged and lead to positive outcomes.

For example, many members of professional sports teams leak their angry grievances to the press in order to embarrass managers and owners into modifying contracts or policies. This sometimes results in the firing or benching of a player, but there are many times when such publicizing of discontent results in the redressing of an unfair labor practice. This most often occurs, it seems, when a team owner or manager believes that the public is highly sympathetic to the grievances expressed by the player in the media.

Thus, when considering the social situation in which one is tempted to express negative emotions, it is normally advisable to determine, as well as possible, whether one would gain more mileage from "having it out" in public or private. Those who tend to favor the public route sometimes do so, not necessarily to humiliate their adversaries, but to possibly recruit allies to their cause from among those who are privy to the conflict. Those who prefer the private route do so sometimes out of genuine respect for the confidentiality of the disagreement. They may also believe that they are in better control of a one-to-one encounter.

Another factor to be considered when expressing angry emotions is the *timing* of such behavior. It is interesting to note that many individuals vent their angriest emotions when they are least able to articulate and defend their feelings. Because their hostility has reached a feverish pitch, they can only express what they feel by helplessly stammering, blubbering, crying, shouting, and convoluting their thoughts and words. Consequently, they compound their sense of misery and futility because they have (once again) failed to say what they truly feel, clearly and emphatically. To make matters worse, the person to whom they have inarticulately expressed their anger is, under the circumstances, likely to either misinterpret or take advantage of their sorry defenselessness.

It makes sense, therefore, to consider one's own state of preparedness before launching into expressions of negative emotions. Do we know reasonably well what it is we are angry about? What is it that we wish to say about how we feel? In the event that objections are raised to our negative emotions, how do we intend to further substantiate or defend our feelings or thoughts? Does it matter to any degree whether our feelings and thoughts are rational or irrational, valid or invalid, insofar as sharing them with another person is concerned? These, and many other questions regarding our state of preparedness, may have considerable relevance when we are considering the timing of our actions.

An additional factor that may determine when we choose to express anger is the emotional state of the person to whom we are directing our feelings. Is this person prepared and strong enough to deal adequately with another individual's anger? If not, this can work either in our favor or to our disadvantage.

For example, let us say you have had a long-standing enmity for your employer who has conveniently overlooked your requests for a raise. You have just learned that your employer has recently gone through a nasty divorce, suffered a whiplash in a car accident, and, for good measure, his house has just been burglarized for the third time. He is sitting in his office, immobilized by depression. Is this an opportune time to express your disgruntlement to him about your salary?

Unfortunately, there are usually no clear-cut answers to this kind of question. Given the employer's Job-like ordeal, it is certainly possible that he will be feeling such intense rage that a request for a raise might well be summarily rebuffed. On the other hand, the employer's misfortunes might cause him feelings of resignation to such an extent that, in an unguarded moment, he will respond with careless generosity to the angry requests of his underlings.

In order to reduce the unpredictability of such situations, it is probably best to take into account what we know about a person's typical reactions to intense stress. If we have observed certain individuals typically react to stress by tyrannizing others, it is probably best not to approach them with our own anger when they are overwrought. Conversely, if a person typically behaves in an altruistic manner when life is relatively tranquil, this should tell us something about the best time to express our displeasure to this individual. If, perchance, we don't have a precise grasp of an individual's mood, we might do well to first consult those who have a better understanding of that person's emotional state before we risk expressing our negative emotions in their direction.

An additional factor to be considered when evaluating our own negative thoughts and emotions is the role of our personal past, including even our earliest childhood experiences, in coloring and influencing how and when we express angry feelings. In my work as a psychotherapist, I have been impressed with how often my patients' problems with their own angry emotions are closely linked to the personalities of their parents. The conflicts ordinarily arise in relation to parents who themselves have had appreciable difficulty in dealing with their own angry feelings. As a result, these parents tend to manifest their anger in either an excessively reserved or explosive manner. Because the patients' parents have not expressed their negative emotions constructively, their behavior serves as an inadequate example for their children. Thus, these patients often fear and misevaluate their negative emotions and thoughts. If, on the one hand, their parents were inordinately emotionally reserved, they may feel that any open and spontaneous expression of anger on their own part is an unpardonable violation of parental values and codes of conduct. Thus, they may at times, quite involuntarily, react to situations in which the open expression of angry feelings is obviously warranted and psychologically necessary by being inappropriately staid and self-composed.

If, on the other hand, their parents were typically volatile and overtly sadistic in the way they expressed their angry emotions, this too could create considerable emotional conflicts for their offspring. If the children have come to think of their parents' irrationally angry and sadistic outbursts as the appropriate norm and behavioral standard for expressing negative emotions, they in turn will perhaps adopt this selfsame mode of expressing anger. This can of course later cause them serious problems in their personal relationships.

The husband of one of my patients is a man who, due to certain conflicts with his parents early in childhood, has a strong proclivity to lose his temper, shout, become verbally abusive, and "go for the jugular" at the drop of a hat and in the most inappropriate social situations. Only gradually and largely because of his wife's insistence that he face and overcome this problem, has he begun to realize that his behavior is inapt and highly offensive to others. Evidently, he had been able to grow up in a home in which verbally abusive behavior met with neither adequate strictures nor penalties. Thus, he naturally felt he had license to tongue-lash his wife whenever the impulse overcame him.

None of the above-mentioned examples is meant to suggest that overly reserved parents automatically beget overly reserved children and explosive parents spawn explosive kids. Children, fortunately, find many adaptive ways with which to deal with their parents' foibles, including finding alternative and healthier forms of expressing negative emotions than their folks. However, as indicated earlier, when people encounter unexpected difficulties in expressing negative thoughts and feelings, it may be well to consider how their parents' personalities and modes of behavior have over time shaped their attitudes toward their own angry emotions.

Now let us return to the second guideline introduced earlier in this chapter: In considering the consequences of expressing or inhibiting angry thoughts and feelings, it is ordinarily important to determine, as realistically as possible, whether our actions will enhance or diminish our self-esteem.

It is suggested that we consider this principle because there is probably little point to expressing angry emotions unless the experience holds the potential for improving our self-respect, self-awareness, and self-esteem. This is why we sometimes feel worse, not better, after having irrationally erupted in rage or even triumphed over an adversary by verbally dismantling him. Actually, it is quite common for people to feel worse after erupting in anger because, after thinking matters over, they despise the manner and method with which they expressed their own negative emotions. As a result, they suffer guilt, humiliation, a loss of self-esteem, and alas, only heap more hatred upon themselves.

The reasons people sometimes lose rather than gain self-esteem as a result of expressing anger are many and subtle. Often it has to do with a feeling that one has expressed his anger too little or too much, considering the actual, immediate provocation. When individuals hedge and blunt their anger too much, it is possible for them to feel that they have done a serious injustice to their own feelings of outrage. Thus, they may regrettably come to the conclusion that they are inveterate cowards, milquetoasts, who should never again presume to express anger.

If, on the other hand, individuals feel they have expressed their anger too volubly or too brutally, they may find themselves beset by feelings of shame and guilt. Consequently, they may come to a conclusion that they are sadists who must divest themselves of all expressions of hostility before they do further harm.

Thus, for some persons, the feeling that they have expressed their anger too much or too little—that is, failed to find a Goldilocks-just-right emotive medium—causes them remorse and loss of self-respect and only serves to deepen their resolve to avoid the future expression of negative emotions altogether.

I mentioned earlier that the angry triumph over an adversary, even one who vastly deserves a good browbeating, does not necessarily enhance one's self-esteem. There are several possible reasons why this is so. First, we may feel that, by strongly directing anger at other persons, we have taken unfair advantage of them. Therefore, we may suffer some guilt as a result. Second, as indicated earlier in our discussion, we may feel that, by verbalizing our anger, we have violated a time-honored parental code and should, therefore, be punished for our actions. Finally, the person who has just absorbed our hostility may cause us to feel even worse by responding either with more intense and vicious anger or by arousing our guilt with a mea culpa comment such as, "Yes, you're right, I'm entirely to blame, but look at how you're hurting me now with your nasty tongue. If I've hurt you, it certainly wasn't deliberate or conscious. What I've done, even if it makes you angry, was only for your own good." Such bromides about the unintentionality of the harm one has committed or, if harm is admitted, that it was carried out for the good of the victim, seem to work wonders in intensifying guilt and emotionally disarming the angry individual.

So, as we can see, the expression of anger in itself, even when it enables people to best a genuine adversary, does not always enhance their self-esteem or embolden them to further assert their feelings in the future.

Validation

What, then, essentially determines whether individuals will augment their self-esteem by expressing anger? The answer to this question seems to revolve around the matter of whether, by expressing anger, a person will come through the experience feeling, if not entirely vindicated, at least partially *validated*. If we listen carefully to people who are feeling and expressing angry emotions, we are likely to discern that their quest is not so much to emotionally hurt or annihilate another individual, but rather to derive validation for their negative thoughts and feelings.

What do I mean by validation? By the term validation, I mean that feeling people have when they realize that their angry thoughts and emotions, no matter how bizarre or extreme (at least to others), no matter how obscure their origins and meanderings, and no matter how inarticulately expressed they may be, have been met with respect and acknowledgement by others. This does not mean that an individual's angry attitudes and feelings are confirmed for factual accuracy and reliability. It does mean, however, that a person's inalienable right to feel and express anger has been nonjudgmentally considered and acknowledged. In other words, individuals who have expressed anger have not been made to feel insane, bitchy, or evil simply because they harbor and air hostile emotions.

In order to feel validated most people do not require that the content or accuracy of their angry thoughts and feelings meet with a scrupulously mirroring approval and agreement from others. Rather, angry persons ordinarily feel validated and appreciated when they receive the decided impression from others that their inviolable right to express their emotions has been met with understanding and respect.

I am underscoring the need for validation of and respect for angry feelings for two reasons. First, the feelings of people are an essential and inextricable part of their very beings. Thus, the negation or invalidation of *any* feelings, including the most hostile, tends to cause people to feel negated as human beings and, therefore, will only serve to aggravate their feelings of hostility.

Second, keeping in mind the importance of the role of emotional validation will enable us to see that when others become angry with us, or vice versa, an angry disagreement will not necessarily mean that someone must "win" in order for that person to come out of an angry encounter with self-esteem and self-respect intact. As a matter of fact, the concept of emotional validation entirely changes the definition of "winning." If we can recognize that the exchange of angry words between two individuals can eventually lead to mutual validation—i.e., each person need not absolutely agree with the other regarding factual matters but nonetheless respects the other's right to feel and express anger—we will cease to regard angry encounters as intrinsically destructive to human relationships. Instead, we can at times consider that the exchange of angry emotions can be a constructive and mutually validating experience, an experience that allows each principal of an angry encounter to feel appreciated and respected; in other words, a "winner." Unfortunately, when the principle of emotional validation is ignored (and it is indeed often forgotten in the heat of an argument), the participants, no matter how factually correct their views, come away from the fray feeling depreciated; in other words, "losers." The mutually respectful and validating exchange of angry emotions, however, produces no psychological casualties, no "losers," only "winners."

At this juncture, the reader may logically ask, "If my angry emotions are invalidated by another person, must I necessarily suffer a loss of self-respect and self-esteem?" The answer, fortunately, is an emphatic, "Of course not." Naturally, we generally feel better about ourselves when others validate our feelings, and correlatively, worse toward ourselves when we are depreciated by others. Yet, it is extremely important to keep in mind that the capacity to adequately validate another person's angry emotions is far from universal among members of the human race. Because of ignorance, fear, insensitivity, or a natural temptation to fight fire with fire, many, if not most, people, react to anger in others by lashing out or withdrawing indignantly and disrespectfully, thereby invalidating the angry individual.

If one does not receive emotional validation from others after having expressed negative thoughts and feelings, it is ordinarily a very good idea to know why. Unless we look into this matter for explanations of the adverse response we have received, it is quite possible to react to an invalidating experience by assuming that our negative thoughts and emotions are in themselves reprehensible and, therefore, we are very "bad" people for having them.

To avoid being overwhelmed by the emotional invalidation of another individual, we might take a good look at the reasons for that person's adverse response. It is likely that this kind of scrutiny will reveal that we have been invalidated, not because we and our feelings are bad, but because we have frightened, offended, angered, cornered, or simply baffled that individual with the intensity of our negative emotions. Or, looking at matters from a somewhat different standpoint, we may be dealing with someone who, due to limitations in his or her personality, cannot, under any circumstances, respond affirmatively and empathically to another person's angry emotions.

If, after examining the matter closely, we discover that some of these factors truly exist, why then should we lose our self-esteem simply because our negative emotions have not been ratified by someone else? If we discover that another individual has little empathy for our negative emotions, we can accept this fact philosophically and, without berating ourselves for failing to get our feelings across, move on to other people who will give us a more sympathetic ear. Of, if we discover that part of the problem is the inappropriate manner in which we have expressed our anger, we need not despise our feelings and ourselves for this, but rather seek to change our means of expressing our emotions. In any case, it is crucial to realize that when our feelings have not been adequately validated, we almost always have at our disposal some constructive means of salvaging our self-esteem. Usually, we can begin the process of reconstructing our self-esteem by seeking to learn the actual reasons, intrapsychic and interpersonal, for our failure to attain emotional validation. This is best done by first avoiding the fallacious reasoning that leads us to believe that it is always our emotions and ourselves that are inherently at fault and cause us to be unworthy of validation from others.

Facing the Challenge

Finally, when confronted with angry thoughts and emotions, it will probably be very helpful to consider the various creative ways—social, recreational, occupational, artistic, political, etc.—that can be put to constructive use. As has been illustrated in the previous chapters, angry, negative emotions and thoughts have untold potential for animating constructive and even stellar achievements. It might be well to keep in mind what Senator George McGovern said in our interview, quoted in the previous chapter: "I've never let a disappointment or setback throw me into idleness or depression. I've always felt that there were challenges to be met. There's always plenty to do, even if you're frustrated in one area."

I realize and appreciate the fact that feelings of anger and disappointment are not always easy to overcome and readily transform into positive pursuits. However, if we can at least keep in mind that negative emotions and thoughts hold the potential, not only to wreak havoc, crime, disorder, and conflict, but to also generate accomplishments of great social worth, we can in time face them and use them more creatively and courageously.

In conclusion, I would like to return to the simple but controversial thesis I put forth earlier in this book. Since all people seem to harbor highly negative emotions and thoughts at one time or another, it is best not to pass moral judgment so much on what any person, including ourselves, thinks or feels at any given time. Rather, let us judge our own moral worth and the moral worth of others according to how well we generally transform our thoughts and feelings into socially worthwhile *deeds*. By this means we can freely and enthusiastically embrace and use all of our emotions and thoughts—negative and positive—for the betterment of ourselves and society and avoid the sad fate of becoming a race of emotional mugwumps.

About the Author

Dr. Gerald Amada is one of the founders and a director of the Mental Health Program, City College of San Francisco. He also has a private psychotherapy practice in Mill Valley, California. He received the M.S.W. degree at Rutgers University and Ph.D. in social and clinical psychology at the Wright Institute, Berkeley, California. He has published seven books and over fifty articles, book reviews, and booklets on the subjects of mental health, psychotherapy, and college students. His latest books are *A Guide to Psychotherapy* (Ballantine Books/Random House) and *The Mystified Fortune-Teller and Other Tales from Psychotherapy* (Madison Books). He has lectured at over fifty colleges and universities in the United States and Canada.

Dr. Amada has been a book reviewer for the *American Journal of Psychotherapy*, University Press of America, the San Francisco *Chronicle*, and the *Journal of College Student Psychotherapy*, of which he is a member of the editorial board and the book review editor. He is the recipient of the 1984 Award of Excellence in the category of administrator, Post Secondary Education, conferred by the National Education Special Needs Personnel, Region 5, which comprises eighteen states.